WHERE DO WE FIND SUCH MEN?

ROBERT N. GOING

and featuring the war-time diary of

Edward T. Hartigan

ISBN: 1438288840
ISBN-13: 978-1438288840

GEORGE STREET PRESS
Amsterdam, NY

Powered by createspace.com

With all best wishes,

Robert M

In loving memory of
Francis J. Going, SK2, USNR.
For historians, his life is of little interest.
From 1942 through 1945 he did his duty,
every day, to the best of his ability.
And then he came home.

Thank God such men were born.

They were, what General Marshall called, "Our secret weapon: the best damned kids in the world."

Where do we find them? Where do we find such men? And the answer came, almost as quickly as I'd asked the question.

Where we've always found them in this country: in the farms, the shops, the stores and the offices. They just are the product of the freest society the world has ever known.

-Ronald Reagan, reflecting on his trip to Normandy for the 40th anniversary of D-Day.

ACKNOWLEDGMENTS

This work could not have been possible without the archives of the *Amsterdam Evening Recorder and Daily Democrat* and the reporters, columnists and editors of the era 1941-1946. Special mention must be made of the late Hugh P. Donlon, whose tireless work during that time kept the paper, and history, alive. One of the truly delightful finds in my research is a social page notice from 1942 indicating that Donlon had been one of a handful of guests at a farewell party when my father was about to leave for the service. He remained a good family friend for the rest of his long life. He was a living Time Machine, an invaluable resource for those of us who wondered how life used to be in our home town.

And I would not have been able to access those *Recorder* files without the friendly assistance of Montgomery County Historian Kelly Yacobucci Farquhar and her wonderful staff who put up with me almost daily during the six months it took me to digest every page of every newspaper from that period. Duly noted as well is the help of Ann Peconie, Director of the Walter Elwood Museum.

Thanks also to Amsterdam City Historian and former New York State Military and Naval Historian Robert von Hasseln for his many clarifications of military terminology of the era and the numerous resources provided.

Noted presidential historian David Pietrusza has been invaluable every step of the way and has offered many useful tips on writing, research and organization.

I spent some delightful hours with the late Jack Blanchfield, fleshing out the details of his incredible story, and he provided not only his own written memoirs, but those of his brother Porky as well, and a most remarkable photograph. To the Hasenfuss, Crouch, Makarowsky, Freer, Hartigan, Kleopfel, Romeo and Watroba families and Nancy and John Mattas and Mark Frey (cousins of Father Anthony Sidoti) and others for the opening of their family archives and memories, words are not enough.

My friend Gavin Murdoch lovingly preserved his grandfather's collection of the *Bigelow-Sanford Uniteds PX*, thus enabling many long-forgotten stories to be retold. Montgomery County Surrogate Judge Guy P. Tomlinson filled me in on a great many details about his remarkable father.

Thanks to Dawn Eden, Mary Anne Luffman, Dr. Michael Hardies, Sister Monica Agnes, CSJ, Richard Redznak and everyone else who persuaded (or even forced) me to write over the years.

And, of course, to Mary, who made it possible for me to spend five of our thirty-five years on this project. What a doll.

-RNG

1. SUNDAY MORNING

Bill Hasenfuss doesn't mind. Sure, he's gotten up early, on a Sunday, no less, and already has his tools and equipment lined up to take care of this B-24 bomber that has just flown in from the states and needs servicing. By this time his well-trained crew could do this in their sleep. Now twenty years old, he considers himself a veteran, and a satisfied one at that, doing what he always loved to do, from the time he'd been a young teenager hanging out at the tiny Perth, New York airport with his friends from Amsterdam's Wilbur H. Lynch High School. His intention had been to enter the Army Air Corps right out of school in 1939, but his junior class buddies Paul Lazarou and Ray "Jinx" Brooks convinced him to wait a year, so they could all go in together.

Not only do they go through basic training together, they end up stationed only a few miles apart, with Brooks with another airplane mechanic group over at Wheeler Field, Lazarou working the shore artillery, and Hasenfuss puttering away, wrench in hand, here at Hickam Field. If you have to work outdoors in December, he can think of a lot worse places to be on this beautiful Sunday morning than Pearl Harbor, Territory of Hawaii.

Another Amsterdamian serves with "Jinx" Brooks over at Wheeler Field, 1st Lt. C.P. Gragg, as head of a ground mechanic crew. Gragg has his family with him in Hawaii. They're not even supposed to be here. They'd been scheduled to ship out to Washington on Saturday, December 6, but the political and military tensions of the moment result in a freezing of the *status quo*. Gragg remains.

Down in the harbor, Chief Machinist's Mate Elmer Ingham goes about his business on the cruiser *USS Phoenix*, while fellow townsman Eugene LaJeunesse relaxes aboard the light cruiser *USS Helena*. The *Helena* sits parked in the berth usually reserved for the battleship *USS Pennsylvania*, now in dry dock.

And then, the skies grow dark from the silhouettes of 353 fighters, bombers and torpedo planes.

Without warning, wave after wave of planes from the Empire of Japan sweep over the harbor, dropping bombs and strafing the decks of the fleet with machine gun fire. One drops a torpedo that speeds straight into the *Helena*. Twenty men die, but the remainder of the crew respond instinctively, sealing off sections of the ship to prevent the in-gushing sea water from spreading. Somehow, she manages to remain afloat.

George Condello, a high school classmate of Brooks and Lazarou, is a crew member of the destroyer *USS Tucker,* in berth X-8, which has the distinction of firing the first shot against the Japs and shoots down two planes. Port-side of the *Tucker,* Arnie Eckelman and Henry Belkowski, aboard the destroyer *USS Selfridge,* swing into action from berth X-9. Within five minutes of the initial attack, every available man is firing away with anti-aircraft and machine guns. A few hours later, they put out to sea.

Paul Lazarou is standing in line for breakfast at Fort Kamehameha near the entrance to Pearl Harbor.

At first, they all just look at each other in total confusion as the explosions rock the mess hall. Only 19, Lazarou has never experienced anything remotely like this. An old-breed sergeant quickly explains and they run for cover.

Though supposedly on war-footing, they have no live ammunition and have to wait a half hour before the supplies arrive from Diamond Head for their small artillery and .30 and .50 caliber machine guns. After that, they fire at everything in sight. He can hear the noise and screams coming from the harbor as the clouds of smoke and fire rise from the wounded ships.

Hit by shrapnel, Lazarou joins the chaos at Tripler Hospital in Honolulu. He looks around, and sees little room to accommodate the wounded. Just bodies. And more bodies. And more bodies.

The Hasenfuss crew members have already been working on the plane for an hour or so when they hear the strange sounds coming up from the area where the American Pacific fleet lies anchored. Momentarily, they think it might be some oddly-timed naval exercise, but a sky suddenly filled with planes bearing bright red circles on their wings quickly convinces them otherwise.

Bombs drop. Machine guns fire.

The B-24 becomes a blazing hulk.

Every member of the ground crew is hit.

An army friend, Pfc. Morton Roth, taking a ten minute break from guard duty, sees Hasenfuss brought inside, blinded and with a shattered left arm. A less-injured G.I. applies a tourniquet to the arm while Roth calls for help.

He can't get through to the hospital, so he runs about seeking any form of vehicle to transport the wounded. Low-flying planes strafe him as he dashes about.

Finally, he spots an ambulance and flags it down.

They load the casualties and drive madly to the hospital.

For William E. Hasenfuss, Jr. it is too late.

He is now one of the Honored Dead.

They all volunteered for this job.

> *Where do we find them?*
> *Where do we find such men?*

Hickam Field, December 7, 1941 (NARA)

2. THE BIG PARADE

I don't exactly remember World War II, of course, being born six years after it ended, but we Baby Boomers somehow managed to pick up quite a bit of critical information by some strange form of cross-generational assimilation. Not a kid in the neighborhood, for example, didn't know the ribald parody of *Whistle While You Work* involving Hitler and Mussolini, which must have been passed from older lad to younger lad for the previous fifteen years before it became our turn to pass it on. Likewise there existed that summer horticulture pest we knew as the Jap beetle, which we looked upon with a certain haughty disdain, as though this miserable little bug had been all the poor losers had to show for the attack on Pearl Harbor.

And there'd be the little cultural things. Songs from the war still played on the radio from time to time, Popeye still licked the Axis on a regular basis and Mom would sometimes break into *Remember Pearl Harbor* while folding the laundry.

And sometimes, but not often, we'd hear our parents and their friends talking on a summer's eve around an outdoor fire when men now in their thirties would quietly recall an adventure or two from when they were just kids, really, usually over a couple of cans of Ballantine beer, the kind you opened with a funny little triangle-shaped tool before flip-tops came on the scene.

Natural curiosity would cause us to make occasional inquiries, like about the guy with the wooden leg who'd come over with his wife to play bridge with the folks, and what you'd get back would be a friendly, but short, reply with "the war" constituting the bulk of the answer.

I remember when *The Longest Day* came out at the Mohawk Theater, which Dad usually called the Strand, a mere eighteen years after the real event, and I asked Dad if he'd been there. No, not on D-Day, but two weeks later. And then he told me about Cherbourg and seeing Charles de

Gaulle speaking from the balcony there when he made his triumphant return to French soil, and about Paris.

But not about the horror of the sinking of the troopship *Leopoldville* on Christmas Eve, 1944. That I had to pick up by listening to him and Ed Bablin talking one day, about where they were and what they saw, and I remember thinking how the hell can anybody see such things and then come home and live your life as though none of it happened.

Nearly every kid I knew had a father who'd been in the war. Parents of two of my classmates, Melrose Freer and Paul Romeo, marched out with the National Guard and two others, Bob Conover and John Armstrong, left with the first batch of draftees in 1940 for one year of military service that ended in 1945. Many of the men whose stories I tell are relatives of my friends and colleagues, or of mine. Or cousins of cousins of cousins. You don't have to travel too many degrees in a small town before you're connected to just about everyone.

Eventually I inherited some old letters and pictures and got a better idea of Dad at twenty, and by and by began pulling these stories together. I found myself in dusty attics and long-neglected archives and absorbing whole library shelves and viewing old documentaries. Sometimes I stumbled into lives of total strangers and ended up knowing them pretty well, even though they had long since passed from this earth. I even attended the funeral of an Amsterdam man who'd been killed in World War II. It's an odd feeling indeed to be forty years old in 1991 and saying goodbye to someone who died in 1944.

One day I went through a box at the Walter Elwood Museum in Amsterdam and came across a scrapbook kept by a high-schooler named Leon Mazanek. I found it quite fascinating. The young naturalist had journeyed around town collecting plant specimens which he glued in the book with careful notations of where he had collected the item and when, together with identification of the item and its utility for mankind. Some of the plants came from my own neighborhood. Some of the species grow in my own yard.

I spent more time going through this seventy year old plus record than I ordinarily would have because I knew Leon Mazanek. Sort of. I knew him as one of the 180 or so Amsterdamians who didn't make it home from World War II.

Leon W. Mazanek. Born in Amsterdam April 16, 1921. Graduated from the Wilbur H. Lynch Senior High School, Class of 1939. Before entering the Navy he'd been an apprentice at the General Electric Company in Schenectady. Enlisted in the Navy, November, 1941. Sent to the Great Lakes Naval Training Station in Illinois for basic training. Assigned to school there and later at Norfolk, Virginia, finally being sent to the Naval Training School at Philadelphia.

He's aboard the destroyer *USS Halsey Powell* on March 20, 1945 off the coast of Japan. The ship is refueling, connected to the aircraft carrier *USS Hancock*, when a *kamikaze* pilot aims his plane at the carrier, scrapes the flight deck, and then smashes head-long into the *Halsey Powell*. Mazanek is killed instantly.

There I am, flipping through his plant book, with the knowledge that I have in my possession a photograph of the moment Leon Mazanek died.

USS HANCOCK   KAMIKAZE HIT   MAR 20 1945

His parents, Mr. and Mrs. Leon L. Mazanek, receive a letter from the commander of the *Halsey Powell*:

> *Dear Mr. Mazanek:*
> *I, my officers and the crew of our ship miss your son very deeply and offer our sincerest sympathy to you, whose loss is so much*

greater. He was hit and killed instantaneously by shrapnel, in action with the enemy off Japan on March 20.

We buried him at sea on March 22 with a Catholic service. We are sending you the flag which we used in the ceremony. If some photographs of the service develop satisfactorily, we will mail them to you later.

We will always remember our friend and shipmate, as a fine, upstanding, competent, hard working man. During the last few months, especially, when we were frequently in action with the Japanese, he performed his duties most creditably and so served his country well. You may be very proud of him. He was a brave man. We consider it a pleasure and a privilege to have known him and an honor to have served with him. We miss him very much.

(Signed)
SIDNEY D. B. MERRILL,
(Commander, U. S. Navy.)

He had three brothers still active in the service: Pfc. Alfred E. Mazanek, then in the thick of the fighting in Germany, Capt. John B. Mazanek with the Army Air Forces in England, and Lt. Henry Mazanek, last heard from in Mississippi. A sister, Kathryn Stella Mazanek, of Amsterdam, also survived.

In preparing this book, and its companion *Honor Roll: The World War II Dead of Amsterdam, NY*, I posted some of the raw research, such as the above, on the Internet.

Nearly sixty-five years after Mazanek's death I received the following message:

Captain Merrill, commander of the Halsey Powell at the time of Leon Mazanek's death, died January 7th, 2010, in his 96th year in Newport, Rhode Island, the result of a stroke suffered on the 29th of December. I thought you might like to know that the week before the stroke, I found this posting and called to ask him about the letter he had written to the Mazanek family after the death of their son, Leon.

> *With no prompting from me, Captain Merrill remembered each of the 12 men lost at that time by name, rank, together with some family info about each man. He knew that Leon had three brothers, each in the service of our country and that Leon died of shrapnel. Over the phone he said to me:*
> *"Some things you never forget."*
> *-Patricia Budd, daughter of SDB Merrill*

If you're not careful when you do this stuff, sometimes you start linking fancy unto fancy and playing the "what if" game. "What if" that *kamikaze* bounced a few feet farther and landed in the drink. Maybe Leon Mazanek comes home to Amsterdam and stays. Who knows, with the GI Bill and all maybe he becomes a biology teacher. I can see his son joining the gang from the neighborhood in a pick-up baseball game on a Saturday morning at the four diamonds behind the Wilbur H. Lynch High School. Heck, maybe I ask Leon's daughter to the Junior Prom.

But there is no future for Leon Mazanek, of course. Just the end, in 1945.

Well. Enough of my musings. If you don't mind, I'm going to step back now and let the tale of my home town in World War II tell itself. It all begins on a beautiful October day.

E very town loves a parade, and never more so than when its boys are marching off to war. Amsterdam, New York is no exception, and the fact that the calendar reads October 23, 1940 and not December 8, 1941 matters not to the folks who line the streets and jam the railroad station and cheer their hearts out for the soldiers of Company G, Second Battalion, 105th Regiment, 27th Division of the United States Army.

Weeks earlier they had just been the local unit of the New York State National Guard, weekend warriors made up mostly of young mill workers and a few hearty veterans. Some, like their captain Peter Rogers, had served in the old Company H chasing Pancho Villa across Mexico, and with the 27th Division as they surged across the front in one of the last great battles of the World War. They had left behind in France a few of their friends, including Lt. James T. Bergen, who had one of the two local American Legion Posts named for him.

Over the years, of course, the boys of Company G had provided the color for many a local parade: Armistice Day, Memorial Day, Independence Day, Kiwanis Halloween parades. But the old-timers know that this one will be different, special. They remember 1917 and the great send-off they got from the town. They remember 1919, and the big welcome home.

America is not at war, but it sure looks like it will only be a matter of time. Franklin Roosevelt, in the middle of a battle for an unprecedented third term, has begun the preparations: expanding the Navy, including plans for a cruiser named for the City of Amsterdam, jacking up the manufacturing capacity, planning for a multi-million man Army, and simultaneously in October of 1940 federalizing National Guard units from across the country and registering millions of men for the draft. A week after the big parade more than 4,000 will sign up in Amsterdam alone, a city of just over 34,000. And that's only round one.

It has been a whirlwind couple of weeks for Company G, with endless private farewell parties, culminating with a big bash hosted by the local Elks Club.

Company G, 105ᵗʰ Inf. October 23, 1940

The day comes, and the troops assemble at the State Armory on Florida Avenue at the head of Bridge Street on the city's South Side (Port Jackson in the old canal days). Like many New York Armories it resembles a medieval castle in red brick, perched on a mount with a clear view of the four hills on the city's north side, densely occupied with a dizzying mixture of homes of all sizes, small stores and 19th century factory buildings which line the Chuctanunda Creek from the edge of the Mohawk River into the far distance. Off to the left, on Market Hill, stands the new high school, named for the long-time Superintendent of Schools Wilbur H. Lynch, which many of Company G had attended.

You can see the steel bridge over the Mohawk linking the vibrant downtown with the South Side, and in the near distance a string of warehouses, lumberyards, bars, restaurants and markets that had sprung up around the old Erie Canal. Most folks can still remember Clinton's Ditch and the mule paths and the big port and canal boat resting area on Bridge Street.

Towering incongruously over the low-level canal buildings is the multi-story Chalmers Knitting Mill along the river, built in the mid-teens, about the same time that the old canal was closing and the new river bridge opening. It employs hundreds of South-siders, mostly first and second generation Italian immigrant families, who had brought much of their culture with them from across the sea. On Sundays the neighbors flock to Our Lady of Mount Carmel Church on Minaville Street, which has long since been out-drawing the old blue-stuccoed Dutch Reformed Church of Port Jackson's first residents.

Wednesday, October 23, 1940 bursts forth in spectacular Indian Summer style, a perfect day for a parade. The eighty-three officers and men brim with excitement.

The senior NCO, First Sgt. Boleslaw "Boles" Knapik understands the importance of the moment and gives the boys a pep talk worthy of Knute Rockne. He wants his soldiers to present themselves neatly, march smartly, hold themselves proudly, and in all things to display themselves in a manner worthy of the adulation about to be heaped on them.

With that, the doors of the armory open and the men set a brisk pace down the stairs to DeWitt Street and then across Florida Avenue to Bridge Street. There they are met by their honor guard, composed of the generation of their fathers, the veterans of the 27th Division who had marched out of the State Armory in 1917 on their way to the first World War.

Several of them, including postal clerk John Curran, will later re-up.

Capt. John Liddle 2d, Grand Marshal, gives the command, "Forward, March!" and the bands and drum and bugle corps filling Bridge Street set off with spirit and gusto, along with waves of veterans groups. High School kids from Wilbur H. Lynch Senior High and the Technical High School and St. Mary's Institute, even Junior High students, hundreds of whom will themselves wear the uniform before too many years pass, join their older brothers, as do a group of girls and boys from the Fourth Ward School, each bearing a flag to honor a departing sibling.

Men, women and children cheer, people hang out their windows and off porches. They pass the bars and eateries and the West Shore Railroad Station and the empty field and DPW warehouse where the old canal port used to be and the Chalmers Mill, then cross over the Mohawk River on the 1916 bridge and on the far side march over the New York Central Railroad and on down to the busiest intersection in town, Market and Main. First Lt. Charles DeGroff keeps his men in order while school kids run along beside them, wide-eyed and hero-worshiping.

—Recorder Staff Photos

They head up Market Street, past the bowling alley and the banks, the Milner Hotel and the Blood Building and the Orpheum on their left, more bars and more eateries and the Larrabee Hardware Store and the Regent

Theater on their right. More offices and shops and then, just past where Division Street comes in on the left, they take a sharp right on Grove Street near the Rialto Theater, an old vaudeville house now showing movies, and then through the Grove Street urban canyon, crossing the Chuctanunda Creek on a narrow bridge, past the old city jail, finally emerging at Church Street with Doc Tomlinson's house and office on the left, and the Amsterdam Free Library, graciously donated by Andrew Carnegie at the turn of the century, on the right. On the far right corner stands the stately Second Presbyterian Church, and if allowed to glance left they would see the brownstones lining Church Street and below them the John J. Wyszomirski Post 701, American Legion, empty for the moment, as every available veteran in town is already engaged in the grand gathering.

The Boys of Company G continue on Grove past the Riley Funeral Home and the Zion Evangelical Reformed Church to Liberty Street, where they turn right again, marching between the Congregation Sons of Israel Synagogue and the Fownes Glove factory, down to East Main Street, where they once more turn right to greet the cheering throngs in the business district and find themselves showered in confetti.

Spanish-American War Vets march ahead of Mohawk Mills Band (Diane Hale Smith)

It would later be billed as the biggest parade in the city's history.

More than twenty thousand people line the route, ten thousand of whom continue with the boys to the New York Central train station, flags flying and cheers raising for the passing troop trains of other units from other home towns. The Mohawk Mills Band strikes up "The Star Spangled Banner" and "God Bless America" as the transient soldiers lean out their windows and wave to the Amsterdam crowds.

(DHS)

By coincidence, a campaign train carrying Republican presidential candidate Wendell Willkie from Chicago to New York finds itself delayed beyond the bridge overpass and then slowly creeps through the mass of people. Willkie does not appear, and reporters speculate he might be taking a nap.

Downtown stores shutter their doors for the duration. The U.S. Post Office closes up and abandons afternoon deliveries so that the carriers can participate.

Even way up on Market Hill a grocery store carries a simple sign in its window, "Closed Due to Respect for Our Boys. We are Americans."

There are a few dissonant sounds. One woman cries, recalling how messed up her son had become as a result of the first war. Now she has four grandsons of age, and is none too pleased at the prospect of another war.

But mostly it it a happy, patriotic, flag-waving, rousing good time.

For many of the men of Company G, this will be their last parade.

The October 24, 1940 issue of the *Amsterdam Evening Recorder and Daily Democrat* contains full-page coverage of the event, including a roof-top view from the Griffin Hotel as the parade approaches Market and Main, in front of the Community Pharmacy, a sea of humanity as far as the lens can grab.

There's another photo near the bottom of the page, bearing the caption, "Oh, Boy! Ain't it Great to Be a Soldier!" In the picture is Pvt. Lewis Dilello, being caught in a kissing sandwich between his mother and a pretty brunette named Ann Dargus.

By 1944 Pvt. Dilello will work his way up to second lieutenant.

Mrs. Dilello will become a Gold Star Mother.

There are many future Gold Star mothers in the cheering crowd that day.

Oh, Boy! Ain't It Great To Be a Soldier!

—Recorder Staff Photo

Amsterdam in 1940 is an upstate New York mill town built on both banks of the Mohawk River in historic Montgomery County. It had been on the edge of the frontier when the King's agent to the Indians, Sir William Johnson, built his home nearby. Sir William, when he wasn't fighting the French and fathering children (he was rumored to have had over a hundred progeny) set up a trading post in what would become the city's South Side. When his daughter Polly married his nephew Guy Johnson, he built them a fine mansion on the north bank of the river.

After the Revolution, when the forfeited lands of the Johnsons escheated to the State of New York (the citizens having frowned upon Sir William's son leading Mohawk Indian raids against their homes and farms in the notorious Burning of the Valleys), budding industrial revolutionaries sought out suitable locations on the fall line to build the water wheels that would power their machinery. Albert Vedder found the Chuctanunda Creek to his liking and built the first mill. Workers, stores, churches and other mills followed.

By 1940 Amsterdam is past its prime, though its citizens can be forgiven for not having noticed, as the march to the top had been breath-taking. A pretty accurate idea of the reasons for optimism, notwithstanding the Great Depression, can be seen from this report to the Amsterdam Board of Trade in 1906, compiled by Thomas Foster:

MARVELOUS STATISTICS.

Amsterdam, located in the Mohawk Valley, beautiful for situation, is about midway between the equator and the north pole. To be exact, it is less than 150 miles south of the dividing line.

Amsterdam's population in 1813 was 150. Since then it has doubled seven times, an average of once every twelve and one-half years. To continue this growth will give us in 1925 a population of 76,000; in 1950 a population of 304,000; in 1975 a population of 1,216,000.

This is ab-so-lute-ly sure to take place, provided every man now a member of this Board of Trade will remain here an active, working member until 1975.

Amsterdam has two pearl button factories. One of them is the largest manufacturer of pearl buttons in the world. They export to Canada, England, Ireland, Scotland, Australia, Mexico, Cuba, Germany, Brazil, and Argentine Republic. During the past six months they averaged 16,076 gross of buttons daily, *i.e.*, 2,314,944 buttons per day, or 694,483,200 pearl buttons per year.

In this item alone Amsterdam gives work to over a million hands daily—in buttoning them in the morning and unbuttoning them at night.

The output of the Amsterdam carpet mills is 10,200,000 yards a year, equal to 5,800 miles. This would carpet a stretch from Amsterdam to St. Petersburg, via London, with a small strip left over long enough to reach from Amsterdam to Buffalo.

The Amsterdam trolley line, the seventh longest in New York state, called for short the *Fonda, Johnstown, and Gloversville Railroad*, carried 3,888,198 passengers for the year ending June 30, 1905. This is the equivalent of the combined population of Chicago, St. Louis, Boston, San Francisco, New Orleans, Washington, and Fall River.

Our knit goods manufacturers use annually 18,401,250 pounds of cotton and a vast amount of wool, making 2,676,300 dozen, or

32,115,600 garments. They could supply the underwear for the inhabitants of a nation of 8,000,000.

Our broom manufacturers use 16,700,000 pounds of broom corn and make about 465,000 dozen, *i.e.*, 5,580,000 brooms, and 160,000 dozen, *i.e.*, 1,920,000 brush brooms annually.

What city on the face of the earth renders more assistance in making this world a clean place to live in than does Amsterdam in this item alone? "Our output of brooms exceeds that of any other city in the world."

We believe more money was spent for school buildings in Amsterdam during the past fifteen years than in the entire 5,894 years preceding—including the years before the deluge.

Our pasteboard factories make 6,000,000 boxes yearly.

Our paper mill produces 6,000,000 pounds yearly, and necessitates the loading and unloading of 600 freight cars, or a train four and one-half miles long. It makes 300 feet of newspaper two yards wide per minute, equal to seven miles one yard wide per hour, or 50,000 miles a year. This would reach twice around the globe.

The streets of Amsterdam if made continuous would reach from here to Albany, then turn and go on to Troy.

Our city has nearly one church for each thousand inhabitants.

Amsterdam is a most attractive place for men with families, as it has such diversity of manufactures that all working members can find employment, and this is one of the causes for its being such a thrifty city. Although we have a population of but 23,943, the Amsterdam Savings Bank has 10,221 open accounts, with deposits of $3,625,391.

The output of the oil mills is 3,000,000 gallons of linseed oil per year. This would fill a canal twelve feet wide and one and one-quarter miles long to a depth of five feet.

It is interesting to know that our freight depot is 700 feet long, and there were handled through our freight department 536,176,000 pounds of freight. This would make a train that would reach from Amsterdam to Chicago, back to New York, and then back to Amsterdam, or a distance of 2,309 miles, or would make 464 trains of seventy-five cars each, or 34,820 cars carrying 268,088 tons of freight.

Our packing house prepares in a year 2,400,000 pounds of dressed pork, 360,000 pounds of sausage, cure and smoke 840,000 pounds of ham. Three hundred cars were placed on their side track during the past year.

The Hudson River and Automatic Telephone Companies answered during the year 3,515,000 local calls and 135,000 toll messages. Owing to a delay, we are unable to present the statistics of our spring manufactories, but we understand that one of them is the largest of its kind in the United States.

A resident of Amsterdam at a dinner in a large city in another state was called on to tell what Amsterdam was noted for. Ignoring all these statistics, he affirmed that Amsterdam was famous for the beauty of its women. We will close our report by quoting from him:

"The typical woman of Amsterdam is prettier than an evening star in the glow of a summer sunset, more inspiring than a thousand songs. She is our hope, our romance, our vine and fig tree, the light which enables us to see a million miles beyond the North Star."

All of which is respectfully submitted.

ISAAC E. LYON
JOHN BARTHOLOMEW
JULIAN DU BOIS
JAMES B. GARDINER
DAVID D. CASSIDY. JR.

Their predictions for the near term are not far off, as the city nearly doubles in size again by the end of the 1920's and may *actually* have done so between the censuses during the Coolidge Prosperity. Headlines of the *Amsterdam Evening Recorder* in that decade warn of the dire economic crisis facing the city: not enough residents for all the jobs that are available.

So when the Great Depression begins to hit in late 1929, few expect it to be more than a bump in the road. The political chatter in City Hall in the 30's is all about the future, not the grim present. Plans are made for improving the water supply, already capable of serving a city of 60,000, and of building a water filtration system, and a sewage treatment plant, and a solid waste disposal facility. New parks continue to be built, and a Robert Trent Jones-designed municipal golf course. The old high school on Division Street becomes the junior high, and the brand-spanking new facility opens on the old Collins farm, with baseball fields and softball fields and a football field and room to expand and grow into the unforeseeable future.

The early Dutch and German and English settlers give way in the 19th and early 20th centuries to new waves of immigrants: Irish fleeing the famine, and working on building the Erie Canal and the railroads. They mostly gather on what comes to be known as "Cork Hill", around what an eighth grade girl, Clara Clizbe, in 1881 quaintly calls "the suburb known as Reid Street." Then, in rapid succession, come the Italians, the Poles, the Lithuanians, the Ukrainians, Jews from eastern Europe and more Germans and more Irish and more English until the mills become a chattering melting pot. Though the city by 1940 is over 70% Catholic, they sit in many different pews, with two Italian churches, two Polish churches, a German church, a Lithuanian church, a Ukrainian Eastern Rite church and St. Mary's, a church of general canonical jurisdiction, but mostly left to the Irish who founded it. Amsterdam supports two synagogues, and name a Protestant denomination and there would probably be at least one, with major Presbyterian, Baptist, Methodist, Lutheran and Episcopal congregations.

An analysis of census and other data shows that by 1940:

Amsterdam is New York State's eighth industrial city, with 10,500 industrial wage earners, 586 stores, 33 wholesale houses, 202 service establishments and 66 manufacturing companies. Somehow, by 1940, it is only the second largest city in the country in the manufacture of rugs and carpets, but still number one in the production of brooms and whisk brooms and fresh water pearl buttons. The standard of living is 6.9 per cent above the average for the country. There are three thriving movie houses, a Little Theater group and even a summer stock show every Monday night in season.

And Amsterdam is a sports town, every sport. Besides professional baseball's Rugmakers, there are the semi-pro football Zephyrs, the amateur Bigelow-Sanford Uniteds soccer club playing in a professional league, and local leagues for basketball, soccer, hockey, baseball, softball, bowling, darts, bocce, marbles, you name it. The era produces a series of national-class boxers. And there are bird-watching societies and garden clubs and women's groups; an endless string of fraternal organizations and veterans' posts. In short, Amsterdam, NY produces not only the exports of its mills, it produces a broad and fascinating culture all its own.

And when the time comes, and the nation requires, it produces heroes.

Irish immigrant Jane Mahoney Nichols, 8 McCleary Avenue. She had two sons in World War I, another in World War II, and a nephew who will be seriously wounded in Normandy.

3. LIFE BEGINS FOR ANDY HARDY

On October 14, 1941, famed government anthropological photographer John Collier slips into Amsterdam to snap some shots to add to his collection of Americana for the U.S. Farm Security Administration. No hoopla, no stories in the paper, no key to the city. Just a guy with a camera, and an eye for the magnificence of the ordinary. Day shots, night shots, rain shots and bright shots. Walking up and down East Main Street he catches glimpses of everyday life: folks hanging around the White Tower lunch counter on the corner of Church Street (soup 15 cents, hamburgers 9 cents); old ladies stopping near Woolworth's to exchange the latest gossip; multiple examples of Main Street window dressing.

Four late-teen kids chat near Railroad Street, a block from the downtown New York Central station. The girl wears a neat fall coat, bobbysox and saddle shoes. Two of the boys are carrying bowling bags. The one with the letter sweater has an earnest look on his face. East Main Street is lined with American flags, still hanging from Columbus Day.

A woman in a fur coat carrying a bag walks down Chuctanunda Street past the office of the Textile Workers Union of America Local office at the back of the Farmers Bank building.

At the corner of Chuctanunda and East Main, Collier spots three mailmen with their big leather satchels deep in discussion while a man in a suit walks briskly by. You can see Amsterdam's skyscraper, the seven-story First National Bank Building, in the background. Here's one of Kresge's (precursor of Kmart for you youngsters), another of the Lurie's Department Store that occupies what had been, at the turn of the century, the Amsterdam Opera House.

A woman steps out of a storefront. A grocer straightens out some bushels of cabbages in his sidewalk display while crates of grape bunches drape invitingly nearby. A couple of pensioners look for all the world like they're exchanging information on the daily street number.

The rains come as Collier snaps two photos of St. Mary's Church, one from the east, one from the west. The latter picks up the clothing stores that line the north side of East Main Street across from the Strand Theater, one of three downtown movie houses owned by the Gloversville-based Schine chain.

The Strand is featuring a mid-week second run of *Life Begins for Andy Hardy.*

(John Collier -LOC)

Could it get any quainter? Mickey Rooney and Judy Garland?

Yet this eleventh entry in MGM's famed series is somewhat atypical of the usual Andy Hardy fare. *Life Begins for Andy Hardy* is, in fact, far and away the most "adult" Andy Hardy movie ever made. The Catholic Church's Legion of Decency had even found it unsuitable for children, and for good reason.

Andy, having graduated from high school, decides to forgo college, at least for the time being, and find a job in New York. He soon runs low on cash, but hides an even worse-off friend in his room. The friend ends up dead in his bathroom, a seeming suicide.

Meanwhile, Andy gets involved with a woman who has seen the world (and, unknown to him, is actually married), alarming Betsy Booth (Judy Garland) who conspires with Judge Hardy to bring Andy to realize what is happening, and to his senses.

It's a story about youth on the cusp of lost innocence.

Like those kids on East Main Street, chatting away, not remotely realizing that their world in less than two short months is about to be turned completely upside-down.

(John Collier – LOC)

On December 4, 1941, William Hasenfuss dashes off a routine letter home to his parents on Amsterdam's Northampton Road from Hickam Field, near Pearl Harbor in the Territory of Hawaii, and sends it airmail. He has a surprise for them, but it can wait. Looking forward to his first Christmas furlough since entering the service, he has been delighted to learn that an

Army reclassification of technical positions had resulted in a forthcoming promotion to staff sergeant.

Airplane mechanic had been a natural fit for Hasenfuss. He'd been tinkering with them for a while at the tiny Perth airport, just north of Amsterdam, even logged thirty-six hours of solo flight from there. He likes fiddling with radios, too, had even built several sets himself. *"He comes from the wide open spaces,"* it says next to his high school yearbook picture.

(*Walter Elwood Museum*)

But the furlough is starting to look iffy, what with tensions increasing between the United States and the Empire of Japan. Indeed, only a few days earlier a local Hawaii paper had carried sensational headlines of an imminent Japanese attack on Pearl Harbor. Those fears proved groundless, of course.

Back in Washington Secretary of State Cordell Hull has been demanding clarifications from Japan about various troop movements. A Chicago newspaper charges that President Roosevelt has a secret plan to send five million American troops to Europe by July of 1943, a revelation that is widely denounced by the politicians in Washington, with words like "treason" being bandied about lightly. The Soviet Union, meanwhile, is striking back at the Nazi invaders and by all press accounts has the Germans on the run. One pundit confidently predicts that there will be no trouble with the Japs until it became clear whether their buddy Hitler is winning or losing.

The Polish government in exile has struck a deal with the Soviets to jointly fight the Nazis, with assurances of Polish independence after the war. (Two years later, when evidence is discovered of the Soviet execution of the Polish Officer Corps in the Katyn Forest, the Polish government cancels the arrangement).

And in Amsterdam, New York, PEACE flows like the lovely Mohawk River on which it stands. The downtown stores are decked out in their Christmas best and geared up for the hordes that descend every Friday night. The Thursday *Evening Recorder* runs over thirty pages during the shopping season. A children's serial Christmas story, *Santa and the White Rose*, appears six days a week. Sam Fariello on Lincoln Avenue supplements his hot fudge sundae trade with Christmas trees, "The Largest Assortment in the City!"

The three downtown movie theaters are getting ready for the new features coming in on Sunday. The Rialto on Market Street has the blockbuster *Birth of the Blues* scheduled, with Bing Crosby, Mary Martin, Brian Donlevy, Carolyn Lee, Rochester and J. Carrol Naish, replacing Wallace Beery's *Barnacle Bill.* Down the street the Regent headlines the Marx Brothers in *The Big Store* along with James Cagney and Pat O'Brien in *Devil Dogs of the Air.*

The much racier Strand, down near St. Mary's Church on East Main Street has another Brian Donlevy movie upcoming, *South of Tahiti*, also with "Brod" Crawford, Andy Devine, Maria Montez and "50 Sarong-Clad Goddesses of Love." *Daring Days! Exotic Nights! In a Forbidden Pagan Paradise!*

Over on the South Side, Lanzi's restaurant features "pizza" on Friday nights, the strange delicacy being so new they feel they have to put it in quotes. Up on Hibbard Street, the Krupczak Pharmacy, decades ahead of its time, offers movie rentals of Castle Films for those people lucky enough to own an 8mm or 16 mm projector. "Amsterdam's Only Rental Library," they proclaim.

On the sports pages, the major league baseball owners are holding their winter meetings in Jacksonville, Florida. Baseball has just finished an epic season, with Joe DiMaggio's never-to-be equaled hitting streak and Ted Williams' still amazing .406 batting average. Plans are already being made locally for the Yanks to come to Amsterdam in July to square off against the Rugmakers. Dom Salamack, a local booster of the New York

Giants, notifies the area that he has available for viewing a National League film recounting the recent season, including clips from the World Series between the Yankees and Brooklyn Dodgers.

Hank Greenburg, legendary slugger for the Detroit Tigers, is released from six months of active military duty (due to an act of Congress exempting draftees over the age of 28) and greatly looks forward to rejoining his team and getting his Army service behind him. (He next picks up a bat professionally in July of 1945).

The *Recorder* emphasizes in an editorial the importance of the annual fund drive of the Amsterdam Community Chest.

And Jack Lanny and his orchestra announce that there will be dancing at Mohawk Mills Park. Admission for men, fifty cents. For women, thirty-five cents. Women arriving before 9 PM get in for a quarter!

Come one! Come all! This Sunday night, December 7!

Early morning in Honolulu is mid-afternoon Eastern Standard Time. Nineteen year old Frank Going does what he ordinarily does on a Sunday after Mass and dinner with his mother: he meets up with some friends and heads for the Strand Theater and takes in the latest features (they go with the *50 sarong-clad goddesses of love* over the Marx Brothers or Bing Crosby). While they sit in the dark watching the fantasy land of the southern Pacific, the news flashes across the Associated Press teletype machine in the downtown offices of the *Recorder*, and from there quickly spreads across the city. The Strand is not spared. The movie stops, the radio news is piped in, the theater empties, and dazed teenagers wander into the streets.

On "Dutch Hill," up at Sanford Field on Locust Avenue, the mighty Bigelow-Sanford Uniteds soccer team hosts the First German FC in the first round of the State Cup tournament. The home town boys are having the time of their lives on this bright, crisp day. One of the greatest teams ever assembled in the fifty year history of the club, they lead 5-0 at half-time.

And then the news.

The boys play effectively, but quietly, for the rest of the contest, then walk silently from the field. There are no post-game celebrations.

Within hours veterans' groups assemble and offer their services, and on their own organize ham radio operators into listening posts to monitor the short waves for signs of subversive communications. Governor Herbert Lehman issues orders to all the state's mayors, including Amsterdam's Mayor Arthur Carter, to take all steps necessary to prevent sabotage of strategic facilities within their jurisdiction, and to protect the safety of Japanese citizens.

The Amsterdam Clubs Association, a loose knit confederation of leaders of the Bigelow Weavers' Association, St. John's Club, Polish National Alliance, Group 113, St. Michael's Club and Sacred Heart Club, meet on short notice at the St. Michael's Club on Reid Street, in the dark, narrow clubrooms on the second floor. There they hear a stirring address from their counsel, Attorney Frederick A. Partyka, urging the organization and their member groups to be devoted to true Americanism.

While the papers make no mention, it is highly doubtful that anyone shows up for dancing that night at Mohawk Mills Park, not even Jack Lanny and/or his orchestra.

An order goes out to New York Central Railroad employees not to sell any passage to anyone who looks Japanese. On Monday, December 8, a ticket agent at the Fonda station, later credited with "quick thinking and intelligent action" spots a Japanese-looking man and cleverly sells him a ticket, then runs a short distance to the State Police Barracks. The State Police alertly determine that the man is carrying papers they describe as "communications in the Chinese language" and "incoherent continuity of English words" which they conclude must be code. He is turned over to the FBI, with the *Recorder* reporting their conclusions that he "at the least is an unregistered alien, and . . . may be a spy engaged in collecting military information."

News of the death of William Hasenfuss hits Amsterdam hard. Massive headlines, stories and even an editorial cover the pages of the *Evening Recorder*. And it isn't even just the rocking shock of the attack itself and the loss of a hometown boy that affects the locals. Some twenty-five other Amsterdamians are stationed at Pearl Harbor or elsewhere in the vicinity also, and quite a few more in the Philippines, also under attack. For days and weeks news and rumors trickle out.

The city grapevine soon reports that Arnie Eckelman has been killed as well. Just a few weeks earlier there had been three Eckelman brothers at Pearl, though Edwin had gone home in November, leaving Richard, in the Army, at Schofield Barracks, and Arnie aboard the *Selfridge.*

But the *Selfridge* had put out to sea shortly after the attack and it is two weeks later before Eckelman and his mates are able to finally telegram home that they are, in fact, safe and not dead at all.

"Safe" is the one word message that families and friends long for, and they slowly make it into the press. Such include an Annapolis grad, Navy Air Corps Lt. William Sampson, and a number of men who had been out at sea with the various carrier groups and submarines when the Japanese struck Pearl.

There is no "good" news from the Philippines.

Still, the parents of twenty-four year old West Pointer Capt. Christopher

J. Heffernan 3rd are relieved to receive that one word cablegram "SAFE" in the early morning hours of December 10. Capt. Heffernan is the son of one of Amsterdam's most distinguished jurists, State Supreme Court Justice Christopher Heffernan, Jr., a member of the Appellate Division, Third Department, and frequently mentioned as a possible candidate for New York's highest court, the Court of Appeals. After that first ray of hope, World War II becomes a long Purgatory for the senior Heffernans.

As it does for so many of the families of our men in the Philippines.

Gen. Douglas MacArthur's forces are overwhelmed, and pushed back to the Bataan Peninsula and Corregidor Island at the mouth of Manila Bay, where they put up a gallant defense for several months.

Privates William Thatcher and Clifford Arnold of Hagaman, two good friends from home, had joined up together in February of 1940, and serve together in the Headquarters Division, 60th Coast Artillery Anti-aircraft, at Fort Mills, Corregidor. On May 2, 1942,[1] during the final Japanese assault, Arnold is manning an anti-aircraft gun. When his gun fails, he leaves the comparative safety of his gun emplacement to man a machine gun against Japanese dive bombers. He is killed, and posthumously awarded the Silver Star for outstanding gallantry in action.

Arnold's death is duly reported, but when Corregidor falls three days later Thatcher's status becomes "missing in action," as it is for Lawrence Covert, and Joseph Revelia, a 42 year old native of Italy and veteran of two world wars, and Walter S. Slawek.

Not until February of 1943 does Thatcher's family learn that he has made the list of prisoners of war, the Empire of Japan not being a firm adherent to the Geneva Conventions. Limited reports of the POW status of Pvts. Walter S. Slawek and Lawrence Covert also eventually reach the United States.

But of Christopher Heffernan, there will be no word at all.

The fall of Corregidor and the striking of the colors is met with especially bitter poignancy by one Amsterdam veteran. On August 13, 1898 John J. Keating, then with Company D, 18th Infantry, regular Army, had helped raise the first American flag over Manila.

For Company G, now in the fourteenth month of their one year of active military service, there are no Christmas furloughs. Instead, shortly after Pearl Harbor the entire 27th Division is transported from Ft. McClellan, Alabama to Fort Ord, California. It doesn't take a psychic to figure out that soon they will be shipping out across the Pacific.

For Sgt. Melrose Freer, Nell Pileckas is the girl back home in Hagaman. And if Freer can not go to Hagaman, Hagaman will go to Freer. Borrowing the fare from her grandfather, Nell trains across the country accompanied by Mrs. Boleslaw Knapik, wife of Company G's First Sergeant. A "quiet and simple" wedding ensues, with First Sgt. and Mrs. Knapik serving as the

---

1 Dating can be confusing with incidents west of the International Date Line. To be consistent, I've tried to normalize these by using the date in the USA, Eastern War Time.

attendants, and essentially the NCO core of the old National Guard company as guests: newly minted Lt. Thomas Quigley, Sgts. Michael Makarowsky, Frank C. Betinger, Pasquale J. Mercadante, Henry Gawlak, Max J. Tracz and S. W. DiSiblio, and Cpl. Edward R. Golenbiewski.

(Freer Family)

The bride and groom pose for pictures with the military honor guard, then all retreat to a downtown restaurant for a wedding breakfast. Laughing, joking, horsing around, the guard then escorts the newlyweds to their hotel, where they somewhat wistfully take their leave and go off to see an Errol Flynn movie.

Before World War II closes, the Best Man, First Sgt. Boles Knapik, is dead.

So is Lt. Thomas J. Quigley.

So is Sgt. Michael Makarowsky. And Frank Betinger. And Edward R. Golenbiewski.

Pasquale Mercadante loses his kid brother, Frank.

Max Tracz gets shot up good in Saipan.

And Nell Pileckas Freer's brother, Allen Pileckas, USMC, will give his life on a miserable piece of rock and volcanic sand called Iwo Jima.

4. THE WRONG PLACE AT THE RIGHT TIME

Adolf Hitler wastes little time in bringing Germany into the war against the United States and Benito Mussolini's Italy soon follows. An undeclared war of sorts has been going on for a while anyway, as merchant fleets bearing cargo from the United States to Great Britain come under attack from German U-boats. Even before the war, American troops had helped occupy Iceland. Air cover from there and from Canada helps protect the fleets for a distance, but a big hole opens up in the middle which leaves the ships as sitting ducks for the German submarine wolf packs. Particularly in 1942 the allies suffer tremendous shipping losses, and the relatively few American destroyers and Coast Guard cutters have their work cut out for them, extremely hazardous duty for them and the merchantmen they accompany.

Coastguard Seaman First Class Joe Litwin has one of those jobs, a crewman aboard the cutter *Alexander Hamilton*. The 22-year-old ranks high on the list of Amsterdam's star athletes of the period. A solid hitter, consistently keeping his average above .300, he had been given a tryout by baseball's Rochester Red Wings. Only his lack of speed had kept him from making the team, his six-foot-five frame hampering his sprint and no doubt making movement aboard a coast guard cutter something of an adventure in itself.

On January 28, 1942 the *Hamilton* has a Navy supply vessel in tow when they encounter a German U-boat. In the exchange of unpleasantries they drop depth charges in the area of the submarine and the ensuing silence convinces them that they are free of their adversary. With the tow of the Navy ship having been passed off to another vessel, they then steam ahead toward Iceland. The next day they come within visual range of the snow-capped mountains of that island nation. The crew feasts on turkey dinner and ice cream as they approach their destination.

Litwin pulls watch duty on the top deck, where he is standing when the torpedo hits the engine room.

Twenty-six men are killed and the *Hamilton* is a wreck. Four of the seven life boats have been destroyed and a fifth one doesn't look so hot either. There are few options, as abandoning ship in icy North Atlantic January waters is pretty much a ticket straight to the hereafter.

The injured are given the lifeboats. The rest of the men cling to the wreck, praying that there are sufficient water-tight compartments to keep them afloat long enough to be rescued.

Later, a telegram reaches his parents, informing them that Joe Litwin is missing in action. Family and friends grieve.

Imagine the surprise of his friends, then, when he walks in on them in Amsterdam six weeks later.

After a frightening two and a half hours, they are rescued and taken to Iceland. They stay a month there, and then make a harrowing 17-day return voyage aboard a ramshackle vessel, sleeping in their clothes and protective jackets, finally arriving in Halifax, Nova Scotia where they spend two days before heading for Boston and a ten day leave which gets Litwin home before all but his family have learned of his rescue.

And then he goes back to work.

There being insufficient war ships for the task, the Navy assigns gun crews to serve on merchant vessels. Stephen Dlugos, 24, is serving as a fire control man on one of them in the early summer of 1942. There is no time for anything when the torpedo hits and Dlugos is suddenly in the water at night without ship, without life jacket, without anything except dim hope.

He takes some small comfort in the fact that he has a companion, fellow seaman John Dick of Elizabeth, New Jersey. When they'd been ashore, Dick had purchased a five cent tin whistle, which he now employs maximally, eliciting a shrill sound with every breath he exhales.

But they are alone, and the minutes turn into hours, which seem like years.

After four of those dark, lonely hours all odds are defied when an alert sailor on a Coast Guard craft hears the whistle. Cold, wet and shaken, they live to fight another day.

In June of 1942 the Japanese Navy takes and occupies the island of Kiska in the Aleutians, part of the United States territory of Alaska. They immediately begin building and supplying a naval base there, and the United States fights back with Amsterdam-born William H. Lansing. The 28 year old Aviation Machinist's Mate First Class has been in the regular Navy since 1934, and had at one time been a member of the crew of the storied carrier *USS Lexington* until, at his request, being transferred to England in 1941, there to meet up with his brother Howard, then serving with the Canadian Army. Lansing is recalled to the United States and has time for a brief visit with his mother before departing for the West Coast on December 6, 1941, where he joins Patrol Squad 43 out of San Diego. War breaks out; the squad is dispatched to the Aleutians.

While flying over Kiska harbor on June 11, 1942, Lansing comes under heavy anti-aircraft fire from ship and shore batteries. Rather than turning away, he takes the battle to them, dive-bombing the Japanese ships and strafing their crews. He stays at his controls, doing as much damage as possible, until finally killed by enemy fire. He is posthumously awarded the U.S. Navy Air Medal.

Upon hearing of his brother's death, Howard Potter Lansing, in the service of the King since shortly after Great Britain entered the war in 1939, volunteers for the Dieppe raid, the disastrous amphibious attack on the coast of France by Canadian forces on August 19, 1942. Howard Lansing is wounded and taken prisoner by the Germans.

To honor the bravery of William Lansing, the navy names a ship in his honor, the destroyer escort *USS Lansing* (DE-388), launched on August 2, 1943 by his widow.[2]

---

2 The *Lansing* escorts supply convoys across the Atlantic to Casablanca throughout 1944 and 1945. When the European war ends, she is reassigned to the Pacific and is enroute to Pearl Harbor when the Japanese surrender. After some mothballing, she returns to active duty in the 1950's, finally being decommissioned in 1965 in Bremerton, Washington where she remains as part of the Pacific Reserve Fleet.

For Henry Smeallie Wheeler, graduation from Columbia University in 1940 had brought with it an interesting trip halfway around the world, a visit to the Philippines with his mother to drop in on her brother, Rear Adm. John Morris Smeallie.

The Philippines in 1940 is then still an American territory as a consequence of the Spanish-American War of 1898, but on schedule to become a free and independent nation. In 1940 Smeallie heads the 16th Naval District, covering the general area of the Philippines. Smeallie had attended the U.S. Naval Academy on a congressional appointment, served in the Great White Fleet put together by Teddy Roosevelt and been an American witness to the surrender of the German High Fleet at the end of the First World War.

The son of Amsterdam industrialist Peter Smeallie, he had served as the

first commander of the *U.S.S. Indianapolis* (that ill-fated ship that will later deliver the two atomic bombs to Tinian Island and ultimately lose more of her crew to sharks than to the Japanese torpedo that sinks her). One of his proud duties had been to serve as host to the Commander in Chief, President Franklin D. Roosevelt.

FDR and John Morris Smeallie (LOC)

Future five-star Adm. Chester Nimitz serves as an usher at the Smeallie wedding in 1912.

Adm. Smeallie loses no time in signing up his sister's boy for the Naval Reserve. Upon returning home, Wheeler works for a while in Bridgeport, and then reports for active duty in November of 1941, attaining the rank of ensign.

Adm. Smeallie shares an impossible task with Gen. MacArthur (then Field Marshal of the fledgling Filipino Army): come up with a plan to defend the Philippines from the nearly inevitable invasion by Japan, knowing that it is likely that neither reinforcements, supplies nor defendable supply lines will be available. Washington knows, and the leaders on the ground sense, that what is not defendable will become expendable.

It all becomes too much for Adm. Smeallie, destroying his health. In December of 1940 he accepts a transfer to the mainland and shortly after takes a medical retirement. He dies not long after war's end.

When war comes, Ens. Wheeler is assigned to destroyer escort service on the North Atlantic route. A furlough brings him home to Amsterdam to visit his mother for a short visit before returning to duty on August 12, 1942.

Ten days later he is aboard the *USS Ingraham*, a destroyer escort plying the North Atlantic waters.

Called in heavy fog to investigate a collision between the destroyer *USS Buck* and a merchant ship, the *Ingraham* itself collides with the oil tanker *Chemung*. The collision causes a chain reaction resulting in the explosion of the *Ingraham*'s stern depth charges. The destroyer escort blows apart and sinks almost immediately. Only eleven men survive. Admiral Smeallie's nephew is not among them.

Throughout 1942 the Japanese rapidly consolidate their hold on the western Pacific, seizing the Philippines, Malaya, Burma and the Dutch East Indies, neutralizing French Indochina with "friendly" occupation with the tacit approval of Vichy, and building up their forces on Japanese-held islands across the Pacific. Their bases in New Guinea and the Solomon Islands serve as a constant threat to Australia, which is being kept armed by a long American supply chain that stretches more than six thousand miles, dipping deeply south to take in New Zealand and to stay beyond the air power of the Japanese. To counter that supply line and extend their strength, the Japanese begin construction of an air field in the farthest tip of the Solomons. This is where the United States will begin its long march to Japan, utilizing the full might of our Pacific fleet and the United States Marines, at an island called Guadalcanal.

Many an Amsterdam lad serves in the 1st Marine Division under the command of Major-Gen. Alexander Vandegrift in that campaign that lasts from August 7, 1942 to February 9, 1943. The initial force of 16,000 infantrymen is armed only with bolt-action Springfield '03 rifles and 60 days of supplies (the European war being given top priority in Washington). Still, they have the element of surprise, and the first landings, the first amphibious attack by American forces since the mid-19th century, and by far the largest such operation to date (though soon to be dwarfed by events in North Africa) proves successful, albeit with a certain amount of inter-service confusion on the beaches. The Navy thinks their job is to deliver the supplies and the Marines to unload them, whereas the Marines are under the impression that their job is to fight. Adjustments are made on the fly.

The fighting Marines and the blasting and delivering Navy receive air cover from three U.S. carrier groups, which helps, but the Japanese have the advantage of land-based planes in the region, when it comes time for the Empire to strike back, which doesn't take long. Before the second day ends, the carriers decide to pull out, rather than risk discovery and destruction. This leaves the supply and support fleet extremely vulnerable, so *they* make the decision that they will pull out as well on August 9, no matter what the condition of the unloading operations.

For Amsterdam's third class electrician Michael Kwiatkowski, the night of August 8/9, 1942 will long be remembered. He's been aboard the cruiser *USS Vincennes* since five weeks after joining the Navy in October of 1940. "She was home to me," he will say later of the ship that disappears beneath him that night.

What comes to be known as the Battle of Savo Island is not the brightest spot in our Navy's history. In fact, it is a disaster, a failure of planning, communication and command of epic proportions. Whatever can go wrong does go wrong, and when the battle ends, four of the six allied cruisers present lie on the bottom and another is seriously crippled.

The Japanese attack fleet has been sailing down the Solomon Islands "Slot" all day, and even though spotted on a couple of occasions by

American reconnaissance aircraft, the reports of same are so spotty, so late delivered, and so slowly passed along that the reports are of no value to the ships guarding the landings. Night falls, and when planes fly by in the dark, the ship captains assume them to be ours, not having been informed that our carriers have already pulled out. Faulty primitive radar equipment, under repair as the enemy fleet approached, proves ineffective.

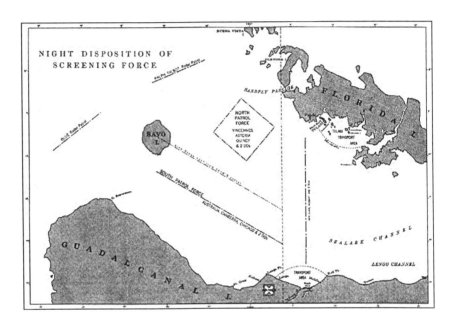

The allied fleet has been divided in two, with the overall command with an admiral of the Royal Navy aboard *HMAS Australia.* Well, actually not aboard, as he has been summoned to a meeting to discuss the carrier withdrawal and has neglected to inform the remaining ranking officers of his absence. Still, his plan remains in effect, with two destroyers criss-crossing the channel and a northern and southern group of three cruisers each and support vessels operating independently of each other. Most of the respective captains have already put in 20-hour days and have passed off control to junior officers when the Japanese torpedo-equipped ships, with incredible blind luck, shortly before 0100 sail right between the (uncoordinated) criss-crossing destroyers south of Savo Island, and between it and Guadalcanal without being detected.

At 0138 they release full salvos of torpedoes against the southern group, then a minute later open fire with the big guns. Once engaged, it takes all of three minutes to wreck the *Canberra* with 24 inch shells. The Australian cruiser is later scuttled and sunk by allied destroyers.

Turning north, the Japanese approach the American cruisers *Quincy, Astoria* and *Vincennes*.

"I was in the sick bay when the Japs struck," reports P.O. Kwiatkowski to his home-town paper two months later. "It must have been the heat of the fire room a couple of days previous, for others were affected the same way. We got out of there when the action started and the smoke of battle didn't help our condition any. They hit us hard."

Two, or maybe three, torpedoes hit the No. 4 fireroom. Another takes out the No. 1 fireroom. No survivors. Pounded by shells, fires break out all over the cruiser, including the three canvas-covered float planes on deck and the one below. The *Vincennes* lasts eighteen minutes, but not before getting off four rounds from its big guns. Capt. Frederick Reifkohl, seeing the ship's colors blasted away by a well-placed shot, orders another set raised. Shortly thereafter the Japs silence the last functioning turret and the *Vincennes* has nothing left to defend herself. She has taken 56 large-caliber hits and probably half a dozen torpedoes.

Reifkohl gives the order to abandon ship.

Kwiatkowski goes overboard and reaches a raft.

Capt. Riefkohl abandons his own raft to swim around through the dark, gathering and encouraging groups of survivors. He quiets shouts for help and whistles, knowing that they are as likely to attract a vicious enemy as a faithful friend. It is daylight, some six hours later, before they are rescued. The destroyers *Mugford* and *Helm* together picked up more than 570 *Vincennes* survivors.

"In spite of it all, I like the Navy," Kwiatkowski tells the *Amsterdam Recorder.* "I've seen a lot of the world and expect to see a lot more. Our skipper, Capt. Riefkohl, is a regular fellow and when he said we were going in to fight we went in to fight. He called a spade a spade and when he got through talking, everybody felt like fighting. It's going to feel strange going back to another ship. I was on the *Vincennes* so long I knew every part of her and it means a lot when the crew knows the ship. It's hard to believe that she's gone."

In addition to *USS Vincennes* and *HMAS Canberra,* the cruisers *Quincy* and *Astoria* are sunk as well, and the cruiser *Chicago* badly hurt. In all, the U.S. Navy loses 1,024 killed and 709 injured in the Battle of Savo Island, the first of five major sea battles off Guadalcanal over the next few months which result in the stretch of water being forever after known as *Ironbottom Sound*.

The Japanese commander, overwhelmingly successful in his destruction of the cruiser fleet guarding the transports, still fails, nevertheless, in his primary mission, which is to eliminate the transport vessels unloading supplies for the Marines. The reason is simple: he needed to high-tail it out of there and out of range of the aircraft carriers. Had he been aware that the carriers had already pulled out, he could have wrecked the invasion of Guadalcanal before it even had much of a foothold, setting the American advance back a year or more, and posing a major threat to Australia and the advance bases of the allies.

And yet, all is not well for the Marines. Deprived of their air cover, early on the 9th of August their naval cover pulls away as well: fighting ships, escorts, and vast amounts of unloaded supplies. Food rations are cut immediately, and for a time they survive on captured Japanese rice, all the while fighting off tropical diseases and dysentery (which hits fully a fifth of the troops). Their heavy equipment consists of one (1) bull dozer.

But these are the United States Marines of the 1st Division, and even though out-numbered with poor supplies and no firm knowledge of when they might get reinforcements and aid, if at all, they plunge ahead, and on the 9th of August, but two days after landing, seize the unfinished air field on Lunga Point and, even while under fire and fending off counterattacks, manage to finish the airfield with their single bull dozer and captured Japanese equipment, sufficient to three days later rename it Henderson Field and try out the new runway with a landing by a Navy pilot, arriving at 10:35 a.m. aboard a Navy PBY patrol bomber.

Whether the idea comes from Rear Adm. John S. McCain, or whether it springs full-blown from the Amsterdam brain of McCain's aide and personal pilot, Pearl Harbor veteran Lt. William S. Sampson, the 1935 graduate of the Annapolis Naval Academy somewhat fancifully reports severe mechanical difficulties and requests permission to land at the not-quite-finished field. The big grin on his face when mechanics find absolutely nothing wrong with the plane suggests to some historians that Sampson may have been conning his way into the history books. Certainly the embattled Marines are happy to see him and he receives a personal commendation from the general commanding.

Lt. Sampson making first landing on Guadalcanal

Marines delighted to greet Navy flier.

Not satisfied with one historical footnote, Sampson takes the opportunity to also conduct the first air evacuation in the Pacific war from a combat zone, a couple of casualties he brings back with him to *Espiritu Santo*.

Six days later the Marines declare Henderson Field officially open for business, and on August 20 a squadron of twenty Marine Fighters from the *USS Long Island* sets up permanent station there.

Though they can not know it at the time, the landing of that single plane by Lt. Sampson marks a major turning point in the Pacific War. The construction of the field had been the "high water mark" for the Empire of Japan. With the taking and holding of Henderson Field as a forward base, the tide has permanently turned. From this point on, though there will be vicious fighting and horrible casualties over the next three years, the American and allied forces march, sail and fly ever closer to the home islands. There will be stand-offs, but there will be no more Japanese victories. Only retreat and destruction.

As early as August 19 the Japanese begin to land major reinforcements on Guadalcanal and are able to supply them by nightly runs down the Slot, which ships are able to retreat safely before daylight can make the American planes at Henderson Field useful. The first serious attempt to retake Henderson takes place on August 21 and the second from September 12-14. Both are beaten back.

On the night of October 7-8, Amsterdam Pfc. Joseph A. Bucci is on patrol with his company at the mouth of the Matanikau River, essentially the dividing line between the two forces. They know an attack is coming, and prepare to meet the enemy on the beach, where they have built up a good defensive position.

All is quiet and suddenly a huge artillery barrage hits them from the rear. The Japs are attacking through the jungle.

It's dark. Very dark. The only light at all is coming from their own tracer bullets. Bucci hears weird screaming and "jabbering" from the dense undergrowth.

He teams up with a sergeant from North Carolina and waits for the shelling to let up. In an attempt to consolidate their position, the two men crawl from foxhole to foxhole to gather the other men.

The foxholes are empty, their company having vacated to a hill on their left. They'd missed the order.

All night long the two men, along with five other Marines similarly situated and widely separated, hold off the Japanese advance, hurling grenades as the the enemy approaches with swords and bayonets, and shooting sparingly to conserve ammunition.

"It was like a World Series pitcher pitching baseballs, only every one of ours had to be a strike," Bucci will say later.

As if the situation isn't deadly enough, the American artillery starts returning fire and they are just as much in the path of the shells as are their antagonists.

At last morning breaks and the marines are able to rejoin their comrades.

The seven men leave 175-200 dead Japanese in front of them.

Bucci, a graduate of St. Mary's Institute and the University of Notre Dame, had been among the first Americans to land on Guadalcanal. The three shrapnel wounds he receives in that battle and subsequent malaria bring him back to the United States and the Naval Hospital in San Diego where he will recuperate over the next several months. The former John Hancock Life Insurance agent finally makes it home in June, 1943 and on July 12 he receives a summons to appear with his parents in the downtown offices of the *Amsterdam Evening Recorder*, there to review with the reporters a wire story of his heroics written up by a Marine reporter. At that meeting he is informed for the first time that he has been awarded the Silver Star.

Says Bucci, "It was just a case of being at the wrong place at the right time."

Right.

Gunner's Mate First Class Leon Markulis, in the Navy since 1938, sails aboard the light cruiser *USS Boise* and takes part in the Second Battle of Savo Island October 11-12, 1942. The next Japanese offensive against

Henderson Field had been scheduled for October 20, so both sides [3] proceed to send reinforcements, which is how they come to meet again.

One Japanese cruiser and a destroyer are sunk, and another cruiser heavily damaged and the Japanese forced to retreat. The Americans lose one destroyer; another destroyer and the *Boise* are heavily damaged. Planes from Henderson sink two more Japanese destroyers after daybreak.

Shortly after midnight, the *Boise* barely dodges a couple of torpedoes. They turn on their searchlights to establish a target to return fire. Instead, they make themselves the target and two shells from the *Kinugasa* explode in the main ammunition magazine between the first and second turrets. A hundred men are killed instantly, but in a bit of serendipity, seawater crashing though the shell-holes quenches the fire before it can reach the ammunition and blow the ship apart. The *Boise* limps out of the battle and is given up for lost. Amazingly, in just three hours the crew brings *Boise* back into line, and a month later she cruises into Philadelphia under her own power while a Navy band plays *Hold That Tiger*.

Also taking an active part in the battle is the cruiser *USS Helena*, that Pearl Harbor veteran still carrying Second Class Petty Officer Eugene LaJeunesse. She survives that battle, but will have an unhappy future.

Though the naval battle pushes the next major ground offensive against the Henderson Field perimeter back a few days in the timetable, it comes nonetheless as the Japanese prepare a surprise attack from the south, through trackless jungle and some of the most difficult terrain of the Pacific. Always ready to improvise, the Marines assign four telephone linemen, a sergeant and three PFCs, including Amsterdam's Francis Murphy, to exercise their skills and climb and remain atop a radio mast at six hour intervals to serve as spotters for the American artillery, all the while being exposed to bombardment themselves. On the afternoon of October 23, while men on the ground are diving into foxholes, Murphy holds his position, even as bomb fragments sever the antenna wire running between the two masts. Though none of the four has any prior

---

3 The Americans were probably aware thanks to our code-breakers.

experience as an artillery spotter, each performs his task with efficiency and courage, and all receive commendations thereafter.

The Japanese fight ferociously, and in vain. Over the next few days they lose 2,200-3,000 troops and the Americans 80.

Among the American casualties is Marine Pfc. Peter Barbagelata.

Serving with Barbagelata, 30, who had run a family confectionery store on Market Street before the war as well as working in several mens' stores, is his hometown buddy Marine Pfc. Albert A. Greco. Greco, hiding in the underbrush, looks on with horror as Japanese troops pass among the wounded Americans crying for help and finishe them off.

He watches his friend die.

There are jobs for just about every profession in the service. Nurses, doctors, mailmen, electricians, photographers, even lawyers sign up. Future Corporation Counsel for the City of Amsterdam Pvt. Joseph Jacobs, stationed in Atlantic City, writes home to his friend Dr. James D. White:

> It's now Thursday about 6:30 P.M. I have just come from chow. I am tired as all hell. It was one tough day, shots in the arm, lectures, drill, drill, and more drill, and if there is any better time to sit down and tell you what I think of the Army I can't think of it.
>
> "Doc", it's a privilege and a pleasure to be here, not only because we could not have selected a better country to serve, but also because they treat you like men. Of course there is a lot of detail and every job to do, and the change in routine from law to soldier isn't the most simple thing to become accustomed to, but what an ungrateful baboon I would be if I were not ready to do my share, and don't you forget it.
>
> This is not being written with a sergeant holding a gun at my back. Maybe I have been fortunate in getting into the Air Corps. It sure is one of the finest branches in the service. Food, all you want and good, too, lodging, hotel rooms and tile baths, better than I could ever afford in civilian life.

Do me a favor, "Doc".

If anyone is beefing about serving Uncle Sam, or if you hear stories about how lousy the Army is, you give them a juicy bird for me.[4]

Joe Jacobs, of course, is not the only somewhat gregarious local attorney to serve in World War II. In *Storming Ashore,* a fascinating memoir of his experiences in Headquarters Company of the Second Battalion of the 531st Engineer Shore Regiment, Kenneth H. Garn introduces one of Amsterdam's most colorful men-in-arms, Malcolm Tomlinson. Only it takes a while to get to that introduction. The bunk next to Garn's has been empty for several days since the arrival at Camp Edwards on Cape Cod of the various troops who will form parts of the new unit. It's not until both men are promoted to corporal that Tomlinson bothers to make an appearance, tossing his duffel on the vacant bunk.

Raised as the son of a doctor, and drafted while in his second year of law school, "Doc" Tomlinson has not exactly worked himself up to the attitude of regular army yet. In all the confusion of setting up the new outfit, no one has noticed that at the conclusion of each day's activities he simply walks off the base and spends the night at a nearby motel, where he has conveniently stationed his wife, then returning before breakfast. It proves to be a very sweet deal until the Army out-foxes him with a promotion that gives him both responsibilities and noticeabilities. The jig is up.

Malcolm's father had assured him he would never be drafted, what with his having suffered a broken ear drum as child. Doesn't matter, and the local draft board doesn't look on lawyering as a vital war time profession, so off he goes. Before the summer of 1942 ends, they are already getting shipped overseas, sailing out of Brooklyn on the *Thomas H. Barry,* an Army transport ship.

---

4 By the time he reaches the Pacific, the accommodations are not quite as accommodating, but Jacobs never grouses and goes on to be awarded a Bronze Star for meritorious service to his country.

Their job will be simple: hit the beaches, remove the obstructions, clear the mines, open the roads, unload the supplies, set up defenses, blow up the enemy and stay alive.

With lots of free time available on the sea voyage, Tomlinson and Garn begin to plot out their vision for the corner of the American expeditionary forces that they will occupy. They develop a series of strict guidelines:

- Carry out all orders to the best of their ability.
- Maintain a soldierly posture during duty hours.
- Soak up as much fun as humanly possible during their off-duty hours.

Next stop: Northern Ireland, and a base near Londonderry, close enough to make passes advantageous after a long day of physical conditioning. One of the favorite destinations of the daring duo is a huge dance hall that caters to allied servicemen. Tomlinson, always with his ear to the ground, gets wind one night of a plan by the American marines to start some action.

"The plan is for each of the marines to stand next to a Limey and punch him out at nine."

They stay for as much fun as they deem humanly possible, and then beat a hasty retreat at 9:01.

By October 1 they are in Scotland, for some serious training, with veterans of the Dieppe expedition giving the practical advice of those who have already been through it. Here, Tomlinson begins to develop a reputation for misplacing and replacing things, stuff you get charged for out of your meager pay if they need replacing.

Like his canteen cup, which he replaces with a rusty tin can in the chow line. He continues using it for several days until Garn one morning finds *his* cup missing and an oddly familiar rusty tin can in its place.

Nor is a Sgt. Nelson particularly amused to have to fall out for reveille one wet morning, slopping through mud with one shoe and one sock. He makes a beeline straight to Malcolm, who, he has correctly figured, had needed to borrow a shoe to replace one he had lost.

Before October of 1942 has ended, with less than three months of preparation, including the sea voyage, the 531st Engineer Shore Regiment sets off for the first offensive operation of the European Front for the Americans: the invasion of North Africa. Thirteen days at sea aboard the liner *Monarch of Bermuda* brings them to the coast of Algeria in the early morning hours of November 8.

They begin loading the landing craft at midnight, scrambling down the cargo nets in total darkness with sixty-five pound packs on their backs, waiting for the precise moment in the rather rough sea when the pitch of the landing craft precisely meshes with the tossing of the *Monarch of Bermuda*, then carefully making the leap with as much grace as they can muster. Once loaded, they speed to shore, the bow ramp drops, and they wade into three foot deep water and make their way to the beach, a bit west of the city of Oran.

Fortunately their only opposition comes from small arms fire laid down by rag-tag defenders from the once vaunted French Foreign Legion. The *Monarch of Bermuda* is not so lucky, coming under fire from the big guns at a nearby French naval base. Still stored aboard are the barracks gear of the men who had just gone ashore, scheduled to be unloaded after the beach head is secured. When his belongings are finally returned to him six weeks later, Malcolm Tomlinson finds that they have been thoroughly saturated with sea water and totally destroyed. This time, the Army issues them new gear without asking for reimbursement.

Their assignment takes them straight into an orange grove, which serves as a nice supplement to their GI rations, and is soon stripped of all that is edible. By the end of the first day they have secured the area and set up a manageable defense perimeter, but the night is an uneasy one, and when guards detect movement towards them, the Americans let out a significant barrage of heavy machine gun fire until everything quiets again.

The next morning they find the lifeless remains of forty goats.

Seaman 1st Class Theodore Lubiniecki, 22, is told with the rest of the crew on his destroyer that they are about to embark on a suicide mission, taking the ship up a shallow North African river to provide support for the taking of a French airfield twelve miles upstream. Every man aboard volunteers, notwithstanding that the pre-battle estimates predict 90% casualties.

To lighten their load they remove all but essential supplies and equipment. The river channel is only nine feet deep. At dawn on November 8, with commandos aboard, they try to slip past the French forts at the mouth of the river, but with a range of barely 25 yards, the French have no trouble keeping them out. The next day the fleet opens up on the forts while commandos attack them. One of the forts is still in French hands the morning of November 10, but Lubiniecki's destroyer is able to slip past it.

They are some five miles up the river when they come under fire from machine guns and anti-tank guns. American troops who had come overland are being held up by the same French defenses, but when they spot the American flag coming upriver, they break out in cheers and storm the defenders. Firing long-range, the destroyer guns take out some of the French guns. Some of the American shells carry over a hill and begin landing, probably accidentally, on French troops holding back an American tank advance. It is enough for the French troops to retreat.

The destroyer continues upriver at full speed, barely making three knots as the keel keeps scraping bottom. Lubiniecki, manning a gun, sees dogfights in the air overhead, but they are unopposed until reaching the airfield, when they come under fire from shore defenses as soon as the first commando boat launches. Lubiniecki and his crew-mates quickly silence the French batteries, the airport is abandoned, and the American tanks they had freed up earlier come over the hill and take the field. By the next day the field is already repaired and landing supplies and troops.

Despite being under fire three times, not a man is lost.

Former Junior High English teacher Corp. Robb Gardiner makes it ashore alright, and meets little military resistance. Not so his company's supply ship, the *Leedstown*, which had carried them across the Atlantic. She succumbs to combined air and submarine attacks from the Axis, and with her go their supplies, personal belongings and clothing. With no other options, for a time they are clothed head to toe in British uniforms until gradually they became "re-Americanized," beginning with Gardiner's receipt of a blanket with the Bigelow-Sanford label, and fresh underwear from the Chalmers mill on Amsterdam's South Side.

The French forces have no particular interest in fighting the Americans, notwithstanding their orders from Vichy, and soon the battle ceases and diplomatic arrangements bring them over to our side, and the 531st settles in for a long occupation. Eventually Garn and Tomlinson are put in charge of squads at various points around the port of Oran carrying out "smoke pot duty." Housed in large packing crates, they wait night after night for orders that never come, prepared to light the pots and set up a smoke screen across the port to confuse the German invaders who aren't there.

Finally the phone rings and in their respective crates Tomlinson and Garn picked up simultaneously.

"Give me a report on wind speed and direction," requests the voice on the other end.

"It's blowing directly over Gobbler's Knob," Garn hears Tomlinson reply, as the caller laughs out loud.

"There's a loose canooting valve on the frammis, so I can't give you the wind speed."

"If you send us a new stassion, we can have it fixed in no time," Garn chimes in.

Though the Major at the other end laughs, their company commander does not when they are hauled into the woodshed the next morning. With respect to that issue, they do thereafter behave.

John J. Kuris tries everything to get into the war. He takes the recruitment route, and is shot down due to a back injury. The Amsterdam draft board classifies him 4-F. He goes to Canada to enlist in their armed forces, but is turned back there. Finally the Merchant Marine takes him, bad back and all, and he lands a job below decks as an oiler on the extremely dangerous Murmansk run to that Arctic Ocean port of the Soviet Union. In late 1942, as the nights grow longer and the weather colder, they are hit by a German torpedo in the Arctic Ocean. Kuris and five others manage to board a life raft before the vessel sinks. What becomes of the other 31 officers and men of the crew they know not.

The six men drift about and await rescue. There is no land in sight or near, so they travel wherever the prevailing current takes them. A day and a night pass. Nothing. Then another and another and a week. Their rations run low. Hypothermia grips them.

They pray.

Two weeks pass on some of the most inhospitable waters on earth. Fifteen days, sixteen, seventeen.

They have long since reached the point of exhaustion.

Then, on the twentieth day, the mist about them lifts. Before them looms a warship.

Kuris lifts his head and sees the Stars and Stripes flapping in the Arctic breeze. Later, he will find it impossible to describe the emotions of that moment.

Despite suffering from exposure, a thirty day hospital stay in Liverpool restores his health. He is allowed two days leave in Amsterdam to visit his mother before shipping out again.

Company G had sailed for Hawaii on March 10, 1942 and arrived on St. Patrick's Day. They will remain there for more than two years, training for the battles to come. But if you have to train for battle, there are worse places than paradise. Staff Sgt. Michael Makarowsky reports in November:

> Received the cake yesterday and it was gone in nothing flat. Too many friends, I guess. We moved about three weeks ago from one of these islands to another and I like it much better where we're at now. It's very hot here and we go fishing or swimming every chance that we get. Caught two lobsters with a spear yesterday and cooked them myself. Had a lot of the boys over at my place for a sea-food dinner last night and what with the cake, well I guess you could call us gluttons at that. I guess I'll makes some woman a good wife someday!

On November 9, 1942 William Marsten[5] has been scheduled to report to the Marines. Previously he had held an agricultural worker deferment, but when the farm is sold his draft status reverts to 1A, so he enlists. His only sibling, Cpl. Leonard Marsten, had entered service on May 19. Their parents live apart and the mother, Lucille Marsten, is distraught beyond words to lose both of her sons to the service, threatening to hurl herself in front of a freight train if he leaves. The father is summoned by William to talk some sense into the mother, but she is inconsolable.

On his last night home, after he falls asleep, Lucille drags a mattress into his room and lies on the floor next to his bed. Early the next morning, neighbors enlist the help of the beat cop to knock down the door where they find the two of them unconscious, a rubber hose leading from the gas stove in the kitchen to the closed bedroom. They also find a note, seemingly intended for Leonard:

> I am not able to mail this message to you because we are dying at this minute. I cannot live without you, my son. At old age I lost everything. I had my sons. I lost one and do not want to lose another. My heart is breaking to separate from them. I am sorry to leave you without your mother. Good-bye, my dear sons.

The Fire Department arrives with resuscitation equipment. Marine Recruit William Marsten lies dead.

Lucille Marsten survives.

District Attorney Charles Tracy ultimately determines that no compelling societal concern requires him to prosecute her for the death of her son. After a period of recovery at Amsterdam City Hospital she is transferred to the State (mental) Hospital in Utica, on the order of Justice Christopher Heffernan, where she is treated for over a year, being released on December 5, 1943 when her husband brings her home to a new apartment on Cady Street.

---

5   Because of the nature of this story, even though the parties involved are all deceased, I have chosen to change the names of the members of the family. Otherwise, this is the way it happened.

Two days later, on the second anniversary of Pearl Harbor, she finishes what she had set out to do. This time the rubber hose leads directly into her mouth.

As for the old age she has been concerned about, at the time of William's death she is 46.

5. NO MEAN CITY

As in every city, town, village and crossroad in America, the Battle of Amsterdam is fought on many fronts. The recruitment offices in those first days after Pearl Harbor (and the swiftly following declarations of war between the other Axis powers and the United States) have no trouble meeting their quotas. Before 1941 ends, Amsterdam has organized its first of many "blackouts". Local Boy Scout troops set up scrap paper drives (38 tons collected in the first month alone), and tin cans are recycled, and used tires and household waste fats and grease. *Recorder* paperboys sell 50,829 Defense Stamps by December 30, at ten cents a pop.

And that is just the beginning. Almost immediately the ladies begin knitting sweaters for sailors, and a book drive produces several thousand volumes on short notice to give the boys something to read. The locals raise funds to purchase and equip an ambulance for our British allies and when that is delivered move on to finance a B-17F bomber, the *City of Amsterdam*, which helps deliver the city's message to our overseas adversaries. Every bond drive exceeds the quotas, by a healthy margin, and the City of Amsterdam and County of Montgomery are always near the top of the state in every aspect of the war efforts.

Not everything that happens in Amsterdam during this time is related to the war, of course, although famed radio priest and future candidate for sainthood Msgr. Fulton J. Sheen does bring up Hitler a bit in his inspirational talk to the locals in the spring of 1942. But people do go about their ordinary business and despite all the bad news, good things continue to happen.

Like a baseball game.

By mid-summer of 1942 Frank Going has already decided to join the Navy. He had turned 20 in April and has a bit of time free before the necessary preliminaries, so on July 20 he does what just about everyone in town who is still there and not working does: he goes downtown and joins four thousand other folks anxiously waiting for a special stop at the Amsterdam New York Central station of the Empire State Express, which ordinarily passes the city by at half-past noon daily. But today the New York Yankees are coming to town!

Not that Dad is a Yankee fan. Far from it. His mother comes from Brooklyn, and their blood runs Dodger blue.

Still, the Yankees! In Amsterdam! Off the train steps manager Joe McCarthy, Lefty Gomez, the Scooter Phil Rizzuto himself, Henrich, Keller, Gordon, Selkirk, Rolfe.

And Joe DiMaggio!

The crowd goes wild.

Yankees Parade, 1942 (AER)

Every convertible in the area gets into the action for the short parade over East Main, where ticker tape and home-made confetti cascade from the offices, and up Market Street to Division and a first-class luncheon at the stately Elks Club close-by the Amsterdam Savings Bank. Special souvenir rugs from the Looms of Mohawk commemorate the occasion and are handed out freely to the participants. Seven-year-old heart patient Johnny Martuscello gets to meet his idol, Joe D.

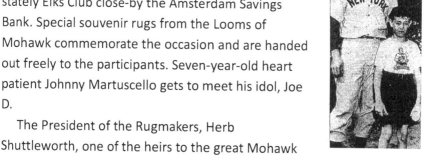

The President of the Rugmakers, Herb Shuttleworth, one of the heirs to the great Mohawk Carpet Company (and Vice President of same), has been working tirelessly for five years to make the arrangements for the local franchise to play the parent club in an exhibition game, and when the details have been almost entirely worked out, the war interrupts and Shuttleworth finds his duty to his country comes first and so he accepts an Army commission and misses the game altogether. 2nd Lieutenant Shuttleworth reports for duty on July 11, working in the business end of the Army in the Material Control Section of the Procurement Division of the Jeffersonville Depot.

Just as baseball is a game of preparing for the unexpected, the locals have to face the unexpected on a grand scale: rebuilding the ball field at Mohawk Mills Park when it burns to the ground on July 12, 1942, eight days before the big game. A small blaze resists the efforts of the caretaker to control it with a garden hose, and the Amsterdam Fire Department can't muster enough water pressure (in the lowest low-pressure area of the city), so in a short period of time the 900 seat grandstand vanishes into ashes, and the adjoining fences, and the concession stand.

Though the neighboring city of Gloversville's club graciously offers to host the game, the Rugmakers will have none of it. They immediately let out a construction contract and not only does every seat get replaced, but the park's capacity increases by 200 more. Some details have to be improvised, like the acres of chicken wire that serve as a temporary back-stop, and war shortages prevent some of the nicer amenities like replacing the grandstand roof, but Mohawk Mills Park gloriously awaits the World Champions.

DiMaggio, Gomez and a couple of other Yanks almost don't make it. They skip out to enjoy a bit of hospitality and spaghetti and meatballs with famed boxing promoter Jimmy Pepe and miss the team bus to the park. They end up having to hitch a ride.

Four thousand and thirty four paying fans fill the stands and every available square foot of standing room. To put some war-time perspective into that, on July 11 the Yankees had hosted the St. Louis Browns at the Stadium and drew only 2,921. The locals make a good show of it, even surviving a DiMaggio blast over the right field fence, and run the game into extra innings before falling 9-5 in the 10th. Jack Smith, sportswriter for the New York *Daily News,* can hardly believe what he is experiencing.

I felt like a red corpuscle the other day, or perhaps it was a white one. My travels with the Yanks carried me through the bloodstream of baseball and finally into the City of Amsterdam, N.Y. (pop. 35,000), pumped me into the heart of the game itself. Rising industriously on the banks of the Mohawk River, the city is deep in the Class C minors. But for sheer love of baseball, enthusiasm and support it outstrips major league owners, officials and fans. It reflects the pure, wholesome attachment of the American people for the game and contrasts with the blasé "give us a winner" attitude of the big cities.

(DHS)

A downtown cynic rejoices at the welcome given the Yanks at the train station. "Well, it's nice to be able to come over here once and greet somebody coming into town. For the past year and a half, it seems, everybody has been going out."

Ann Wyszomirski, whose brother John had been killed in the first World War (and after whom American Legion Post 701 is named) commences sewing a giant flag, the City of Amsterdam Service Flag, at the behest of a committee of World War I veterans of the Post, headed by Desmond F. Nichols. She adds a star for every Amsterdam boy then in the service, with room for many more.

Service Flag Parade (RNG)

Presented to Mayor Carter with proper pomp, ceremony and parade down East Main Street on Saturday, July 25, 1942, the flag is carried horizontally down the street, escorted by various veterans groups and bands, held on the edges by the ladies of the Post 701 American Legion Auxiliary, with Des Nichols marching in front.

As the flag travels on its march, people begin throwing coins at its broad center star, ultimately adding up to $111.45, money which is turned over to City Treasurer Frank Howlan for his administration of the popular

"Smokes for Yanks" program, by which cartons of cigarettes are sent to our boys as a gift from the folks back home.

The combined bands of the Senior High School and the Mohawk Mills Band (courtesy of Musicians' Local 133) play *The Star Spangled Banner*. The crowd joins in the singing. Mr. and Mrs. William Hasenfuss, Sr. are presented, and Mrs. Fred Morse and Mrs. F. Leslie Morse, mother and widow of another deceased Amsterdam lad. The flag is then strung over East Main Street on the Market to Chuctanunda block.

Three days later, on Tuesday evening July 28, the city Recreation Department dedicates its new Upper Locust Avenue playground in memory of William Hasenfuss. Previously known as Patrick's Field, the Recreation Commission has recommended the name change which meets with solid approval by the Amsterdam Common Council. Playground equipment, sand boxes and a softball diamond memorialize the fallen hero of Pearl Harbor.

Mayor Arthur Carter presides over the ceremonies and an inter-playground choir sings patriotic tunes, followed by a talent show. A sidebar in the July 27, 1942 *Recorder* recounts the hero's legacy, and includes that the family has been informed that he had been "given a military burial in a flower-studded cemetery in Hawaii and they will await the end of the war to decide whether or not to bring the body home."

Eventually, that information from the Army will seem somewhat suspect.

Wars can be expensive, and so the nation holds war bond rally after war bond rally, and Amsterdam participates in numbers and amounts that are staggering. But everyone can use a little encouragement, and so Hollywood sends Ann Rutherford and Charles Laughton to appeal to the folks cascading over a Church Street blocked to traffic in front of the Post Office in September of 1942. Mayor Carter introduces Miss Rutherford, who appears, she says, not as a motion picture star and entertainer, but as just a plain American.

> We must buy bonds, and more bonds, and again more bonds before we shall be anywhere near victory. . . . We haven't won a major victory in this war yet and we are fighting for our very lives. We have laughed at the Japs and the Germans, but history plainly shows us that the Japanese haven't lost a war in 2,000 years, and the Germans have taken country after country in Europe while we have been laughing at Hitler's funny mustache. . . .We've got to earn our right to be citizens of this glorious country. Then and only then shall we achieve victory!

Laughton speaks next.

> Some time ago, I spoke at a bond rally similar to this in San
> Francisco. Speaking from the same platform with me were eight
> American sailors who had been at sea for 187 consecutive days on
> the ill-fated *Yorktown*. That means they were forced to put up with
> poor water and poor food. And seven of those days were spent in
> open water which had two inches of oil and grease upon it. When
> these men came ashore, they knelt and prayed. They ran the soil
> of their America through their fingers, and kissed the ground upon
> which they knelt. Then, in the most disgraceful scene I ever hope
> to see, these men, unaccustomed as they were to public
> appearances, were asked to make monkeys of themselves before a
> large crowd in an attempt to sell war bonds, attempting to sell the
> American public the idea that some effort is required to achieve
> victory. These men not only were asked to go out and fight the
> war, but were required to plead with us to back themselves up
> with the funds required to finance this war. I repeat, it was the
> most disgraceful thing I have ever witnessed. America's last hope
> and democracy's last hope is to keep the flame of liberty alive.
> And don't allow yourselves to be kidded. That flame is now
> flickering. If it flickers out, your lives will not be worth the living.
> You haven't begun to fight yet. Get in there now and give us all
> you've got. We need it!

He concludes with a recital of Lincoln's Gettysburg address. Ann
Rutherford then receives a large bouquet of red roses, donated by florist
Raymond Gumuka. Spontaneously, she decides to auction it off for the
war bond effort.

Immediately someone shouts out a bid of two hundred dollars. From
there, the competition gets vigorous and the price goes up and up until
finally settling at ten thousand dollars, and that is just a very small piece of
the action raised that day.

By October, the local scrap metal drive has accumulated over 178 tons.
Included in the pile are the cast iron fence and the heavy metal doors
from City Hall, trolley rails uprooted from Vrooman Avenue, Forbes Street

and parts of Division Street, and eleven "one-armed bandits" of the nickel variety confiscated in one of the Amsterdam Police Department's periodic gambling raids.

War Bond drives are conducted at every level, even little school kids. By the first Armistice Day of the war, the children of St. Mary's Institute, by nickels and dimes, have raised $1,538.50. At a patriotic assembly that day, those who have given as much as one dollar receive the rare privilege of a handshake from Uncle Sam himself. Pandemonium breaks loose as he enters Dugan Hall.

The ovation drowns out his singing of *Any Stamps Today?*, a variation of Irving Berlin's *Any Bonds Today?* (which itself had been an adaptation of his more innocent-times *Any Yams Today*). Played by six foot four Francis "Dutch" Howlan, popular senior basketball star, sporting a stove-pipe hat, the tall, lean son of the city treasurer cuts quite a swath as the nation's symbol, whiskers and all.

Ninth grader Edward "Ned" Wilkinson entertains with his essay, "America Goes in Singing" and quotes Irish poet Arthur O'Shaugnessey:

> *Three with a new song's measure*
> *Can trample an empire down.*

He then leads the assembly in rousing and sentimental renditions of the World War I songbook: *Over There, Pack Up Your Troubles in Your Old Kit Bag* and *Keep the Home Fires Burning*. With the able assistance of Kathryn Egan at the piano, they conclude with the always popular *Marine Hymn* and the songs from the contemporary Hit Parade of 1942: *Remember Pearl Harbor* and *Praise the Lord and Pass the Ammunition.*

Ned's older brother George had gotten the jump on everybody, joining the Royal Canadian Air Force in June of 1941, and by the time of the SMI assembly he is already piloting bombers out of England. In March of 1943 he transfers to the American Army Air Forces and engages in numerous bombing runs at Nazi targets and the city of Rome as part of Col. Edward J. Timberlake's squadron, "Ted's Flying Circus." In August of 1943 he pilots a heavy bomber in a highly successful, though disastrous for our men, raid on the Ploeski oil fields in Rumania. Only three planes return, including Wilkinson's.

Second Lt. George B. Wilkinson's luck runs out on October 1 of that year, "missing in action" over Austria.

By 1943 less than 1% of the industrial companies engaged in the war effort have received the prestigious Army/Navy "E" Award for excellence, so it is a very big deal, hugely celebrated in song, speech and cheers when the award comes to the Mohawk Carpet Mills on March 5, 1943.

One of the largest manufacturers of carpets in the world, Mohawk arises from dual origins. The earlier, founded by the Shuttleworth family, begins in Scotland when a Scottish weaver sends his son, William Shuttleworth, to France to display their wares. William returns with a certificate of merit executed by the Emperor Napoleon III. In 1878, William sends three of his sons with some second-hand looms, to establish their rug business in Amsterdam. They are later joined by their younger brother, Herbert L. Shuttleworth, who dominates the business and carries it to great heights.

Meanwhile, over at the rival Stephen Sanford and Son Carpet Mills, around 1886, the head of the rug department, John Howgate, the head of the weft department, William McCleary, the head of the designing department, Samuel Wallin, and the head of the dying department, David Crouse, bolt and form their own company in Port Jackson (soon to become the Fifth Ward of the new City of Amsterdam), operating as Howgate, McCleary and Company. The night before their first shipment is to be made, their plant burns to the ground. Fortunately they carry insurance, and with the proceeds they resume operations along the Chuctanunda Creek in the then Village of Rockton (later the city's Eighth Ward). When Howgate dies, the firm became McCleary, Wallin and Crouse and with the merger with the Shuttleworths, the "Upper Mills" in Rockton became known as the McCleary, Wallin and Crouse Division and the "Lower Mills" in the city's east end the "Shuttleworth Division."

Mohawk Carpet executives proudly display the Wheel of Life carpet at the company plant before it is shipped to the Waldorf Astoria Hotel in New York City. Guy Murdoch is at left. (Murdoch Family)

The most magnificent achievement of this innovative company is probably the famous "Wheel of Life" carpet that for many years graces the Park Avenue lobby of the Waldorf Astoria Hotel in New York City. Installed in 1937, it weighs three tons and measures 48 feet 11 inches by 46 feet 11 ½ inches, containing 15,000,000 individually dyed tufts to form the design.

Wool from more than 35 countries is shipped to Mohawk for their carpet production.

But that is before the war. The company in a short time retools its entire operation, and looms that had been manufacturing rugs for generations begin kicking out thousands of miles of canvas duck for the Army and Navy, and wool blankets that keep the boys warm all over the world. At the time of the award, ten percent of the total payroll of Mohawk is being subscribed for war bonds by 90% of the employees. During the summer and fall of 1942 the plant's 90-voice choir gives five concerts for the war effort, raising $135,000. More than 1,000 Mohawk employees serve during the war.

Amsterdam native Brig. Gen. Allen Kimball, who counts on his staff Capt. Herbert L. Shuttleworth II (grandson of his namesake), presents the award. Mayor Arthur Carter then speaks on behalf of the people of Amsterdam:

We gather today to publicly acknowledge one of the most significant events in the history of our city. One of Amsterdam's leading industrial concerns, Mohawk Carpet Mills, Inc., has been cited for outstanding accomplishment in the field of manufacture of essential war material. Today they receive the Army and Navy "E" Production Award for their contributions to the war effort.

All members of the Mohawk family have just cause for pride in this fine achievement. Management and workers all are to be heartily congratulated on this award, representing as it does recognition of their total fidelity of purpose on the home front which is indispensable to total victory on the war front.

As most of you know, I have frequently used as my civic text, if you will, the words of Saul of Tarsus, who many years ago said: "I am a citizen of no mean city."

Today's ceremony is indicative of the aptness of such words. As Americans and fellow Amsterdamians, we each have reason to be proud of the signal honor of this day paid to the Mohawk Carpet Mills. On behalf of the men and women serving in the various branches of the armed forces, and in the name of all the people of Amsterdam I salute and congratulate you soldiers of production for making the civilian's contribution to our country's date with destiny.

As I speak to you, brave American soldiers, sailors and Marines are fighting all over the world. On the home front America, too, is engaged in a gigantic battle—the battle of production, to back up the boys who are fighting the actual battles on the far flung, flaming battle fronts of the world.

We are a people of many races, of many creeds, of many callings, yet a people who are realizing individually and exemplifying collectively the most enlightened way of life. It is a splendid thing to be a part of a great wide awake nation. It is a fine thing to know that your own strength is infinitely multiplied by the strength of other men who love their country as you do. It is a noble thing to feel that the wholesome good of a great country can be united in common purposes, and that by frankly looking one another in the face and taking counsel with one another, prejudices will drop away, ample understandings will arise, a universal spirit of service engendered, and that with this increased sense of community of purpose comes a vastly enhanced individual power of achievement; for we are strengthened by the whole endeavor of which we constitute a part.

We are fighting today not because we originally wished to fight. We are fighting because we were attacked. We are fighting to preserve our very existence, fighting against the attempts of the Axis powers to enslave the world. Our foes, the arch enemies of individual freedom, are at war with the human spirit, the spirit of decent men crying out for release from tyranny and demanding for themselves and their children a world of justice and hope. Mankind has never before witnessed such a deadly conflict as now confronts us. One between barbarism and civilization, between slavery and freedom, between evil and the forces of decency and good.

As Americans it is inspiring to know that we are the champions of liberty and right, and to realize that America asks nothing for herself except what she has a right to ask for humanity itself, and to understand that we are privileged to stand for what every civilized nation would wish to stand for, and speak for those things or which all humanity must desire. And that is a firm adherence to the belief that the world has a right to be free from every disturbance of its peace that has its origin in aggression and disregard of the rights of peoples and nations.

America is not merely a name. It is not merely a country. America is a symbol; it is an ideal, the hopes of the world can be expressed in the ideal—America. I believe the glory of America is that she is a great spiritual conception and that in the spirit of her institutions dwells not only her distinction but her power. America came into existence to show the way to mankind in every part of the world to justice, and freedom and liberty. The one thing the world cannot permanently resist is the moral force of great and triumphant convictions.

The man in America, with the opportunities afforded, with the right of expression, with the right of determination, who will not or does not appreciate that it is his duty to stand by such a country in times of storm or stress, who is unwilling to stand up and be counted as a man in this fight for the maintenance of these ideals, is unworthy of the privilege of living in this country.

As we revere the memory of the founders of this country, so the men and women of the future will regard those of our generation who devotedly enlist each in his or her own way for the duration of the war. It is a privilege indeed to feel the satisfaction of wholeheartedly contributing to a great cause, the greatest that has ever been presented to the people of any country and in any time. It is a privilege to live in this time and to have the opportunity to help in this common cause and crusade to free men of every nation from every unworthy bondage.

Ours is the priceless heritage of American citizenship, its freedoms, its liberties, its rights, and its responsibilities. Let us so crave a part in the victory necessary to its preservation, that we will gladly sacrifice our comfort, our pleasure, our convenience, to sustain our fighting forces to the utmost. Future generations will call blessed the name of everyone who makes any contribution to this great cause of human justice and freedom.

Let each of us take as our individual pledge, the words written in the diary of Martin Treptow, a young Iowa soldier killed in action during the first World War. Here is what he wrote:

My Pledge.
America must win this war. Therefore, I will work—I will save—I will sacrifice-- I will endure-- I will fight cheerfully

and do my utmost as if the issue of the whole struggle
depended on me alone.[6]

> Let this message of hope and encouragement, of true
> inspiration, be our guide and watchword until total victory is ours.

No man heeds those great words more than Mayor Arthur Carter himself. A veteran of the First World War, he has served as Amsterdam's mayor since the early 1930's, through the darkest years of the Great Depression, and currently holds the position of Chairman of the Democrats for Montgomery County. A close ally of first Governor and then President Franklin D. Roosevelt, Carter serves as New York State Chairman for President Roosevelt's favorite charity, the March of Dimes, fighting infantile paralysis. It is said that as a personal favor to Mayor Carter, the president himself has directed that a new Navy cruiser be named the *USS Amsterdam*, the only known instance that FDR has ever been involved in the naming of a ship.

Born in Kidderminster, England, in the heart of the British carpet-making country from whence came many a skilled laborer to spark the rug industry in the New World, Carter had come with his family to Amsterdam at the age of 9 in 1906. No rugs for him, he goes into the wholesale food business instead, later working in the State Comptroller's office in Albany, during which time he first meets the future president. Initially terrified of public speaking, he eventually overcomes his fear and, despite three early political losses, becomes the most-elected man ever to hold the title of mayor of Amsterdam.

In his tenth year in office Carter rejoins the Army, there to engage in applying his municipal talents to the occupation of conquered territory. His letter of acceptance received on April 16, he sets out to clean up some city business before reporting for duty.

---

6   If the Treptow quote sounds familiar, the likely reason is that it was used to great effect in the first Inaugural address of Ronald Reagan almost forty years later. Though both men are solid Roosevelt Democrats in 1943, and may possibly have met in the old days, it is unlikely they ever exchanged speeches. We'll call it coincidence.

Along with the city corporation counsel, he sits down with Republican Governor Thomas E. Dewey and Dewey's counsel to go over the logistics. A new law has been passed by the legislature, allowing elected public officials to enter the armed services without vacating their offices, providing a means of temporary replacement for the remainder of the term, or discharge from the service, whichever comes sooner, and requiring that the temporary replacement be of the same political faith as the departing office holder.

For his final Common Council meeting on May 25, Carter arrives dressed in his captain's uniform, and joins in the salute to the flag before taking his seat at the head of the chamber.

What should be a great and joyful *ave atque vale* moment soon degenerates into a free for all. The Council is split 4-4 and the Democrats on the Council further split 2-2 as all jockey for position to fill the power vacuum. One Democrat places the name of City Clerk Thomas Tighe in nomination for the vacancy, while another nominates Alderman John Klobukowski, who, if successful, would thus become the first Polish-American mayor in the history of the city. A Republican puts up retired school superintendent Wilbur H. Lynch, who is so old he already has a high school named after him. Carter rules the Lynch nomination out of order and all hell breaks loose.

Someone questions the ruling of the chair. Carter and the city attorney carefully restate what had been explained to them by Governor Dewey and his counsel. Their word is challenged. A recess is called, and the eight aldermen retire to a side room in City Hall to question each other's parentage for about fifteen minutes, while Carter sits and waits.

Red-faced legislators return, and a motion is quickly made to table the resolution. Though the two Tighe supporters vote *No,* the motion carries. A motion to adjourn follows with an identical vote and Carter watches in amazement as the aldermen angrily file out without a word of farewell.[7]

---

7   No consensus ever emerges and Klobukowski, as Vice President of the Council, serves as acting mayor anyway, though the bitterness left among Polish-American Democrats by Carter's perceived slight of Klobukowski will follow Carter the rest of his political career and sabotage his efforts for a comeback twenty years later. When a Polish-American mayor is finally elected for the

The war comes to Amsterdam in a most startling way on the evening of October 13, 1943. At about 9:45 P.M. Fireman Frank Mazur, standing outside the Central fire House at West Main and Pearl Streets, hears the sound of an airplane engine sputtering and looks up to see the tail light of the plane descending rapidly toward Amsterdam's South Side. What follows is even more astonishing: four billowing nylon parachutes headed straight into the Fifth Ward.

The No. 1 Pumper and the Fire Chief's car speed immediately across the bridge to find the wreckage and assess the situation. Meanwhile Police Headquarters on Chuctanunda Street is deluged with calls, and soon cops and ambulances, sirens blaring, race to the scene as well.

Capt. John Pope, the last to exit the plane at about 500 feet, is found wandering on DeWitt Street, near the top of the hill behind the State Armory. The other three crew members all land safely in and around the grounds of the Fifth Ward School. The exit door from which they had escaped is found in the city's East End.

The twin-engined Army plane had been on a routine run between Rome and Schenectady and return when the engines went out. The crash site is in a rural area about a half mile south of the Armory. Incredibly, there are no injuries either to the crew or anyone on the ground.

Capt. Pope and Lt. Charles Thompson, another member of the crew, are both experienced and heavily decorated combat veterans from the North Africa campaign. Thompson's plane had been shot down 45 miles behind the German lines, but all four crew members survived and found their way back to allied territory. Still, bailing out over Amsterdam must rank with the greatest of his war time adventures.

Capt. Pope has lost his beat-up old hat in the hasty exit, a hat that had been with him in England, Ireland, Scotland, Gibraltar and all over North Africa in his 108 combat missions. Fortunately, Fifth Ward School second

---

first time in 1967, a plaque in City Hall is quietly amended to recognize *nunc pro tunc* Klobukowski as the real mayor from May-December of 1943. And on January 1, 1944, the war not having ended in the interim, Wilbur H. Lynch is sworn in as Carter's elected replacement.

grader Peter Marcucio finds it and is rewarded by the grateful Pope with a junior set of pilot's wings to wear proudly for the rest of the war.

Throughout the year 1943, each of the Eight Wards dedicates an Honor Roll for their men in service. Prayers are said, bands play, patriotic songs are sung, flags wave, veterans march, Gold Star Mothers are introduced and admired. It is a continuous outpouring of affection, support, defiance and determination.

The last of them, the Second Ward monument on the grounds of the

Eighth Ward Memorial, Lyons St.

Academy Street School, is unveiled on Sunday, November 21, 1943, with the principal speaker being New York Supreme Court Justice Christopher Heffernan, Jr., whose son had been reported missing in the Philippines. His words carry that burden, and responsibility:

> Today the world is gripped by war. We are in the midst of the greatest war of all history. It has been brought on by the personal ambition of wicked and corrupt men. It is not a struggle for national supremacy. Its roots go far deeper. It is in very truth a world revolution that challenges all those principles of personal freedom, equality of right, impartial justice and popular sovereignty that are so dear to the hearts of all free men everywhere. In all the sorry pages of human history never has despotism stood forward more defiantly, never has it more brazenly announced its foul purposes, never have the rights of men and nations been more brutally assailed.
>
> The present war is not merely for markets and territories; it is a struggle for the possession of the human soul. The civilized world is threatened by a sinister power which strikes directly at its moral foundations. Two philosophies of life are involved in deadly combat— the one based upon law, justice and human dignity; the other upon arbitrary will, violence and human slavery.

When a ship is battling through a storm of hurricane violence and has sprung leaks that the pumps cannot keep up with, there is sometimes one chance of keeping it afloat — throwing overboard its heavy cargo. Plainly we are now in the midst of such a storm and plainly, too, our ship is a leaky one. We would like to save everything that we value in our civilization, the small dear toys of our children no less than the canister of food, the deck chairs we relaxed in no less than our life belts.

But the inexorable conditions we face win not permit it. We must save what is most worth saving, that which will ultimately serve our humanity, that which will guarantee that our children will have toys again and the aged a place where they may quietly stretch their feet. In short, we must save the vessel itself,—our civilization and the institutions and habits of free men.

Some day our children, perhaps only our great-grandchildren, will find a safe anchorage in quiet waters within sight of a green coast and white buildings. This saying is harder than the figure of the storm-tossed vessel indicates unless one remembers that those who stick to their posts in a storm to work the vessel may be caught in an avalanche of water and swept overboard, for we cannot do our job if we seek first to save our lives or even to protect our children's lives, once they are old enough to take their turn at the watch. We cannot save bodies. We can only save the spirit that makes those bodies significant. In the long run, it will not matter for humanity if London is ruined as completely as the heart of Rotterdam, provided that those who die in the ruins pass on to the survivors the spirit that is capable of building a greater London. Nothing whatever is saved if only the bodies and the buildings are saved, to crumble stone by stone; to die drop by drop.

Similarly, nothing is lost if the spirit lives, for a little leaven will leaven the whole loaf. It is not those who sought safety first or who surrendered quickest who will carry on the work of our civilization. It is those who barely escaped with their lives, the Czechs who continued the struggle, the Poles, the Norwegians, the French, the British, our own brave men who continued to fight. As for the rest, most of them were, pitiably, the appointed victims of Fascism because they thought that their material goods mattered and their bodies were worth keeping alive. That is the conviction of corpses; to that degree, the most brutal Fascist who risked his life was still a better man.

What we need, to get to port finally, is the ship itself, a few hands to navigate it and above all the compass, the chronometer to give us our bearings, and if the violence and carnage spread, nothing else can be saved. We cannot preserve ourselves against this barbarism and worry about the cost of our effort; we must give beyond the ordinary power of giving. Nor can we insure seven per cent profits or the eventual redemption of all our bonds and mortgages at par value; nor can we hold fast to the particular patent monopoly or a particular hourly wage scale. Only one need counts—the need to save the institutions of a free civilization, the institutions of democracy founded on a profound respect for the personality of all men, and for a Power, not ourselves, that makes for righteousness.

We in America shall not work swiftly enough, ruthlessly enough nor shall we have the means of striking back against Fascism hard enough, if we think we can baby ourselves through this crisis. We are working against a barbarian power that has demanded, and exacted, years of bitter sacrifice from every man, woman and child in Germany. Fascism's power is great just in proportion to the unwillingness, on the side of the nations they threaten, to depart from their comfortable bourgeois routine. Mr. Walter Lippmann has well called those who think that they must give up no vested interest or privilege whatever, "the sleepwalkers," and that is the most charitable name one could apply. Some of these Rip Van Winkles fell asleep before 1933.

The mistakes of Europe, above all, the mistakes of France and England, are a warning to us who survive: if we cling to the cargo, we may lose the ship. We must strip for action. Nothing is sacred except our ship— our democracy itself— the civilization we share with all men of good will, the ideals that have shaped us, the heritage of immaterial things we hope to hand on to our children. We Americans must struggle for democracy; that is progress, experiment, adventure, innovation—a ceaseless war that brings no promise of security, a war of the spirit against all that obstructs the spirit. Fascism promises peace, Fascist peace which is death. While democracy lives, that is the one kind of peace we will scorn to accept.

I speak now to those Americans who love life but are willing to face death so that life may go on. I appeal to those who have experienced love but who know that no smaller love than that of humanity will enable the love of mates and friends to be secure. I appeal to those who still carry on the tradition of immigrants and pioneers; those who dared much to create a new world. The task our ancestors started is not finished. The struggle is not over. We have a job to do, the hardest that ever faced a generation. Our job is to restore our own faith for living and to lay the foundation of a world in which life, love, freedom, justice, truth, will once more be sacred. If we rise to the task, we will have our good moments; the sacrifice will not be unrelieved. Though much will be snatched from us that is still precious, the moments that remain will be keener because of the very threat that they may be near our last.

Nothing is sure; not death, not victory. To those who would abandon the very hope of struggle, I would repeat the counsel that Krishna offered Arjuna on the eve of battle, as told in the Bhagavad-Gita. Like the slack liberals, Arjuna hesitated, debated, had specious moral scruples, clung to the hope of safety in a situation that did not permit him to enjoy it. Victory, Krishna pointed out, is never guaranteed beforehand. What is important for man is to attend to the overwhelming duty of the moment in a spirit of emancipated understanding. "Counting gain or loss as one, prepare for battle."

Counting gain or loss as one, knowing that gains are losses and losses are often gains: there lies a truth to take us through these hard days. In that spirit, only in that spirit, can our civilization be saved.

Man's destiny is a great one because the essence of it is tragic. All that he builds crumbles; all that he embodies turns to dust; all that he loves most he must one day leave behind him. That which alone endures on earth is the spirit in which he understands and meets his fate. This he passes on to his children and his comrades —only a breath indeed, but the breath of life. Death comes to all but death comes best to those who are ready to die so that Man may live. The words of Jesus are ultimate in the wisdom: "He that loseth his life shall find it."

That applies to individual men; it applies to nations and peoples. No smaller faith will console us for temporary defeats, sustain us in the hours of despair or give us the strength to push through to victory. Today we must have the will to resist and the courage to give battle in order that liberty and justice shall not perish from the earth.

6. GENUINE "OUR TOWN" FEELING

Father Edward Whelly is a long way from home. He's Lt. Whelly now, on leave from the Diocese of Albany. The accommodations are, to say the least, primitive. But all the better to appreciate the glories of God, he thinks, as he gazes at the beautiful mountains of New Guinea, towering to the edge of heaven itself. So tranquil. So peaceful.

And then the bombs burst and the deafening ack-ack firing of anti-aircraft guns quickly reminds him of the other side of the human condition.

He dives into a muddy slit-trench. *Our modern catacombs.*

And yet, out of all the evil of man's inhumanity to man comes some good. His duty, after all, is to provide for the spiritual needs of his men. Faced with a possibly imminent court martial before the judgment seat of God, even those who have been long away from the Church find themselves easily reconciled.

The necessities of war require some bending of the rules. The Sunday Mass obligation of his Catholic soldiers may be satisfied on Monday or Wednesday, or any other day, but the spiritual ardor required to meet that obligation is no problem. Here on the front lines, with often just the sky for shelter and two blankets for covering, most of the men would gladly receive the sacraments daily if possible. Chaplain Whelly does his best to accommodate. He labors as hard as any other man, from dawn to an hour past dusk, seven days a week.

He ignores the noise and the cries and the fear for a moment and looks around him, at these kids who are even younger than himself.

He's heard the saying many times, of course, but he knows it to be true. In spite of Hell's best efforts, there are no atheists in *these* foxholes.

In January of 1943 Malcolm Tomlinson and his buddy Ken Garn begin beach training in earnest a bit down the North Africa coast, and later in Tunisia.

It takes a while for their mail to catch up with them. In January, Tomlinson receives a pile of *Amsterdam Recorders* from October and is delighted to get them. He writes his parents, "So far as I can make out, Dewey and Bennett are running neck and neck for Governor of New York." The suspense is killing him.

When the folks back home ship him a carton of cigarettes for Christmas under the "Smokes for Yanks" program, he can hardly contain his enthusiasm as he sends his thanks to City Treasurer Frank Howlan:

> Received your Xmas package and take this opportunity to express my thanks to your committee, and especially my sponsor, Albert U. Karner of Lincoln Avenue.
>
> Beyond a doubt, I'd love to relate some of the experiences I have had so far in this war, but censorship forbids it. Nevertheless, Amsterdamians abroad in the Services can experience nothing but gratification and a certain thrill in the support they receive from the home front. Tokens of this sort, such as the packages your organization sends to us are morale support no end.
>
> When my buddies read the *Daily Democrat* (as they call the *Recorder*)[8] they are amazed at the interest the paper and the community take in the boys overseas. Since the majority of them are from the larger cities throughout the country this is quite a compliment. The usual booster to me is here, but this genuine our town feeling festered by the *Daily Democrat*'s recording of the ways and doings of the home folks and groups such as yourselves is more than just boosting, it is the American way of life as we daily live it.
>
> I have followed with much interest the accounts in the paper of the North African campaign and been surprised by the accuracy of these stories, even when they deal with the small details. For example, the mad rush of the urchins for chewing gum, calling

8   The merger of two papers resulted in the officially named *Amsterdam Evening Recorder and Daily Democrat* quite a few decades earlier, and what was once, in part, a semi-official organ of the Democrats by the 1940's actually leans Republican in its editorial policies. It's likely that Tomlinson, a Republican, is here playfully schmoozing the Democrat City Treasurer.

chewing gum Jawnie instead of the usual Yank. As I have had this experience myself many times it gave me quite a kick to read of it in the home town paper. When you can be on the ball as the Army has it, on these small details which are of no great importance, there can be no room for doubt about the larger issues. And I think that our families should realize that they are getting the truth from the papers at home, even if it is a little late. Unfortunately, censorship prevents us from proving this point in our letters home. From my small corner and knowledge, my observation is that the Free Press at home is still really free.

Sincerely, Sgt. C. Malcolm Tomlinson

By July they are ready to head out for Sicily. This time, because of the relatively short distance, Garn and Tomlinson's Headquarters Company take the landing craft all the way. In rough waters they become separated from the rest of the convoy and begin to wander aimlessly in the Mediterranean.

A submarine suddenly surfaces.

Fortunately, it is one of ours (British) and they are soon back on course and manage to get in line in time for the invasion in the early hours of July 10, 1943. This time when they hit the middle of the three American beaches they meet some serious resistance, coming into direct danger from small arms and machine gun fire, while our naval ships blast away at the enemy emplacements. Tomlinson marvels at the ability of those guns to blow holes right through the dunes and open up pathways for the motorized armor that follows.

Morning comes and along with it the German planes. Sheltered in a gully between two dunes, the men don't feel quite so safe after a fighter flies parallel down their line, strafing them with bullets and dropping a single bomb which hits the sand with a thud, skidding a great distance over the ground and coming to a halt not fifty feet from Tomlinson's position, unexploded.

No one moves for a full five minutes, after which they carefully dig a hole and place the maybe-dud into it.

By the second day tank battles further inland decide the issue, but not without cost, and men of Tomlinson's company dig the ditches with their heavy equipment and assist in the temporary disposal of the dead.

From that point on they take part in the endless unloading of supplies for the troops moving inland, and so remain until August 19 when more convenient harbors are freed up closer to the action, and they then sail back to Tunisia.

Three weeks later they are back at sea.

Another D-Day.

Flight Officer Thomas Cooley, 22, is flying just off of Sicily on July 14, 1943 when he's hit by an anti-aircraft shell. He can smell the smoke, and immediately prepares to bail out over the Mediterranean, but exits with a broken right leg as it catches on the elevator stabilizer.

The first thing he does on hitting the water is to ditch the parachute before it can drag him under. He pulls the emergency cord on his life jacket and it quickly inflates. Next he tears a rubber dinghy out of the parachute seat.

The emergency valve is broken. Still he manages to pump it up by hand and, despite the broken leg, pulls himself in. He looks up and sees other planes in his squadron circling overhead. He knows his position is being reported and that help is on the way.

Only it isn't.

After a couple of hours search planes come looking for him, but somehow don't spot him. He watches despairingly as they fly away. The same pattern follows for three days.

He has no food and no water.

The thirst finally overwhelms him and he drinks the salty sea water, as much as a quart. It's the wrong thing to do.

By the time the sun rises on the fourth day only his arms and left side are not cramped. He does not expect to survive the day.

Then, he sights a ship about four miles off, and, more importantly, they sight him when his dinghy is lifted on the crest of a wave when they are but a mile away. It's one of ours.

They lift him to safety, a doctor sets his leg, and he recuperates in an English hospital in Egypt.

"I know the good Lord was with me out there or I would never have survived," he writes his parents on Pulaski Street.

Captain Arthur Carter is mostly hanging out in North Africa waiting for assignment in the military governance of captured territory. Out walking one day, he hears, "Hello, Mayor Carter," and turns to find Dr. John Butkus, from Hagaman and Amsterdam, one of a great many local doctors now serving their country. They no sooner finish exchanging pleasantries and news of home and part when he again hears, "Hello, Mayor." This time it's one of the Dargush boys from John Street.

September 9, 1943. Salerno, just south of Naples, just about the farthest limit for the Allied fighter planes in their new bases in Sicily to provide air cover.

Even as the invasion forces cruise to their middle-of-the-night landings, word comes that the government of Italy has surrendered. Rookies are overjoyed and some even begin to throw equipment overboard. The veterans know better, that a long, hard, miserable fight lies ahead of them. And the Germans, who could not care less whether they have permission of their former allies to be there, are waiting for them.

Artillery, mortars, machine gun fire, small arms, big tanks. The rule of the day is get ashore and get cover. Follow the beach exits and get out of the way while our big guns come ashore and the Navy blasts away overhead. Every landing craft is a target, but the sheer might of the allied forces moves them forward. By daybreak the Germans bring out their fighter planes; the smoke cover provided to block the view of our ships creates confusion for both sides closer to shore.

Malcolm Tomlinson is still on the beach on the first day when an enemy plane comes roaring toward him with guns blazing. He dives into the nearest trench and the cover protects him.

Unfortunately he has landed in the company disposal pit and his heroic face receives multiple lacerations from the jagged tin cans and broken glass.

For whatever reason, Tomlinson refuses medical treatment. When his buddy Garn finds him later the next day, Tomlinson says he doesn't want the medics to rip the scabs off because it would hurt too much. As Garn tells it, he shames Tomlinson into getting help by pointing out that he is a doctor's son, and what would the good doctor think of his behaving like that?

The infected scabs come off. All that he is given to deal with the pain is a bottle of smelling salts.

And then, halfway through the treatment, four Messerschmitt 109s come down the pike on another strafing attack and they all hit the dirt again. When they get up, Tomlinson is missing.

They find him 200 feet away, hugging the ground beneath a truck.

Do you believe this bullshit? He rhetorically inquires of the author decades later. *They give me a G-D Purple Heart because I was too G-D dumb to stay out of the garbage dump!*

His version of the tale, by the way, leaves out the part about the planes.

No point in going to Italy without getting a decent plate of spaghetti, so Garn and Tomlinson finagle a couple of passes and hitch a ride to Naples, where they befriend some kids who take them home to dinner, where they are most welcome and very well fed. All they have to exchange for the hospitality is their good will and some packs of cigarettes.

On November 18, 1943, they board a ship in Naples harbor and head west. Excitement grows as they pass through the Straits of Gibraltar and into the Atlantic. After three D-Day landings, maybe, just maybe, they are heading home.

Then the convoy turns north.

They are needed again.

For the BIG ONE.

Down at Gulfport Army Air Field a dance at a service man's club draws teen-age Pvt. Leo McNamara. The young man, along with his brother, had been adopted into Amsterdam's McNamara family at the age of five, while their two sisters had been boarded out in Vermont. They had never seen each other again in the thirteen years since.

A pretty WAC private catches his eye on the dance floor.

He gathers up his nerve, and with the music still playing he cuts in and dances with her.

"What's your name?'

"Leona."

"I thought so. I'm your brother."

It is a most wonderful reunion.

7. IT COULDN'T BE DONE, BUT WE DOOD IT

Louis D. Hartigan is the son of Amsterdam's late Chief of Detectives, revered by his family and friends as sweet, quiet and kind to his mother. One of four unmarried adult children of the Widow Hartigan, he is the only one subject to the draft in April of 1942.

He has a sister, a brother who's a priest in St. Louis, and a much older brother, Edward, who at 38 is certainly not private material. If the Hartigan family is to be represented in this war, mild-mannered Louis will have to do the job.

But on Monday, April 13, 1942 Louis D. Hartigan is killed in a train accident in Highland Mills after spending the weekend in New York City.

When he leaves for service in September, Pvt. Edward T. Hartigan had, according to his own self-evaluation, not done much of worth up to that point. The love of his life, Genevieve Orsini, waits for him while he begins his great adventure. It is against military regulations to keep a diary while in the field, for security reasons. Fortunately for us, Ed Hartigan never has cared much for rules.

It's not until July 3, 1943 that he begins the journal, lying on his bunk in a barracks in Trinidad, where they have been undergoing exhausting jungle training. Maybe it's the tropical storm raging outside the screened opening that passes as a window, or the laziness of the afternoon with the men all stretched out dozing or reading, but he gets reflective and picks up his pen.

I don't know where to start this thing. I've been in the army for over 9 months and naturally a lot of things have happened. Things that seemed terribly important when they occurred are now only vague, dim memories.

As I remember, I left Amsterdam on Sept. 18th of last year [1942] and reported at Camp Upton that same day. After a very enjoyable ride in the club car, during which time several highballs were taken care of in an effort to cure the hangover of a week's round of parties, we arrived in N.Y. and were herded into a L.I. train and brought to Upton. That is the worst day I have ever spent in the army. For 8 hours they marched us from one place to another, physical inspection, tests of every description...all this time we carried our grips. We'd set them down, pick them up, go here, go there, until I thought we'd covered all of Long Island. That night when we finally were taken to a barracks where we were to sleep, I found a sink and put my head under the faucet and let the water run down my throat for what seemed an hour. Never before or since have I tasted anything as sweet as that luke warm water.

We stayed at Upton a couple of days, then off to Alabama. Said goodbye to Monaghan and the rest, probably for the last time to a lot of them. Willie Greenspan went with my bunch, and Willie and I were together until he left Butner for California and I for New Orleans and ultimately, Trinidad.

On the morning of the third day, we arrived in Fort McClellan, Ala. We pulled in there about 6 A.M., and the train hadn't come to full stop before a pint sized 2nd Lt. was in our car yelling, "Come on, Goddam it, get out of those seats. You mugs are in the army now." It didn't take long to find out he wasn't kidding.

For a guy well into his fourth decade, twice as old as most of the other recruits, boot camp proves tough. Necessity has crammed the normal thirteen weeks of training into seven, every day, every night, even Sundays. Hartigan is bruised head to toe from the obstacle courses, hitting the hard Alabama ground, and smacking himself with his rifle trying to master the manual of arms.

> We had a sergeant named Edanin who was universally detested by every rookie in his outfit. Simon Legree in his palmiest days never drove poor old Uncle Tom like this guy did the soldiers in his platoon. But at the end of the training most of us realized that it was his job, and that he sure did a good one. Someday, tho, somebody is going to shoot him.

After Basic, Hartigan moves on to Fort Butner, North Carolina.

> There probably are places in the world more dreary and God-forsaken than North Carolina, but I hope I never see them.
> Greenspan got placed in an Anti-Tank outfit, but we saw each other quite often and managed to get to town together a couple of times.
> I met some more pretty good fellows at Butner and formed a lot of friendships that will be fun renewing some time. Hendrikson, who got hurt in N.O., Shorty Haverwas, who is here in Trinidad, a bunch of others. Ed Gorman, too, who left Amsterdam with me and is here in the Tropics. I don't see much of him, tho.
> This Shorty is something. Five feet tall, a little curly headed lad of 20 and the greatest villain unhung. We had a great time in Durham one week and ever since then every place I'd go, there would be Shorty. Dale E. Haverwas is his full name, and when they'd call the roll for any formation, the sergeant would yell, "HAVERWAS," and the answer would roll back, "DALE E.!" in voice that a train announcer would envy. Then he'd laugh, an infectious burst of laughter that you just have to join in. He would get drunk every night and then have nightmares. Jump out of bed, fast asleep and yell bloody murder. I'd wake up and talk to him, then he'd set on the side of my bunk until he calmed down and would go back to bed. This was an every night occurrence.

He had an odd way of taking care of his correspondence. He was telling me of a girl friend of his one Sunday and said, "By Gawd, I'm going to write her a letter right now." He sat down and composed a very nice letter, read it to me to get my opinion of it and seemed very pleased to hear that I thought it was well written. Then he put it in a box in his foot locker. I asked him what the idea was, and he said he always put his letters in that box. It was his own private mail box. I said, "Shorty, let me see that." In the box were all the letters he had written his sister and father since he joined the Army. When I asked him why he didn't mail them, he said he would some day when he got around to it. His conscience was clear as long as he wrote. He still has the box.

The time went by fast enough in Butner, and altho everybody hated the place, we got along so well together that we all regretted breaking up.

The week before we pushed off, Connolly came down to visit me. He looked dapper and healthy in his uniform, and we had a good night. The first face I'd seen from home in all that time, and he sure looked good to me.

Greenspan left a couple of days before me, and he hated to go. We had been together all thru those tough training days, and he felt pretty lonesome pushing off alone. I felt the same way. He's a good lad.

I'll never forget the day we left Butner, with its red clay, its swamps, its dismal climate and its collection of hillbillies. All of us took a good look at it receding as the train pulled away, and the kindest thing you could say about the gestures we flung at it was that they were indecent. To top it all off, Henrickson and I went broke in a crap game just before leaving, and we got on the train for a three day ride without a dime or a pack of cigarettes. We had to do a lot of maneuvering to get smokes and candy, but we got our share.

New Orleans looked like the Promised Land as we pulled in there at the end of the trip. The barracks were clean, the people friendly and the weather perfect.

The food, after Butner, was delectable. I remember one day back in Butner, we had stew, and it tasted pretty good until someone discovered a mouse in his portion. I improvised a little ditty to the tune of "One Dozen Roses," and we sang it that night.

Take one dozen Mousies
Put some slum in beside them
And feed them to Company D.

For that inspired bit of verse I did K.P. 18 hours straight.

The stay in New Orleans is short, and soon they board a troop transports for parts then unknown.

The first night we slept in a hold down in the middle of the ship. It was stifling and when two hundred sweating men removed their shoes it wasn't exactly fragrant. The port holes had to be closed of course at dusk. The entire ship blacked out at night, the submarine menace at that time being no joke.

Everybody was a bit jittery and when the hold lights suddenly went out, Shorty, who was sitting on my bunk put his fingers in his mouth and gave out with a long drawn out whistle, sounding all the world like a shell on it's way. That didn't help any. Those boys just took off in every direction of a hatchway.

The rest of the voyage I spent the nights on deck listening to the waves lap against the sides of the ship as we sailed along like three ghost ships.

It was pleasant and restful lying back on your life preserver, looking up at the Southern skies and dreaming of Jenny and home.

Not long after arriving in Trinidad, Pvt. Hartigan takes in a USO show.

Pat O'Brien was the star. Had a very good troupe with him, among them Will & Gladys Ahearn, an act I had played several times back in the old Vaudeville days. I renewed acquaintance with them after the performance and we had a hell of a nice visit. Will introduced me to O'Brien and he's everything in real life that he is on the screen, a fast talking, happy, lovable Irishman. We had quite a talk about prize fighters and horses, meeting on a common ground on both subjects.

The training now becomes even more intense, with commando tactics, amphibious landings, scaling and descending ships. They are set to ship out to the Pacific on short notice, but something happens and the plan is sidetracked.

Two of our heroic ships lost in the Pacific war are quickly replaced and Hartigan gets an early look at them.

One of the grandest and most majestic things I have ever viewed was the sight of the two new aircraft carriers, the Lexington and Yorktown, riding at anchor in Maracagras Bay out at Chaugaramas. But right now I'd trade it for a look at two dingy tug boats chugging up the Barge Canal.

Nearly a year into his service, Hartigan is at last promoted to Private First Class.

Today I am a P.F.C. At this rapid rate of promotion I should be a sergeant by the time I'm seventy. But the extra dough will buy a case of beer anyway.

And then the news.

Everybody in the Company was called in the Day Room today. Capt. Bozandus, more excited than I ever thought he could get, told us he had good news for everybody that was fed up with this place. Then he said, "Everybody who doesn't want to volunteer for immediate combat duty, raise their hands. Excellent. Take all their names, Sergeant. We may move at any hour. That's all men." And away he went, leaving a bewildered company looking at each other. So, thank the Lord, it looks like action at last. We may leave at any time by planes. Wonder how we'll shape up when we get there? Hope that there's some good liquor.

...Well, we're all ready. Stine just walked over and knocked the book out of my hand. Just a hangover from last nite. What a nite. Everybody taking farewell and getting drunk. Sympathizing with the ones left behind. Toomb & Mike didn't make it. They're both heartbroken. In his rage, Conrie near wrecked the N.C.O. club last night. According to the dope, we go all the way by plane. Some 7000 miles.

There's a chance we may hit the states to be equipped but I'm not figuring on it.

You don't allow yourself to think of home on occasions like this. Too much let down if it doesn't pan out.

But if I could see Jenny for one hour, they can put me in a fox hole for the next two years.

They don't get any leave. Just a view of the USA out the window of a troop train.

We left Camp Stoneham September 20th, going by boat down the river to San Francisco. Lot of grumbling about no furloughs but as the boat passed Alcatraz on the way to the transport and the boys got a look at the rock, they figured they were a hell of a lot better off than those boys in that jug and felt a little better. We got on the transport that night, the *S.S. Lurline,* a former luxury liner on the Matron Line with a run between Frisco and Hawaii. A beautiful ship, which could accommodate some 800 passengers very nicely. There were about 5000 of us. They gave us quite a talk before we left, telling us that the misfits and undependables were all weeded out at Camp Stoneham and we were a group of picked men, selected for a special mission and a lot of other horse manure that was to take our mind off the fact that, all promises to the contrary, we would get no leave.

We left port early the next morning, no escort, the ship being fast enough to make a run for it from subs. Pretty heavily armed with a tried gun crew.

Out into the Pacific, continually changing our course, down into dangerous waters, through the Coral Sea, stopped at New Caledonia for a day to land some troops and pick up some more, then to Australia, stopping at Brisbane for supplies and to pick up some Aussies (we had crossed the Equator some time before this), then out to sea again in the South Pacific, all the way around Australia into the Indian Ocean up to Freemantle where we stopped two days, then out again into the Arabian Sea and finally landed at Bombay day before yesterday. Had a light cruiser and two corvettes as an escort from Australia to India as the territory was pretty dangerous at this time. Ceylon had just been bombed pretty well and I suppose they were a little worried.

We immediately got on a train after leaving the ship and rode about 8 hours into the interior to this British camp where we'll get our rifles and then push on. It was quite a trip, about 40 days in all.

Highlights of the cruise. The food was all right, only two meals a day, but as a rule, they were very good.

Only lost five men on the entire voyage, one man fell overboard, one was killed in a fight in Australia, one died on the operating table, and the other two just died, I guess.

Crossed the equator twice, boiling hot one day and three days later you'd freeze at night.

When we crossed the International Date Line, on Sept. 30, the next day automatically become October 2. A great amount of the troops are from below the Mason-Dixon Line and they're still trying to figure out where that day went.

Saw a couple of whales one day, sharks were around us a few times but outside of these very little marine life.

Had to wear a life jacket and our cartridge belt and canteen full of water at all times during the voyage. Had boat drill and abandon ship drill about every day.

The ship took on the aspect of a four-decked gambling casino as soon as we left. Crap games by the dozen, poker games, chuck a luck. Black Jack, Crown & Anchor for the British and Aussies, everything. Some pretty good scores made, too. One Greek lad won 15 grand, several of the boys won two or three and a good many won pretty well into the hundreds. I never got very far but there was a hell of an opportunity for anyone who got lucky.

The saddest news I got on the voyage was when the Yanks beat the Cards 4 out of 5. I don't know what the hell happened. I figured St. Louis was a breeze.

The prettiest sight of the trip was pulling into Brisbane. Up a long winding river, rich green land and spotless white dwellings on either bank, into a beautiful harbor with hundreds of craft dotting the waters. English, Dutch, French and American ships by the score all with their colors and pennons fluttering in the wind.

I've seen many a sky that was beautiful at day's end, the Golden Gate in Frisco, the Tropical sunsets in Trinidad and Puerto Rico, but when the sun goes down over the horizon in the Indian Ocean, for my money its the grandest spectacle in the world.

We ran into a hell of a storm at sea before reaching Australia. Makes you feel pretty small watching those huge waves break and listening to the angry swish of the sea against the ship. Quite a few of the lads got sea sick but it didn't have any effect on a stomach that has stood up under Prohibition and bath-tub gin.

We figure that with all the maneuvering and dodging we did around the various oceans, we must have covered about 15,000 miles on the water. That's enough water for me.

Now, our hardships start. We're at a British camp and live on British rations. No coffee, no American bread or fresh vegetables, nothing that an American camp supplies. The only meat is water buffalo and that's tougher than Oscar Bush's place and show prices. There's a country wide famine here, millions starving and all the while there's some 200 million cows walking around.

They're sacred, you can't kill them, there's even a prison penalty for hunting them. And as they can't be butchered, and as cows will be cows, I suppose, you can't even sneeze in India without a cow saying "Gesundheit" or it's bovine equivalent.

The beggars are terrible. Armless, legless, blind, diseased, horrible looking creatures all clutching at your arms or falling on the ground grabbing your legs, begging for alms. When we docked at Bombay kids came out in boats and begged for food to be thrown over the side where they'd dive for it. Then on the train ride, all along the tracks, thousands lined up with their arms outstretched, on their knees, imploring you for *annas*. Kids three or four years old and ancients of 90 all begging. And it's all a racket, I'm afraid.

We got into a small town last night, and their Holiday Season is on. New Years, I think. Boy, oh boy. Whirling dervishes, native pipers with screaming pipes, a painted sacred bull led around the town, mongoose and snake fights, and hundreds of merchants crying their wares and bargaining down to the last *anna* for each sale. They start asking 30 *rupees* for something you finally get for 6. If you don't jew them down, they think that you must be crazy. One merchant asked 15 *rupees* for a knife and when a soldier gave it to him, he fell off his bench in sheer amazement. It stunned him.

You can ride from town back to camp in a *tonga* which is a two wheeled cart for 4 *annas*. That's 8 cents. And the infidel of a driver whips the horses, little ones about the size of our ponies, every foot of the way. I guess there's nothing sacred about the horses.

...The latrines in camp are right in keeping with the rest of the accommodations. They're made of stone, with a hole hewed in the middle, a ledge on each side, and an opening at the back where the native attendant reaches in and removes the old reliable pot when he considers it quite full enough. When natures call comes, you spring up on the ledges and straddle the opening, right through your knees and pray for speedy success as any more than two minutes in there without a gas mask would probably result in asphyxiation. One of the reasons I keep this diary is that if in the future I should ever tend to get romantic and wistful about places like this I can always refresh my memory as to exactly how sweet it all was.

We are now at Deogarh, a camp carved out of the wildest part of country I've ever been in. Composed of tents, put up by Indian workers in an area about two square miles that was cleared by the engineers in less than three weeks. Left Saturday night and arrived Monday afternoon at about two o'clock after the god-damdest train ride I ever want to have. Forty hours in a dirty, vermin infested rattle trap coach, baking at day and freezing at night, thru a hundred towns, mostly populated from the looks of the stations crowds, by beggars, cripples and starving children. About 600 miles into the interior, thru forests and deserts. The wildlife is abundant, peopled with beautifully colored birds of all descriptions, spotted deer, bands of monkeys, jackals and what not, all visible from the train, which averaged about 15 miles an hour. When we arrived, we set right out for camp, about ten miles from the depot, thru woods and brush carrying a full field pack. It was pretty dark when we got there and starting to get cold. We got a tent, put up our cots, and went to sleep but not for long. Cold? These tropical jungleers woke up screaming from it then piled every bit of covering they could find over them but still no soap. By three o'clock there were a dozen fires going in the area with half frozen, cursing dog-faces bewailing the day they ever volunteered for anything like this. Nobody got thawed out until two hours after the sun got hot and then it was about 100 in the shade. What a joint.

India, my ass.

Thanksgiving Day, 1943 arrives, and for some reason, Hartigan fails to get into the spirit of the holiday.

There never was a colder night than last night. About two o'clock the jackals started howling in protest and were shortly joined by the wolves and from the roars, an occasional tiger. They were born and raised here and when they kick about the weather, you can imagine what these G.I. gripers say about it. Before turning in last night we sat around talking about things in general and someone ventured the opinion that if those of us got back ever started telling some of the screwy things that happened to us here, no one would believe it. I said that I had kept a diary and that they'd better believe. Dempsey, a dissolute, wise-cracking harp, who sleeps beside me asked "no kidding, do you keep a diary"? I said yes and he said "That's fine. Leave me two quarts of Grade A every morning." For some reason that struck me as the funniest thing I've heard in years. I laughed so hard I forgot about the weather for fifteen minutes.

This morning we fell out in the cold darkness at 6:15. Everybody stood there and forgot to shiver as they listened to the most astounding Thanksgiving address any American, soldier or civilian, ever heard. We were told that anybody who had any field rations left over from our train ride and were found hoarding them would be subject to a court martial. This is on a Thanksgiving morning 12,000 miles from home and roast turkey.

Invoking the Articles of War for concealing a can of cold beans and three soda crackers.

It has taken awhile, but gradually they begin to learn the purpose of their presence, beyond being poster children for the joys of dysentery.

12 January 1944
Up and around altho still a little wobbly. Lord Louis Mountbatten, Supreme Commander of all the Asiatic Forces blew into camp last night and talked to the men this morning. Had a barrage of camera men and correspondents with him in addition to his staff which was composed of more generals than I've ever see in one place. He gave a hell of a nice talk, told us what we were

scheduled to do in Burma and took a very optimistic view of the war in general.

Lord Mountbatten and Gen. Frank Merrill (Hartigan Collection)

A fine looking man, about 45 I should judge, but looks much younger, has a nice easy way of talking, a ready smile and a good sense of humor, you can easily see why he's so popular with everybody. Has one of the most enviable records of any soldier in this war, head of the Commandos, Admiral, and active in 3 or 4 different theaters. Told us that there was plenty of help on the way in the line of men, ships and modern aircraft. Said that the Japs take great pleasure in dying for their country and that he counted on us to make a lot of them well pleased. This looks like the last pep talk before we hit into the jungles for actual combat. Hope my strength gets back quickly. Had a few slugs of grain alcohol that one of the boys stole somewhere, 180 proof. Whew!

16 Jan.

Preparations are being made to move. All the loose ends are being tied up and the tremendous detail of getting ready for the final phase is taking place. The mules and horses have arrived, have been broken (a hell of a lot of fun watching them throw those packs and drivers around the area while they're breaking them) checking of arms and equipment and a million other things that have to be done. This Gen. Merrill is a fast moving guy, gets things done in a hurry. He practically reorganized the whole camp in 3 weeks time. Only awaiting transportation now on the long way to Burma and if lucky, China. This damn stomach of mine still gets cramped up and is pretty sore yet from that dysentery episode. Still weak but able to get around. Visited a couple of temples in the neighborhood yesterday, one built in the fifth century. Gives you a strange feeling at night standing in the ruins of a civilization that flourished 1500 years ago. Some of the figures are in remarkably good condition. You wonder how they could have withstood the ravages of centuries of this Indian sun and rain and cold.

Feb. 2, 1944

We arrived here on Jan. 30, at Panitola , a little village in Upper Assam, near the Burma border. Were delayed a day en route due to a train wreck just ahead of us. Don't know whether the wreck was planned for us or not. Suppose so. Anyway we spent the day and night at a British camp near by, bivouacked with a Chinese Artillery Co. and part of the 7th Air Force, composed of American and Chinese. Cole and I had an Indian soldier who ran errands for us and did everything to make our stay pleasant. A hell of a nice little fellow, stayed right with us and when we left went with us to the train and seemed genuinely sorry to see us go.

Crossed another river by ferry, then further into N.E. India for three days on another ramshackle train crowded as bad as ever. The people look different up here, cleaner and brighter. This is the big tea country, plantation after plantation.

Had to work like hell after getting here, unloading all supplies, setting up tents and getting organized.

A cemetery right near camp and I had a hunch when I see it. Climbed the fence and walked past a hundred crosses right to Don Wemple's grave. He's buried right in the midst of a group of fliers, the inscription on the cross reading

Donald L. Wemple
0-793470   2nd Lt. U.S.A.
Died June 26, 1943

The cemetery is fenced in, bordered with hedges, quiet and peaceful.

This is a tough country for fliers. The Himalayas stretch all around us and visibility is generally very poor, most of the flying has to be done by instruments so there's many a crash. The big field is at Dinjan about two miles away. Planes are in the air all the time, we had our first alert already. The bombers work out of here everyday. This is a combat area, the Japs are twenty minutes from here by air, and they have patrols out all the while. The rest of the outfit must have left Deogarh by now, they will push into the jungles and hills as soon as we establish proper communications. There's some liquor around but they want 40 rupees a qt. Too goddam much for a P.F.C.'s pay.

Lt. Donald Wemple grew up in Gloversville, but married an Amsterdam girl, Doris Johnson, who lives at 9 Mohawk Place when his plane goes down. He had been engaged in transport work from India to China, flying "over the hump." An engine catches fire while transiting the mountains, and he tries to bring it home on one engine rather than abandon the ship. The plane crashes. He survives long enough to chat with the Catholic chaplain, who later writes to the widow. Though not Catholic himself, Wemple prays with him nonetheless. And though they have never previously met, the chaplain already knows all about him, for Don Wemple had earned a pretty decent reputation before the war in the National Football League as a "crashing end" for the old Brooklyn Dodgers.

Feb. 7

It's rained every day since we've been here. A cold, steady downpour, makes everything miserable. Mud up to your knees everywhere you go. The monsoon can't be a hell of a lot worse. One of our officers got killed the other day when a reconnaissance plane was shot up but got back all right but Capt. Farley and another guy got hit with a burst of machine gun bullets. Nice guy, too. The columns are about ready to move. The natives here are a strange bunch. A lot of them are supposed to be Jap sympathizers so we don't mingle with them. They're all barred from the camp, just in case.

Feb. 10

The 10th Air Force is sure getting a workout. The squadrons at these fields, anyway. Every day they take off, the Liberators and Mustangs and hours afterward they come home, sometimes all in one piece, sometimes limping and with one or two missing. The little cemetery is filling much too rapidly. Two more yesterday and they are only the ones that manage to get back. Of course we don't hear any news of other activities but judge from what goes on around here that the Burma campaign is on in full swing. The columns have set out and must be a good ways into the brush. Soon we'll know just how good the unit is.

Hartigan stays behind in the Headquarters Company as Merrill's men perform the near-impossible, pushing their way through hundreds of miles of jungle to attack the Japanese forces in Burma from the rear. The goal is to clear the enemy from northern Burma so that the old road link to China may open up a flow of supplies to the embattled Chinese who up until now have been surviving on the limited cargo flights from India.

Merrill's forces are supplied from periodic air drops into jungle clearings.

Feb. 21

The first air-dropping to the columns took place today. That's the job of this rear echelon, to get supplies to the lads in the jungle. We have communications all working now, they let us know their position and the biscuit bombers take off with food, ammo, etc. Seven C-47s took the first load out and made it OK. Ran into some trouble and one ship limped back with about 30 holes in her frame. No casualties, tho. Hell of a rainstorm last night, damn near blew the tents down. But at least we have tents. That's more than those guys in the columns have. Afraid they're in for a tough time.

The food is surprisingly good, right now. Get fresh meat twice a week which is made into stew of course but it's not bad at all. And we get eggs right along. They're not like eggs back home, but they resemble them enough to satisfy us. And oatmeal. I used to wonder how people ate it. I could never look at it in the morning, especially after a hangover, but it sure is a delicacy now.

Melvyn Douglas, who is a Captain in Special Service in this area, showed up with a swing band of G.I.'s from Karachi the other night and they put on a hell of a good performance. A real, hot, orchestra, who if they manage to hang together and live thru this, should do something in the U.S. after the war. That other troupe, who gave the show in Deogarh, were all killed in a plane crash last week.

The jackals howl all the night around the camp and they sound pretty weird when you're working the night shift, which I'm doing. And wildcats sneak right into camp when they smell the meat, and drag away bones. A couple of them jumped a G.I. at Khanjikoa and clawed the hell out him the other night. Didn't kill him but didn't do him any good either. There are tigers and leopards in the hills but haven't seen any yet. And don't particularly care if I never see them. The jackals are bad enough, yelping outside your tent, if a tiger should ever stick his snout in a flap, I'd probably have dysentery all over again.

Feb. 25
One of our biscuit bombers knocked down today. Everybody killed. Young Painter, a nice kid and a good friend was among them. R.I.P.

March 3
Busy week. Communications pretty fair with columns who are now behind Jap lines. Supplies are flown out daily, the only way they can get them in the jungle. Have lost two of the big transports so far as its pretty dangerous flying. The other night, supplies were to be dropped around midnight but were signaled back when over the troops, owing to the nearness of Japs and the danger of flares lighting up our area. But yesterday 45 tons were dropped without a mishap and now with plenty of ammunition Merrill is planning on attacking, one battalion from the left, one from the right while the other cleans up in the rear. He moves

pretty fast and everything so far is going according to his schedule. Tomorrow should tell a lot. Several casualties so far, mostly from patrols. If this mission shows up the way Merrill thinks it will, and we are able to move on steadily, supplied entirely from the air, it means that these tactics will be adopted for jungle fighting by everyone for the balance of the war. It's all right here at present only the food stinks.

6 March

Merrill is raising hell. Using the planes from Dinjan, 51's and Mitchells, to good advantage. He deployed the columns in such a way as to take a good sized town, knock off plenty of Japs and escape with only a few casualties. The Japs are sore as hell at the Burmese in the area and have fined every home ten pounds of rice and shot one member of every family in any area suspected of giving help to our troops. Merrill doesn't want any prisoners. Kill the bastards, he says.

The drops are going along o.k. now, getting plenty of ammo and other supplies to him. He radioed us today saying that the cooperation made it possible for the success of the raid. These guys have worked like hell, packing those chutes and then flying over and kicking them out. Communications are kept up pretty good, altho it's a tough country for these radio sets. Everybody has his own special job which has to be done but I miss those guys in the column and hope to hell I get a chance to get out there with them pretty soon. No chance right now, tho, as our set-up here is going along smoothly and they want it kept that way.

11 March

Everything okay. Merrill claims plenty of Japs. And Hancock giving us the report of the movement says the verified Jap casualties are over 2000 of which at least 1200 are killed. Seems impossible but it's down in the official records. Merrill has out-foxed them every move he made and we dropped enough stuff to enable him to throw everything he wanted at them. These jungleers have finally found something they can do besides getting drunk.

12 March

The correspondents have filed their stories on the outfit and we are known as "Merrill's Marauders." Lots of praise for the boys, called the toughest infantry outfit in the service. Stillwell says they're the goddamndest roughest looking bunch of bastards he's ever seen! The papers marvel over the box score, over 2000 Japs against fifty or sixty of our men. They mess the Japs up pretty well, too. Kick their ugly little faces in. If there's any atrocities committed, they do their share.

And then comes the news from home. The war, for the moment, is forgotten and Hartigan is inconsolable.

14 March

Mother is dead.

Got a letter from Jenny today, the first mail in weeks.

I'm sick all over.

Don't know what to do.

I'm going to take off somewhere and get plenty drunk.

I could stand anything, I thought, but not this.

The only reason I kept my nose clean all this while was to see the look in her eyes when I came home, without a black mark against me. To give her the first chance she's ever had to be proud of me.

Now, the hell with it.

Here, understandably, the diary stops for a while, even as Merrill's Marauders keep doing their stuff.

15 April

Went up the Ledo road with Capt. Benfield yesterday. The wounded are in the 20th Gen. Hospital, about 130 of them from my battalion. When we got there and I walked in, there was one concerted yell. They're all there, Stine, Arback, Zaino, Hughes, Hahn, Reed, Cadamo, and all the others that came from my outfit in Trinidad. All shot to hell but all in pretty good spirits. 13 days they were cut off in those jungles, no water half the time, dug in their foxholes with the Japs pouring artillery fire to them all the time.

Our Japanese interpreters did wonderful work, calling the shots perfectly when the nips made their changes.

Hahn, on a heavy machine gun mowed down over a hundred Japs on one charge alone and accounted for a good many more until a heavy shell exploded near him and broke both eardrums and put him out of commission. . . .

When he saw me, his face lit up. But when he found out I didn't have any whiskey with me, he was heartbroken.

Zaino was so glad to see me, he threw his good arm around my shoulders and did everything but kiss me. His right arm is shattered.

All the others have shrapnel in them, some pretty bad. They had a hell of an ordeal.

A correspondent told me they were the cruelest bunch of soldiers he's ever seen in action.

I'm going to Tinsukia today and buy some native whiskey and try to get it up to them tomorrow. That's all they want. They used to call us the "Stew" regiment but they've found out what these boys can do when the chips are down.

I had some dough saved to buy Jenny some Indian jewelry but when she realizes that it went for liquor for these kids who really need it, she'd rather I did that.

I guess we won't get home, after all. It's tough, but it looks as tho they need us for the next campaign.

There were official photographers here to take moving pictures of the way the columns were supplied from the air. The War Dept. said it couldn't be done but we dood it.

17 April
Got up to the hospital again yesterday and brought the liquor. Boy, did that stuff go. While I was there, the air raid sirens started and we had to put the badly wounded under beds and the others had to go out and hit the trenches. They didn't get near us, tho, the interceptors chased them the hell home. Hahn & I took a quart to the shelter and had a very nice air raid.

26 April
The boys have joined forces with the chinks and are mopping up before moving on Mainwing to take that air field there. Had another alert the other night and did all right. The N.C.O. has a club, a *basha* that they've thrown up and serves liquor. When the alert sounded, the lights went out and I found myself right beside a qt. of booze. Took it to a trench and enjoyed the attack fire immensely.

A train hit a G.I. truck the other day and piled freight cars all over our area.

This morning a P-51 failed to pull out of a dive and hit the ground about 500 yds. from the tent, doing about 700 M.P.H. Not much left of it.

I seem to have lost about all the interest I had in the Army. Things have been pretty empty since I heard about Mother. Don't feel like doing anything except grab what whiskey might be floating around.

18 May
Transports landed yesterday on the air strip at Myitkyina, the main objective of this campaign. After 4 months of bitter jungle fighting it looks as tho Merrill's Marauders have accomplished their mission. Capt. Benfield's bunch, known as Benfield's Bastards,

have been flown to guard the field while fighting still goes on around that area. About 3000 Japs still around there but we've got artillery and Stillwell's chinks and some fresh infantry to mop them up. Everybody's pretty happy about it. Plenty of casualties, of course, but it was well worth it, taking in the nips at their own special warfare and pasting the BeJesus out of them. In a short time we'll be leaving for a new spot, a rest camp and training center where they'll figure out the lessons learned in the campaign and get ready to head into China in the fall.

An Indian officer died the other day and his company piled up a bunch of logs and burned the body about 50 feet from where I was sleeping. Don't know what they sprinkled him with but it smelt terrible all night. In the morning the GI's were poking around the ashes for souvenirs. Nice lads.

This climate is a bitch. It rains for days until there's a sea of mud. Takes an hour to walk half a mile, you sink right in the slime up to your knees. Then the sun comes out and the temperature goes up to about 120. Too hot to breathe and no shade anywhere. If you drink any of the liquor, when the sun hits you, it makes your head spin and turns your stomach every which way. I've had some goddam tough days, but if I don't drink, I get pretty lonely. I still got that empty feeling when I think of Mother.

Whiskey helps, even this stinking native rotgut.

22 May

Lovely day yesterday. Was routed out early with a fierce hangover from the Dekam Death. A hot sticky day and the smell coming from a couple of Indians that they cremated during the night didn't help any. Then had to take shots for Cholera & Typhus and Smallpox, leaving both arms sore as hell. Then an air raid, which didn't amount to anything but was inconvenient. In the afternoon we got a preview of the monsoon. A rainstorm with the wind blowing things thru the air like a Kansas twister. In the middle of the storm a bolt of lightning struck the camp, knocked about 15 G.I.'s out but no one was killed. There was a foot & a half of water in our tent, everything we own floating around like toy boats in a pond. Together with this, I got an attack of the ?????????????. Beautiful.

25 May
A high class Burmese family father, mother, & 6 children who had been Jap prisoners for 2 years were flew by one of our planes from Myitkyina to the camp yesterday. They sure were thrilled to see Americans. He was a high Govt. official in Rangoon and when the nips invaded, they fled to Myitkyina where they where eventually captured. Nice people, well educated. They'd better get those girls out of here, tho. They don't know it but they're in more danger here than they were from the nips.

29 May
The Japs are putting up a stubborn fight for Myitkyina. They've dug in pretty well and have to be blasted out of every hole. They know better than to surrender.

Lost two more transports. Both evidently got caught in those treacherous winds and were smashed into a mountain side. Parker and his crew and Ross and his crew. All good guys. Drinking and laughing one night and the next piled up on a mountain in Burma where you never can get to them.

Everybody is sour on Stillwell. Now that we've done all we were asked to do, he's claiming all the credit for his chinks. Nobody wants any pats on the back but it's funny to see Vinegar Joe decorating Chinese by the dozens and telling correspondents what wonderful fighters they are and never mentioning a word about Galahad. Merrill is in the hospital again and I guess he's pretty disgusted. The minute he was evacuated Stillwell put his own men in charge and nobody likes the idea. He's been in China and Burma so long he looks and acts like a chink.

When the Catholic chaplain of Merrill's Marauders dies in the jungle of scrub typhus, Albany priest Father Edward R. Glavin is immediately recruited to take his place. They fly the future pastor of St. Mary's Church from New York straight to India and into the jungle to serve with the American forces in Burma. Facing every kind of physical deprivation and hardship, he marches with the men some 750 miles on foot through largely trackless wilderness, and this without having undergone jungle training.

On his 80th birthday, in 1992, Msgr. Glavin tells the *Evangelist*, the newspaper of the Albany Roman Catholic Diocese, "I never talked about the war. It's impossible to picture unless you were there. I was concerned for soldiers of every faith. I would conduct Mass when there was the opportunity. It was rough physical service. My experiences were so bizarre and varied that I never talk about them."[9]

But on one occasion in 1996, a year before his death, he writes to a younger brother of a Merrill's Marauder who had died in the war:

> It was next to impossible to describe how dangerous and difficult our operation was. The unit cut its way through uncharted jungle and over mountain ranges; through territory where there were no roads and no trails. Conscious that we were in Japanese occupied territory, there was the constant danger of ambush. In an ambush, the Japanese always killed first anyone who seemed to have any authority. So we wore a special jungle fatigue and everyone dressed alike from private to colonel. We wore no insignia of any kind because of that. I wore no Chaplain's cross, but looked the same as any other soldier. In that I was fulfilling the orders given by the commanding general. We crossed the Schweli River at flood stage on a bridge made of bamboo and jungle vines. When we arrived at the Burma Road, we were too small a unit to go out and block it, so we set up our units on five little mountain tops along side the Road from which we could interdict the Road. When the Japanese withdrew south, we were flown over the Hump into China to serve with Chinese Combat Command until the end of the War. We were spread out all over China. The 475th had

9   http://www.evangelist.org/archive/hm/0626glav.htm

marched single file through the jungle and achieved a great victory over the Japanese.[10]

Glavin would serve as National Chaplain for the China/Burma/India and Merrill's Marauders veterans for the rest of his long life.

Chaplain Glavin is just one of many replacements brought in to augment the beleaguered troops.

12 June
Our replacements are here and a bunch of them were sent right into action. Flew them to Myitkyina, where fighting is still going on. The Japs are dug in deeper than we thought and it's a hell of a job smoking them out. The new troops are green and are having a bad time so far. They don't keep down and it's suicide when you walk in on these bastards; they're pretty good with those knee mortars and .25 machine guns.

We still have about 500 men around Myitkyina and when they get out, we'll probably move to a rest camp. Lots of talk about going home, but that's too much to expect.

The outfit is pretty well shot, tho. Typhus is taking a big toll. All the hospitals in the area are treating our men but they keep on dying. They can't seem to stop it, once it shows up. It probably comes from the leeches which get into your skin pretty deep, the only way you can get them out is to burn them with the end of a cigarette. The men's resistance is pretty low and they just kick off. We're going to lose more thru typhus than thru battle action, I'm afraid. Plenty of malaria, too, but that's never fatal. The medics think we should be sent home for a long rest. Well, when Myitkyina falls we'll probably know just what the story is on what we're to do. Cole won a chunk of *rupees* at Shaduzup and we had a hell of a time visiting the towns of Dubruganh and Tinsukia, got plenty of gin and ate a couple of Chinese restaurants out of business.

---

10 http://lippertbrothers.com/files/Glavin.pdf

27 July

Things have been pretty quiet. The boys have started to go home on the 2 year rotation plan. Fonda left with the first group this morning. They're all pretty excited and no wonder. Some of them haven't been back for over 3 years. We are still blasting away at Myitkyina. The nips are dug in there right. And they won't quit. They sure got plenty of guts, this bunch. If they're not killed, they've got to starve eventually, as we got them shut off. The town should fall this week, but you can't bet on it. These monkeys are tough and crazy.

16 August

Lots of fun lately. Myitkyina fell the 3rd of Aug. after banging away at it for 78 days. The Japs held out to the last, had to kill all of them that didn't get out. All of the boys are back together and the gin and rum has been flowing freely. The men with two years overseas service are going back to the States. Don't know what's in store for the rest of us. Probably a campaign that will extend to Rangoon. Stillwell has been made a 4 Star General much to everybody's disgust.

Their mission over, Hartigan and company spend nearly three weeks building up fuzzy memories.

20 Sept. 1944
CALCUTTA

I've been here in Calcutta now for 10 days. Finally got a furlough and on Sept. 10 we boarded a plane in Chabua and after 4 hours of flying through rain storms and fog over a country that is flooded from the monsoons, we arrived in Calcutta. What a town! We got here at night and as we couldn't wait to start carousing. Kenny and I didn't report to the rest camp where we're supposed to stay but immediately started looking for drinks and fun. The entire city is blacked out at night and it's amazing how people get around.

Thousands of rickshaws, *gharrys* and taxicabs weave in and out of the streets and go like hell in total darkness. We managed to get something to eat and some drinks and when the drinking places closed, went to Park Circus where the camp is, checked in and got a bed. The camp is nice but too confining so the next day we took off with our stuff and got a couple of beds uptown in the Red Cross right in the center of things.

Called Dennis right away, but he was in China on business. The next day he returned however and got in touch with me that night. What a reunion!! He looks great, has an important navy job, a warrant officers rating and a beautiful setup. Knows a lot of prominent people, progressive, intelligent Indians, whom I've met and enjoy. They certainly know how to entertain, your glass is never empty. Every day we've gone somewhere and have a few favorite drinking places where we sit and cut up old torches over tall gin drinks. We had some scotch saved and we got rid of it the first day. But gin is the best bet. They have 2 or 3 good brands and it's the best thing to drink in this climate. Was out to the Naval Bldg. a few times and met a lot of his associates and friends. All have ratings and all are swell guys especially Frank's immediate superior, Vic Ellis, a Chicago boy, who goes down in the book as a real two fisted drinking man.

We rode around the city a few times and took in the historical spots and points of interest. Did this rather hurriedly as it interfered with our drinking. The port is something to see, the river is literally choked with ships. The Black Hole of Calcutta, the Burning Ghats where they incinerate the dead a hundred at a time, the Thieves Market where everything that is stolen one day is put on sale the next, the old cathedrals and mosques and obelisks, the crowds of a half million men worshiping *en masse* on the holidays, the balloons strung all around the city, the picturesque Sikh cab drivers who tear thru the city at breakneck speed, the Holy Men lying on the sidewalks, the miles of bazaars and jewel houses, all these things are interesting but none so impressive, to my mind, as the sight of a bearer coming toward you with a tray containing the gin, lime, and soda, and a bucket of ice. Oh, that blessed ice.

21 Sept.

Nice quiet night for a change. About 7 p.m. we went to the Great Eastern Hotel, one of the showplaces of the town in peace time. Had a couple of drinks in the lounge and then dinner in the main dining room, a huge place with gleaming chandeliers, hundreds of fans and paneled mirrors on all sides. The food was good, also the drinks, and a damn fine orchestra! At the close of the evening they played a flock of American folk songs and Dennis and I harmonized just as tho it were Coogan's, 10,000 miles away. The orchestra finished as usual with the American and British National Anthems and everyone stood stiffly at attention altho I found it difficult as Frank kept pinching my bottom all thru "God Save The King." Drove thru the town afterwards. The natives sleep on the sidewalks by the thousands in this hot weather and when we'd turn the jeep lights on, you could see droves of rats, big grey ones, scampering over the sleeping forms. It doesn't seem to bother them a bit, tho.

Sept. 30

Back in Dinjan. Our leave was cut short. Left Calcutta the 27th and had to make the trip back by rail. A lousy ride and I do mean LOUSY. A million roaches in every car. But I didn't mind. The vacation was well worth it. Had one of the swellest times I've ever spent. Sorry as hell to leave, but when we arrived here, found out that all the old outfit is going home and that we may leave here for the States within a week. Sounds pretty good.

Oct. 20

KARACHI

Well, we're on our way. Left Dinjan Oct. 11 and arrived here yesterday at noon after 9 days travel on these Indian railroads. Pretty rough trip but interesting at times. Went thru New Delhi and other big cities, had two river crossings by ferry, the Ganges and the Brahmaputra and crossed the Sand Desert, which was goddam dusty and hot. Thousands of camels and elephants along the route, all working. We will leave here by groups, fly all the way.

Oct. 26

Still at Karachi, awaiting our planes. This is all right, good food and bunks only it's about 20 miles to town. Nice city, probably the most modern in India. Had a swell time the last two days, went down to the harbor and hired a sailboat and went fishing and then swimming in the Arabian Sea. Caught 64 fish the first time out, you just drop in a line and pull it in with a fish on it. All small, of course but a lot of fun. The beach is grand, miles of level ground with the surf breaking in tremendous rolls as far as you can see. Met an old Indian sea-faring man who had lived in America for a time, a Capt. Jackson, very interesting and very friendly to us. Has some presents to give us when and if we go down there again.

Nov. 7

FORT DIX

Well here I am in the U.S. again, in a hospital.

We left Karachi the morning of October 28 in a C-46, first stop was at Abaden, Iran. The biggest oil refineries in the world are there, on the Persian Gulf. It's also the hottest place in the world, gets 180 at times according to what some officers were telling me. After lunch we took off again, over Iraq, Palestine, the Syrian Desert, Suez Canal, and landed at Cairo that night. Lovely city. The next day we went on a tour through the town and then out to visit the Pyramids and Sphinx. Very impressive. Around the airport and camps they have Italian prisoners of war doing all the work. Seem happy enough about it. We took off that night, stopped at Tripoli for fuel and coffee, then on again, over the N. Africa battle grounds and landed in Casablanca around noon on the 31st. Went to town, looked over the old and new Casablanca, saw the hotel where Roosevelt and Churchill had their conference, also went thru the Sultan of Morocco's summer palace, the grounds are beautiful and set in the center of it is a tea house, supposedly the finest in the world, of thousands of pieces of mosaic and crowned by beautiful sandalwood roofing, where F.D.R. and Churchill were entertained by the Sultans. The weather got cold at Casablanca and I wasn't dressed for it and caught a bad cold. Left Casablanca Nov. 2, stopped at the Azores, then on to Stevensville, Newfoundland, my cold getting worse all the while. When we hit N.Y., I had a temperature of 104 and after getting to Dix instead of coming home was thrown in the hospital.

Here Pfc. Hartigan's war journal ends. He quickly recovers from his illness, and after an absence of over two years, he returns to Amsterdam and promptly marries his sweet Genevieve that December.

And they live happily ever after.

Genevieve and Ed Hartigan

8. UNITEDS ON THE BALL!

Upon the fields of friendly strife
Are sown the seeds
That, upon other fields, on other days
Will bear the fruits of victory.

                    -Douglas MacArthur

When the men of the Bigelow-Sanford Uniteds walk off their soccer field on December 7, 1941 they know what they have to do. Sure, they're vying for the championship of soccer's National League and the State Cup, but duty comes first. Some of their teammates are already serving: Paul Sykes under the draft in 1940 and Hank Whitney in February of 1941. Some of their biggest fans, social members of the club, like Arnie Eckelman and Eugene LaJeunesse, have been in the Navy for a while already and had front row seats at Pearl Harbor.

Bernard Cooper is the first to go after war is declared, on January 3rd, to the Navy. He ends up protecting those dangerous supply runs to Murmansk to relieve our Soviet allies. In early February the "Four Horsemen," Johnny Campbell, "Bus" Murdoch, Pierce Tolson and Louis Sykes all enlist on the same day, and Jim Jasper two days later, and "Peanuts" Brown, Tommy Wood and Eddie Fretchner before the month is out. Many, many more follow.

Almost as an after-thought, the younger guys left behind, some of them the younger brothers, go on to become the first non-New York City team to become champions of the National League. Then they start joining up, too.

THE UNITED'S P. X.

ISSUED MONTHLY

For the Members of Bigelow-Sanford Soccer Club in the Armed Forces

AMSTERDAM, N. Y.

Back Row (left to right)—Sam McDade, Manager; Edward McKnight, J. Arthur Campbell, Howard Dynes, Stewart McKnight, William Slagus, Carl Russo, Donald Campbell, James McKnight, James Conner.

Front Row (left to right)—Warner Wicke, Milton Yates, William McKnight, Captain; Lindsay Johnston, Thomas Guest, Pierce Tolson, David Guest, Cecil Holland, Daniel Murdoch, Walter Campbell.

Players Not in Picture—Harold Brown, John Campbell, Harry Tolson, Jr., Orville Smith, William Hrycaj, John Hanna, Edwin McKnight.

So many of the boys from the club and the Dutch Hill neighborhood have gone that the folks behind start a monthly newsletter to keep them up to date on the happenings back home and each other. *The Uniteds PX* becomes so popular that club membership expands dramatically, and what starts out as a two-page ditto sheet grows to a polished sometimes 20-page printed letter from home with original graphics, poetry, jokes and a continuing "Bible Story" by Editor in Chief Gavin "Guy" Murdoch, an executive at Mohawk Carpets (and father of Daniel "Bus" Murdoch), writing under pseudonym, tracing the history of the Uniteds and the origins of the families involved, as though it had been written by the authors of the King James edition.

Even by 1941 the exact origins of the Bigelow-Sanford Uniteds Soccer Club have been lost in the mists of history. Some of the players have grandfathers who had played with the club in the decades before the turn of the 20th century, skilled mill workers who had come from England and Scotland and Northern Ireland to work for the Sanfords and the Shuttleworths and McCleary, Wallin and Crouse making carpets to be shipped out all over the world. It's altogether possible that in their home countries their families had been playing variations of the game for hundreds of years, as recorded references in the British Isles date back to the ninth century.

Around the turn of the 20th century the fathers of the World War II era guys had begun playing in the Central New York Soccer League, taking home 14 championships starting in 1904-05, and so dominating the league in the 30's that by 1940 they are somewhat politely asked to leave and give somebody else a chance. They also field a city champion hockey team (1940).

The surnames of McKnight and Campbell and Dynes and Tolson and others have been legendary in local sports circles for some seventy years. Only the faces change.

John "Soup" Campbell is pegged early as officer material and is sent off to OCS, where he emerges as a 2nd Lieutenant, leading a platoon in Company M of the 105th Regiment of the 27th Division, composed mostly of the former National Guard company from Gloversville. He even has a couple of Amsterdam guys in his platoon. Sykes and Tolson are quickly trained as gunners on B-26 bombers. Sykes goes east, Tolson goes west.

G. Pierce Tolson, maybe the shortest guy in soccer's National League, more than makes up for his structural disadvantage with raw courage on the field, the same as he displays as a gunner. In May of 1943 his assigned B-26, piloted by 1st Lt. William Crawford of Niles, Ohio, engages in an armed reconnaissance flight over New Britain Island in the Southwest Pacific. Six enemy planes sit parked on an airfield, perfect targets for their bombs. They score a direct hit on one and two near misses.

Then, the plane lurches violently, struck by anti-aircraft fire. The pilot heads into the clouds as smoke begins to fill the cockpit. One shell hits just beneath the pilot's seat, another lucks its way through the partially open bomb-bay and explodes inside the airship.

A fire breaks out on the floor. Staff Sgt. Tolson yells for a fire extinguisher.

He grabs for the extinguisher, but the pressure is gone. The fire is dangerously close to the ammunition. There being no obvious option, Tolson beats the flames with his bare hands.

Crawford, worried that the fires might ignite a fused bomb, tries to manually fully release the bomb-bay door. The handle comes off in his hand. Finally, with the help of the rest of the crew, they are able to push that fire overboard and, with a functioning fire extinguisher, put out the blaze in the nose fire.

The 23 year old Tolson's prior employment experience had been as a clerical worker in the Shuttleworth Division of Mohawk Carpets. Eventually he completes 47 missions between February 23 and December 18, 1943, receiving in addition to his Purple Heart, for the burns to his hands, a Presidential Unit Citation, Air Medal and Distinguished Flying Cross for extraordinary achievement.

Meanwhile, over the Mediterranean, Tolson's counterpart as a gunner on a B-26, teammate Louis Sykes, flies raids against the Germans and Italians while based out of North Africa with the 12th Air Force. He, too, has his plane shot up in action, over the Gerbini Airdrome in Sicily on the 4th of July, 1943. Later, they count seven holes, including one fist-size in the top of the aft bomb bay ten feet forward of his turret.

"The B-26 is good enough for my money any day," he tells a reporter. "We were lagging in formation and started losing altitude when we were jumped by a bunch of JU 88's and other enemy pursuits. It was pretty hot for a few minutes, but we managed to stay up until our ships knocked most of the enemy planes out of the sky." The bomber is back in business within a few days after getting patched up.

On a later raid over Italy the flak bursts overhead and fragments drop from above like rain on the fuselage, causing no damage.

He gets a bird's-eye view of the American landings at Salerno in September, can see German dive bombers dropping down on the allied ships supporting the Fifth Army beachhead, and the ships' guns throwing up flak, notes the flashes of the big naval guns blasting German shore positions, and the return fire of the German defenders.

Sykes receives the Air Medal with seven Oak Leaf Clusters representing his forty completed missions, and two battle stars for his ETO ribbon before returning stateside in August of 1944. He writes to the *PX,* "What a bull session we'll have when the war is over!"

By late 1943 Edwin McKnight is cruising in the submarine *Mingo,* somewhere beneath the Pacific, Dick Hayden and Bill Graham are in the Pacific with the Marines, Lindsay Johnston in North Africa and John "Soup" Campbell in Hawaii with the 27th Division.

And Bill Slagus, goal keeper of the Uniteds, though not in uniform, serves his country in one of the greatest and most remarkable construction jobs of all time: building the Al-Can highway through rugged wilderness under incredibly trying conditions to link Canada with Alaska to speed the transit of men and supplies to hold off the Japanese who have already set up bases on some of Alaska's Aleutian Islands.

And then comes the bad news. Walt Weidemann, a crew member of a B17 Flying Fortress, makes front page headlines around the world when his plane goes down over Germany. Not because Walt is aboard, but because the pilot's name is John G. Winant, Jr., whose namesake father, a former Governor of New Hampshire, serves as the American Ambassador to Great Britain throughout the war, having replaced Joseph P. Kennedy in the Spring of 1941.

News of the telegram announcing Weidemann missing in action since October 10, 1943 spreads quickly over Dutch Hill, and the neighborhood grows ever closer. And then they wait. And wait.

Finally word comes in November that he is alive and a Prisoner of War, as is Winant.[11] It is not until the following February that a letter from the POW finally reaches home dated November 24:

> *Well, Mom, I am feeling fine and doing all right, and sure do hope that everything is O.K. by you. I suppose by the time you receive this letter, the holidays will be over. At any rate sure do hope you all had a fine time and are all well. Please do not worry about me, Mom, as I really expect to be home soon. Here I am passing the time O.K. with fellows that I knew from away back in the States. Please write soon and as often as possible. Please give my regards to all. Take good care of yourself and take things easy. Don't forget to send me a package or two. Be seeing you all. God bless you, Mom.*
> *Your loving son, WALT.*

Amsterdam boys get a taste of offensive action in the Pacific on November 20, 1943, when selected elements of the 27th Division participate in the taking of Makin Atoll in the Gilbert Islands. The *Uniteds* 2nd Lt. John J. Campbell, lives to tell his story:

> The Navy began shelling Makin about dawn and poured a heavy barrage of shells into their shore positions for more than three hours. Then the troops moved in to shore. I was in the first wave. We had to wade through the surf waist-deep and had no opposition until after hitting the beach. Then the snipers began operating from high in the coconut trees which fringe the island.

---

11 Winant got singled out for special treatment, being considered a potential bargaining chip by the Nazis. He became a personal prisoner of Heinrich Himmler, who ultimately ordered him to be executed in the Black Forest near the end of the war. His captors would not carry out the order, however, and helped arrange his escape through the Red Cross, and he safely reached an American outpost in Austria on May 7, 1945. (*New York Times*, November 2, 1993).

They let us move up well on shore before they opened up, then began picking us off.

I was heading a machine-gun squad. We managed to get some distance inland when I saw a Jap officer come jumping over fallen coconut trees toward us. He had a sword held high over his head in what I thought was a token of surrender. I advanced cautiously toward him and motioned him to drop the sword. He kept coming and so did I.

Two of my men were on each side of me. The Jap suddenly lunged forward and brought down his sword with a sweep. I put up my arm to ward off the blow and he slashed me across the left wrist. The power of the blow continued until the point of the weapon struck me on the left foot. Before I knew what happened one of my men let the Jap have it, right between the eyes. He was deader than a mackerel.

Campbell reports the Japanese had dug deep underground zig-zag tunnels with auxiliary off-shoots. Americans need to go into the tunnels to knock off the Japanese one by one, which is why it takes three days to take the island from a relatively small defensive force. Says Campbell:

They were just as treacherous as we'd been told they would be, and just as ruthless. It was our first action, but it didn't take our men long to get "trigger happy" once they saw their buddies dropping around them. The men of the 27th went to town.

Although I was struck down a little more than four hours after hitting the beach, I learned from others before I was evacuated that we took very few prisoners. We killed every Jap in sight.

Of course, what he says to the press carries a somewhat different tone from his missives to his teammates.

UPX, December, 1943 from Johnny Campbell: *Howdy folks,-- A few lines to say hello and let you know that I am as well as to be expected. As you must know* **[censor excision]** *the 27th Division* *and I am now in the hospital. I had a tussle with a Jap officer and he sliced a hunk out of my wrist and drove his sword through my foot before I got him. I have been awarded the Purple Heart decoration, and feel pretty good. It's really beautiful. I feel fine and the nurses are pretty as L. Nothing like a little rest, you know. Let the gang know that I will write as soon as I can. How is everybody on the hill? They brought my mail in yesterday and the October issue of the PX was among the 26 letters (back mail). I'm sorry I have to make this so short, but I'm a little tired. Merry Christmas and a Happy New Year to all and give my regards to the True Blues. I doubt if soccer will be in my line after this is all over. Bye now, as ever, Johnny Campbell.*

A later letter: Howdy fellows-- Just a line to say hello and thank you for the swell package I received from the club. It's funny – I'm not the sentimental type, but when I received it I realized the importance that is attached to organization back home as well as here. Damn it – I felt funny as the devil. Here in the hospital, little reminders of home and the fellows seem to have a different ring than when you are up and around and can go places and raise L. I can recall that when I was home last January I attended a club meeting. The main issue at that time was if the club was going to be discontinued for the duration or try to carry on. Well, I guess the decision was the right one in more ways than one. We have a club paper now, a Women's Auxiliary and closer contact with the members in the service than any other organization I know of. I guess it took a war, though, to get the old members to come out of their shells and show us how the Club should be run. It shouldn't be too long now before we are all home again and have some good arguments. No doubt you are wondering just how bad I got it. Well, all I can say for now is that this has been my life-long ambition – to lie in bed all day and go to sleep when you want to, wake up for meals, and have a pretty nurse give you an alcohol rub. L -Jimmy – you ought to take some lessons from the little brunette I have here, or maybe it is the feminine touch that is the secret, eh? My foot – the right one, there's a wee bit of a question as to the shape it's in at the present but I'm not worried. The sword went through the side and came out the bottom on a slant. He sliced a fair sized piece out of my wrist, but it is forming up fast and they might be able to sew it up in a couple of weeks. It is already three weeks since my little mishap. I have enough bandages on me to wrap up the whole team. Tell all the boys I'll write soon, until then I'll have to close. Merry Christmas and Happy New Year. This one will be kind of dry for me – but I'll be with you in spirit. Bye now and God bless you. As ever – Johnny.

UPX, January, 1944 from Johnny Campbell: *I was released from the hospital today. Being laid up for 49 days is no fun. . . . I'm going to join my men in about a week. I have to get In shape, ya know. I gained a lot of weight while in the hospital, 175 pounds now. . . . I'm also sorry I can't get home for a while. It looks like the duration down here. The experience I've had is really a corker and now I'm actually mad at the Japs. Terrible – ain't it? I'm even liable to work myself up into enough of a frenzy to start out again very soon.*

UPX, February, 1944 from Johnny Campbell: *Hello, everyone – I just received the December issue of the PX and once again the old home town and the club is pushed ahead of everything in my thoughts. We just had a parade and the General awarded the outfit its combat recognition. It's a wonderful ceremony. Sometimes I wonder what all this is worth – the unhappiness and agony that people back home go through when their loved ones are a little less fortunate than the majority of us – and then we have something like a parade and the haze is cleared up. You see Generals and Colonels, etc. hobnobbing with the men and a few slapping each other on the back and comparing this war to the last one. You see the democratic way that the higher ranking men "let their hair down" and show the human side, not the "official in charge" attitude that predominates in the armies of other* *countries. Then you notice the soberness and the grief that shows on the faces of the men that recall a personality or a little act that included a man that has been killed and is being cited posthumously. It will never bring him back, but it points out clearly that he is not dead as far as these men are concerned – he just can't make the next "trip." I've watched them when I called them to attention while paying tribute to someone, and you realize that we could never lose this war in a million years. Men. You folks could never come close to understanding the meaning of that word, because most of you never had the pleasure of seeing fellows, like those that raised cain in the club a year or two ago, who have grown older mentally a long time before their time, due to existing circumstances. You won't know them when they get back.*

The foot wound will ultimately end Campbell's soccer-playing career, but not his combat duty. After months of medical treatment, he returns to his regiment in time for the invasion of Saipan.

The letters from the servicemen have such a freshness, immediacy, intimacy and poignancy that they will be sprinkled throughout the remainder of this book. In a very real way, they tell the story of America in World War II better than any historian could.

> **UPX , November, 1943 from Arnie Eckelman in Washington State:** *All it does up here is rain. Can you imagine-- you can't get liquor across the bar, no mixed drinks and the lousiest beer you ever tasted.*

> **From Davie Thompson:** *We have been expecting to move out, but something always comes up, and therefore orders are changed. You know, after spending damn near three years in the service you have a craving for a little action. I can hardly wait until the day comes that we go for that long-awaited boat ride.*

From Pete Ruback in India: Being situated here in the middle of the jungle among wild animals that most people would have to go to the circus to see is really no joke, and getting news from good old Dutch Hill surely takes my mind off of things.

Christmas of 1943, already the third Christmas of the war, finds club members in places with exotic names like Attu, Bougainville, Biserti, Sicily, Salerno. . .

UPX, February, 1944 from Bill Slagus, somewhere in the Yukon Territory: I'm told the girls' dresses are getting shorter. They would get that way, just as soon as the fellows go away.

From G. Terry in New Guinea: I now have to live in the jungle, somewhere in New Guinea. It isn't too bad here. The weather is very hot and the days are overcast. We have a little bit of rain now and then. . . . We have a lot of natives around here. I was up in their village the other day and there was about a hundred of them playing soccer. They don't have only one man in goal, they have three.

UPX, March, 1944 from Capt. Jimmy Lindsay: We're setting up on a nice island with a few good swimming beaches.

From Paul Sykes: After 3½ years in the states they are sending me over. About time, eh? Now I am going to take up where my brother left off.

From Roger Ruback: I have been seeing quite a bit of China lately as we are flying supplies there regularly. The weather has been real hot these past few days but still a flying suit feels damn good at twenty-five thousand feet going over the Hump.

From John Geib: After this war the Nips will be the greatest cross-country runners in the world. They're already getting plenty of practice.

From Johnny Campbell: I'm back with my men now . . . . I played basketball tonight with the regimental officers team . . . We beat the Fighting 69th officers team 51-25. The foot is ok to run around on, but I can't kick anything. My big toe on the right foot is stiff and useless, making it rather awkward. In time it will loosen up, no doubt.

From Arnold Eckelman: I am back out in the battle zone again, just coming back from a bit of action which lasted about six days. Not much time for sleep there, averaging about 3 or 4 hours a day . . . . You don't find a hell of a lot of spare time on a destroyer.

From Milt Yates: Well, Blues, I'm somewhere in England at present, have seen a few sights when they had the Blitz, sorry I can't say just what I'd like to but it seems the Nazis sure picked on the churches over here. It's hard to find one that has not been hit.

From Joe Cionek: Finally my conscience has caught up with me, and there's no place to hide from it on a destroyer. In fact, no place to go, just pace up and down the decks. I see that my brother has written to you. Do you remember him? He left for overseas duty around December 7, 1941 and has never come back. It's going on three years that I haven't seen him, and it will probably be much longer. Just about everything I have to say is more or less confidential but I think I can tell you that our ship while in battle with the Japanese has shot down two enemy aircraft and probably missed many more. I've got some souvenir pieces of Jap plane in our first engagement. As I sit here looking at the picture on the first page of the P.X. I can just vision those fellows who are pictured there, just wishing to get back into that *uniform where they can tell the referees off and where the goal is only a hundred yards down the field and not a couple of thousand.*

From Paul Sykes in New Guinea: *I guess once an M.P., always an M.P., so with all my police experience, who knows, I may be a cop when I get back home. But I don't think so; the Rug business is in my blood so it looks like Mohawk will get my services. And incidentally both firms are doing a swell job for the armed forces. And here's an incident to prove it. Of all things, I have two G.I. Blankets and I'm proud of them. Why? Why? Not because of their superior quality, but because one has a Mohawk label and the other a Bigelow label.*

From Johnny Campbell: *Pierce will need a wheel-barrow to carry all those citations around if he gets any more. I had the pleasure of seeing a few major league stars play baseball a while back- Pee-Wee Reese, George Dickey, Johnny Mize, Johnny Lucadello, Berney McCashey, Tom Winsett and a few others. They are over here with the Navy and beat the devil out of an All-Army team, made up of kids out of the different units. It seems that the Navy grabs all these pros and puts them in soft jobs to play sports. If they gave half of them guns – this war would be over a helluva lot faster. OOPS! 'Scuse me – the Navy is our Ally, isn't it? Jack Geib seems to be seeing more than his share of this thing. I met Art Shanahan down here – he seemed to think that we were lucky in beating Bigler's out in the softball league. I asked him if the Hawaiian sun was sending him out of his head. If this war lasts much longer, I'm going to get married – almost an old man now – 24 next month. Everyone seems to be doing it and who am I to steer away from the common trend? But then again-- it means putting up with a woman after the war – which, I believe, would make my life a continual battle. I had better stay single and then I'll have only the Japs to worry about. We had a dinner for some WACS one night and let me tell you – I wish that I had stayed a G.I. We can't even breathe in their direction – unethical they say. I am* *willing to forget ethics in this case – but quick. There can't be many more fellows left around town, can there? One of the fellows in my platoon – Sal Morrone, a South-side boy – gets the Recorder – and every night I have noticed a new list of potential Jap chasers. Send them over here – We'll get this over in no time.*

UPX, June, 1944 from George Shields: *Saw Pierce Tolson over here in my travels. Pierce sure is a hero in my estimation after going through all he has. What with receiving all his medals. Have been around some myself, but not the hero he is, or John "Soup" Campbell. But nevertheless doing my little part for the war effort. Trucking supplies and men, up in the forward areas. No stripes on my upper sleeve, but did not come in the service for that reason. Had other reasons, and now I can prove those reasons and not doing too bad at it either even though I am not receiving any medals. Have been overseas close to thirty months. Know enough about Australia and New Guinea to write a book on. Have been thinking about taking out citizenship papers for one or the other. I have been over here so long it actually seems as though I've always been here. But of course I am only kidding for I love my country just as any true American does. The Aussie girls are very nice and plenty friendly and the hospitality of the Australian people is of the highest caliber. It sure will be a great day when this terrific ordeal is over with.*

From Bruno Petruccione: *I'm over in England not doing much of anything in particular. We're living in hotels. Rate liberty every nite. Beer and whiskey. Who said this is a tough war. However, it won't always be like this. . . . I've managed to see some of the island. They certainly caught hell over here during the blitz. Whole blocks of houses leveled. The countryside itself is beautiful and the majority of the people are very friendly. And the girls aren't bad, either. We get to play softball now and then. The rest of my off duty hours are spent in pubs, the movies or in the sack.*

From James Jasper: Seeing I am only a rookie amongst all you veterans I do as a rookie is supposed to do and that is to be seen and not heard. I do want to send my congratulations to both Lou Sykes and Pierce Tolson and hope they are having a nice rest after their fine work. Lou, we are sort of trying to to take over where you left off and deliver those bombs Hitler ordered. Of course, we accept no cancellation and stand there with our punch to punch his T.S. Card. As for milk runs, they are few and the flak heavy but the show must go on.

On July 5, 1943, while engaging the Japanese in the Battle of Kula Gulf off the northwest corner of the island of New Georgia, the light cruiser *USS Helena* is hit three times by torpedoes and sunk. Then follows an incredible saga of courage and survival as rescue ships (two destroyers) are forced to pull back, leaving 275 men behind, including club member Eugene LaJeunesse and fellow Amsterdamian Warrant Officer Elmer Ingham (who has been a shipmate of LaJeunesse for some five months), with four boats manned by volunteer crews from the destroyers. Eighty-eight men make it to anchorage after an all-day ordeal. The remainder cling to the still floating bow of the *Helena*. A Navy B-24 drops four rubber life boats and life jackets for them. The wounded occupy the life boats, while the rest surround them and try to propel themselves to nearby Kolombangara, but the wind and current carry them away and further into enemy territory. Another day and another night pass before they finally land on the island of Vella Lavella where they are taken ashore, and the by then 165 survivors, including Ingham, are hidden from the Japanese by coast watchers and loyal natives, who radio news of them to Guadalcanal. Finally they are rescued in a daring run on the night of July 16, 1943 by a destroyer that includes on its crew Amsterdam's Seaman First Class John Babrowicz (who'd himself been in six major battle engagements up to this point). Of the *Helena*'s crew of 900, 168 lose their lives.

Eventually the local paper gets wind of some of these details, nearly a year later, and writes up Ingham and LaJeunesse as home town heroes. LaJeunesse, who is rescued after spending three hours in the shark-infested waters, responds in a manner typical of the Amsterdam men of World War II:

> **UPX, June, 1944 from Eugene LaJeunesse:** *I was just a kid of 17 years when I signed up in the Navy. As far as that goes I am still just a kid. Only 21 now. . . . You probably all read the articles in the paper about it while I was home on survivors' leave. Although they gave me an entirely false build-up, my whereabouts was correct anyhow. But let me give it to you straight, fellows. I'm no hero. I just happened to be on a good ship and she had a "nose for trouble." Any lug who was and is as scared of this sea duty as much as I am and have been is certainly no hero. Mind you, I'm not a coward, but I am far from being brave, too. Now my conscience is relieved. I dislike false impressions.*

When Mr. "I'm no hero" gets a trip home after the sinking of the *Helena* he has already earned thirteen battle stars. Looking forward to having a good time tooling around in his car, he is startled to learn that furloughed soldiers and sailors are only allowed five gallons of gasoline under the rationing system then in place.

He need not have worried. When the news of his predicament hits the papers, offers of extra gas come pouring in. He is a citizen of no mean city.

9. A SAMPLE OF WHAT WE HAVE

The sinking of the *Helena* has a rather strange connection with another Amsterdam man, F.C. (2c) Kenneth W. Osborne, who is the son of Capt. Lester Osborne who took over the reorganized National Guard Company G when the original company marched off to federal service. The younger Osborne is aboard the *USS Gwin,* a destroyer that gets hit (for the third separate occasion) on July 13, 1943 in the Solomons. He is one of thirty volunteers who stay aboard after the order to abandon ship is given, in an effort to keep her afloat. Despite the fires, they are able to provide an orderly disposition of secret radio gear and equipment and get the *Gwin* in tow. They fight off three torpedo bombers, but it's not enough. The crew and the captain evacuate and another of our destroyers plunks a torpedo into her and she goes down.

But here's the strange part. When the Japanese torpedo hits earlier, a Seaman named Nichols is in the ammunition room under the No. 3 gun. The subsequent explosion blows away the gun and opens a big hole in the deck. Nichols is blown right through the hole through two decks and overboard.

After the Gwin sinks, the rescue ship takes off back down the Slot, rounds a point, and comes across a motorized whale boat heading in the same direction with one man aboard.

It is Nichols, "stark naked and black with oil from head to foot," reports the *Gwin*'s captain.

He'd been in the water for six hours when the empty, abandoned whale boat from the *Helena* sinking a week earlier floats to his rescue. He's headed in the general direction of San Francisco when pulled aboard the destroyer with only minor flash burns to one arm.

Osborne, with eight battle stars, gets a trip home for a while.

Back in his early days, before the glory years of his Warner Brothers contract, actor George Raft struggled to get chorus parts in unmemorable New York shows. To supplement his meager income he'd spend his after-hours playing cheap clubs with a dance act. One of his dance partners in 1921 is Edwin DaShell.

By and by Raft goes to Hollywood and DaShell works himself all the way up to sales promotion manager for Mohawk Carpets in Amsterdam. In his mid-40's when the war comes, he's way too old for standard entry-level military fare, a role he had already played in the first World War, so he joins up with the Red Cross and gets sent to the South Pacific. A few days after Allied forces land in Bougainville, in the northwestern end of the Solomon Islands, in November of 1943, DaShell is there, as Director of Red Cross operations.

"You'll have to find your own job," the commanding officer tells him. "The moment you decide you're not doing any good, let me know. I'll see that you don't stay on the island."

DaShell stays.

Though entitled to the same respect shown officers, the civilian volunteer endears himself to the fighting men (Bougainville will not be entirely secure until the Japanese surrender in August of 1945), who nickname him "Curly" in honor of his hairless dome. He parks his tent in the area of the field hospital and starts most days when the patients start to wake. Moving from cot to cot, he dispenses fruit and vegetable juices, tobacco and candies. He greets old friends and introduces himself to new ones. He writes thousands of letters for the boys. When a new edition of the *Torokina Times* (named for their beachhead), billed as "Bougainville's only English language newspaper," hits the stands, DaShell reverts back to his performing days and reads the news to his charges in the staccato style of radio journalist H.V. Kaltenborn.

"Naturally, I make it sound as good as I can. To the boys, good news is like a shot in the arm."

He even organizes shows in a make-shift outdoor theater with halved 55 gallon drums as seats.

And he makes frequent trips to the front, delivering candy, writing paper and chewing tobacco, and while there collects the personal belongings of the casualties.

His Red Cross guarantees no safety. Unlike the European front where even Nazis respect the ministering of aid to casualties, the Japanese view same as some kind of weakness and freely target health care workers. It starts on the very first day when a Mitsubishi bomber is shot down over the prow of the boat delivering him to Bougainville. He continuously dodges bullets and shells. An artillery shell duds out eight feet from him. During a Japanese counterattack, a guerrilla guard from Fiji watches over him in his office, shooting bursts over the top of his desk.

During that assault, in March of 1944, DaShell and his workers are at it day and night, helping with blood transfusions and surgical operations, even pulling wounded men off the battlefield.

Nothing glamorous about this job. Mosquitoes and centipedes, bombs and foxholes, mud and misery. These islands are a long way from the storied paradise of the exotic south seas.

But there is some satisfaction knowing that he brings a small touch of humanity that brings a little light into the darkness.

On December 26, 1943 the 1st Marine Division lands at Cape Gloucester on the island of New Britain, part of the territory of New Guinea, and with them is Pfc. Chester Watroba. The battle goes on for a bit over three months as part of *Operation Cartwheel,* a series of island maneuvers designed to isolate the major Japanese base at Rabaul, which guards the western end of the Slot through the Solomon Islands.

The men have a knack for providing their own romantic place names for the terrain they engage in, and one of these becomes the Battle of Coffin Corner.

Watroba is manning a machine gun on a pitch-black night, guarding a steep slope. The Japs sneak quietly up the slope and one leaps into his foxhole before he can even see him. There is no room to wield weapons. All he has are his bare hands.

He grabs the man about to kill him by the throat and does the only thing he can. He strangles him to death.

Before the night ends there are 78 dead Japs and six dead Marines.

And the battle goes on for another six weeks, during which he also earns a Navy Commendation ribbon for an action in which he single-handedly recaptures a heavy machine gun emplacement previously overrun by the Japanese, picking up multiple wounds to his face in the process, requiring his medical evacuation.

But not for long. He comes back to fight again on Peleliu and Okinawa.

Fighting Seabees is more than a John Wayne movie. The navy construction battalions are called in right after the Pacific battles to set up air strips and bases and such while the guns are still firing.

General MacArthur's decision to speed up the plan to capture and hold the Admiralty Islands, some two hundred miles northeast of the New Guinea mainland, brings Carpenter's Mate Third Class Stanislaw Gokas into a dangerous spot in March of 1944.

They're told that the air strip has been secured, and it is, for the moment. But Japanese reinforcements turn the builders into defensive fighters quickly as they are tasked with fending off an enemy attack.

The ground is coral, so hard that when building airfields the Seabees frequently have to employ explosives where bulldozers can't move. Hence, foxholes are virtually impossible, and Gokas has only a shallow slit trench to dive into when the shells start falling. An enemy mortar lands one directly into a nearby trench where eight of his friends are seeking cover. Moments later a second, closer shell explodes and Gokas feels the searing pain as a sliver of shrapnel plows into his leg.

It feels like a log has fallen on him. He cries out in pain, but the firing continues and no doctor or corpsman can reach him.

The leg is broken. Finally the enemy attack is repulsed and he is evacuated to a destroyer to have the leg set.

Oddly, it all happens so quickly that he hasn't time to experience fear. But when he's sent back ashore to a field hospital to finish up the treatment of his leg wounds he realizes that he is scared. Very, very scared.

As psychologically effective as the Doolittle raid on Japan had been in 1942, the Allies have been unable to repeat that success for more than two years, and the Japanese home islands are free from attack. But then, in the spring of 1944, we begin shipping our brand-new long-range B-29 Superfortresses into China by way of India, and suddenly we have a forward base capable of inflicting just reimbursement for Pearl Harbor.

2nd Lt. John L. Cowsert is co-piloting one of 68 B-29's that take off from Chengdu, China on June 14, 1944. The big, heavy bomber has trouble getting off the ground, and right away one of the landing wheels gets stuck and they have to use an emergency motor to retract it for the flight.

As they approach their target, the Yamatas Imperial Iron and Steel Works, they are caught in an enemy searchlight. Bursts of enemy anti-aircraft flak rock the airship, and the on-board gunners hold off enemy fighter long enough to unload their package for Hirohito. As soon as the bombs are off, Cowsert applies full power to the motors and their job is done.

On the way to home base, Cowsert patches up a malfunctioning generator and emergency motor so that they can lower the landing gear for a safe and happy return.

The B-29 raids will continue steadily, in ever-increasing numbers, until August 14, 1945.

At long last Mayor Wilbur H. Lynch receives word that the cruiser *USS Amsterdam* will be christened on April 25, 1944. Originally designated in August of 1940 at the personal direction of President Roosevelt, the Navy had shifted gears when war came and what started out as the cruiser *Amsterdam* became instead the carrier *USS Independence*, CV-22.[12]

Mayor Lynch is given the honor of designating the person to christen the ship, and according to local legend, the competition is fierce, and the names of many prominent women in the community are suggested. Urged

---

12 The "first" *USS Amsterdam*, the *Independence*, had a glorious career throughout the Pacific during World War II and even survived the atomic bomb tests at Bikini Atoll after the war, before finally being sunk in target practice off the coast of southern California.

even. Lynch will have none of it. The honor goes to Amsterdam's first Gold Star Mother, Mrs. William E. Hasenfuss, Sr.

Along with Mayor Lynch, Mrs. Hasenfuss is accompanied by a large group of her extended family to Newport News, Virginia for the ceremonial smashing of the bottle of champagne that sends the Cleveland Class cruiser on its way. Whistles blow from all over the yard. Crane operators, riveters, workmen of all sorts halt what they are doing to pay tribute as the fifteen members of the Amsterdam party and other dignitaries look on.

"I was thinking of William when I smashed that bottle," Mrs. Hasenfuss tells a reporter.

At a country club luncheon that follows, the Gold Star Mother is presented with a diamond-studded watch, a gift from the workers of the ship-building company. As she rises to express her thanks, her emotions overcome her, and Mayor Lynch salvages the awkward moment by coming to her side and gently speaking for her, expressing thanks in her name, and in the name of the city, explaining that Amsterdam is a splendid city, in the same way that her namesake is a splendid ship.

> The *Amsterdam* is bound to be a success. She cannot help but be when named after such a city. Amsterdam is filled with just such fine people as Mrs. Hasenfuss. She is only a sample of what we have.

The hopes for an early end to the campaign in Italy following the formal surrender of the Italian government are soon dashed, and by the end of 1943 both British troops on the east coast and the American troops on the west coast are bogged down (quite literally; the weather is miserable for months) at the German defensive "Gustav Line" that runs across the rugged spine of the Apennine mountains through the ancient hill-top monastery at Monte Cassino, blocking the way between Naples and Rome. In an effort to break through, the allies try an end-around with a landing in late January of 1944 at Anzio, on the west coast below Rome. But that project proves a disaster, as the Germans quickly seize the high ground and begin a rain of artillery on the beachhead that lasts four months.

> *UPX, April, 1944 from Lins Johnston, somewhere in Italy: Right now I am sitting on my own bed, why I say my own is that I built it out of trees, and a lot of chicken wire, for a spring. I wish you could see it. The mattress is not the floating type, some good old straw from a farmer's straw pile; it is better than sleeping on the ground. We moved since the last time I wrote. We are back out in the field again, where the big guns sing us to sleep every night. I remember seeing Lou Sykes and his buddies go over our heads when I was in my fox hole sweating out the jerry planes, and I must say it was one of the nicest feelings a guy has, when he sees those birds in the air, especially that day. We were sure in need of their help, which Lou probably knows. I wish you could hear me try to speak this Italian language, you sure would get a laugh. I saw one of the most beautiful sights I ever saw in my life one night. I never saw so much fire come out of a hole in the ground, I should say mountain, as I did that night. I thought all hell was busting loose, I guess you all know what I am referring to.*

> *UPX, May, 1944 from Harry Musloff: I'm not allowed to tell you where I am. . . . I'm keeping my eye open for Lins Johnston.*

Capt. Arthur Carter has a decade under his belt as Mayor of Amsterdam, so looking after the civilian affairs of captured territory in southern Italy seems like an easy assignment. A friendly population, with most everyone having relatives in the United States, a simple lifestyle and virtual dictatorial powers make things a bit more pleasant than, say, your average Amsterdam Common Council meeting.

They give him a quiet area a bit southeast of Naples containing small villages, farmland, orchards and grape vines. Overlooking the Bay of Naples, the region includes the ancient ruins of Pompeii, its most prominent geographic feature being Mt. Vesuvius.

By the middle of March, Vesuvius begins acting a little frisky. A GI taking a midnight walk to answer nature's call on the night of the 17th/18th gets hit by a piece of flying rock and all the next day the rumbling and roaring and shaking begin as hot lava flows from the crater and heads down the hillsides. By the 21st of March the lava stream, now 50 feet high and two hundred yards wide, has buried the villages of San Sebastiano and Massa di Somma and threatened Cercola.

Mt. Vesuvius Erupts (LOC)

With relief forces from Naples, Carter helps evacuate the villages, as the lava approaches at a rate of 5-10 feet per minute. Unlike Pompeii and Herculaneum in 79 A.D., few lives are lost, though some 88 American planes are destroyed at the Pompeii airfield. And the meager personal belongings of the peasants in the path of destruction are lost forever, along with their crops and livelihoods.

"First there was the war, then we were hungry, and now there is this!" cries one Italian woman.

Food dumps are established, and the people sheltered, fed and clothed.

A further eruption on March 23 leaves a cover of ashes two feet deep. Inhabitants of the Pompeii area flee with washtubs over their heads and blankets over their children. Cinder-covered roads are blocked for a time, hampering evacuations from the large towns of Torre del Greco and Torre

Annunziata. As the lava stones rain down, Capt. Carter tells an Associated Press reporter that he worries that the sheer weight of the millions of tons of lava might crash through the crust and be hurled out again as "black snow."

Carter will not see an idle day for a long time after.

Captain Arthur Carter, former mayor of Amsterdam, points out some of the devastation from Vesuvius' lava at San Sebastiano, Italy, to 2nd Lieut. Helen R. Mumford, (left) of Atlanta, Ga., and 2nd Lieut. Nedra Smith, Logan, O. The town was ground to bits, entombed. (Associated Press Photo).

Elsewhere in Italy, Lt. David Shuttleworth has a harrowing experience piloting a P-40 Warhawk.

> We were putting on our third dive-bomb run of the day, on a cluster of German artillery pieces entrenched in a quarry. The boys who had laid on the first two missions came back with the information that the three rings of flak surrounding the target were about the worst they had met since they started to operate in this neck of the woods. But just how concentrated this stuff was I did not realize until we nosed in for our run. It was so thick, as I dove down on the pinpoint, I got the impression it was raining flak out there. Just before releasing my bomb I heard a funny sort of "plunk." I think it was from the fragment that spiked my selectors-switch for gas. Before I turned the ship up high enough to join the returning formation, more of the stuff bounced up inside the cockpit, but it didn't do any serious damage, and I was able to bring the plane back OK.
>
> The payoff came, though, when I got back to base and took a look at the damage. Boy, did I get a surprise then! A couple of 88 millimeter chunks had penetrated the cockpit, pushed up through the seat, dug into my parachute, where it ripped a couple of pretty slits, and settled right there in the parachute. Close? Mighty, mighty.

Next day Shuttleworth flies two more missions against Nazi gun placements.

Sgt. Michael Borodojkiewicz is the nose gunner on a B-24 on a bombing mission from Corsica to Italy in early May, 1944. They call their plane *Big Fat Mama*. Just short of their target, they run into a bit of trouble.

> I am in a nose turret all eyes and trigger fingers, when something slams into the left side of my coupe. Something bigger than the whole world is spiked to my nose guns and slamming my left side where the glass is gone. It's the tail section of another B-24. The

bail-out bell is ringing and I am trying to get out of that cage to my 'chute pack which is on the floor of the bombardier's compartment.

I turn and there is the bombardier out by the nose wheel flattened out like a guy in a long swan dive and then his 'chute blossoms. It's the prettiest thing I've ever seen. After him comes the navigator.

I guess the ship is about out of its dive by now because I am worming down the hatchway to the flight deck to get out through the bomb bay. I think I am alone in the ship. Then I see the radio man's legs. I climb up and there's the skipper alone and fighting the wheel. I climb up beside him and he's leveling her out. He yells, "I thought you had gone. If you want to jump, then jump!"

"I ain't jumping," I yells. "I am sticking."

A spare navigator is also aboard and joins them. All the maps had been blown out in the crash, most of the instruments are out of commission, and the pilot is near-blinded by the wind rushing through the broken navigator's compartment.

"Where the hell is Corsica?" the pilot wonders aloud as they head out over the sea. The navigator points him in the general direction.

German fighters annoy them for a while, but a squadron of P-47's comes to their rescue and chases them off.

The pilot, Capt. Robert Wingfield of Shreveport, Louisiana, takes them safely home, "creasing the runway like silk, with that barn door dragging under our nose," says Borodojkiewicz.

For Capt. Felix J. Aulisi, being stationed in Italy proves more than just an assignment. It gives him an opportunity to come home. Born in the small town of Laviano, some 50 miles east of Naples, he had left for America while still a boy in 1912. He is the son of a humble shoemaker, but in America all things are possible and two sons become lawyers, and later judges. Felix Aulisi had left his position as Montgomery County Surrogate Judge about the same time that Mayor Carter joined the Army, and the two would sometimes run into each other throughout their training and overseas assignments. Aulisi takes part in the governance of Sardinia and later oversees the civilian judicial system in parts of occupied Italy.

After receiving permission from his commanding officer, Aulisi makes his way to Laviano, a difficult journey at most times, but even more so when the retreating Germans have destroyed bridges and roads on their way. He arrives, unannounced, at the home of his aunts, whom he has not seen in 32 years. Soon relatives and neighbors descend, and as he walks through the streets he is able to point out where various people had lived in his youth. People inquire of their relatives in Amsterdam, for the war has cut off most communication.

When it comes time to leave, some impoverished women of the village approach him and insist that he take some fresh eggs with him for his breakfast. He knows it is all they have to offer, and it moves him to tears.

The breakouts from Monte Cassino and Anzio finally take place in May of 1944, and when Gen. Mark Clark's 5th Army enters Rome on June 4, Amsterdam attorney Lt. Frank A. Dziduch, who had been bogged down with the troops at Anzio, marches right in with them, greeted by the cheers of the crowds and the laughter of children. According to Sgt. Clarence Kiuber, who also enters Rome that day, they are buried in flowers and kisses and gifts of all sorts. Many of the men receive free haircuts and shaves (and doubtless really need them) and many a signora invites soldiers in for a plate of spaghetti. With some others, Dziduch heads for the Vatican, where Swiss Guards hand him a rosary and two pictures of Pope Pius XII.

But then they reach a particular closed door.

"The guard would not let us go further and he told us that the Pope was in there," Dziduch writes to his wife. "When most of the crowd had gone, a priest came out saying that if we would wait, he would find out if the Pope would come out and see us. We waited and, lo and behold, the Pope soon came out with his guard.

"There were about 25 of us who remained and he gave us each a rosary after the Catholics in the group had knelt and kissed the Papal ring. The Pope asked me where I was from, and I told him. He said a prayer, blessed us and said a few words in English that ended the audience."

Dziduch continues northward with the troops and more hard fighting, and, when the war in Europe ends, takes an assignment on the legal team at the Nuremberg war trials.

And then, after all the slogging and ferocious fighting for nine months, the news of the capture of the first enemy capital gets quickly swept off the front page. Something even more significant happens but two days later.

Amsterdam Evening Recorder
AND DAILY DEMOCRAT

Vol. LXV., No. 245.   Amsterdam, N. Y., Tuesday, June 6, 1944.

INVASION LAUNCHED

Paratroopers Dropped Behind Nazi Defenses, Troops Landed by Sea on French North Coast

Allied Troops Advance 5 Miles Beyond Tiber In Pursuit of Germans

British, Canadians and Americans Compose Great Invasion Force; Substantial Progress Reported

Allied Ship Loss During Operations Very, Very Small

4,000 Vessels Used to Move Invasion Army

Patriots Told To Be Ready, Await Signal

Russian Troops Believed Ready For New Drive

Bomber Sinks Jap Warship

Sees Invasion From Bomber

Warships Shell Invasion Areas

Bad Weather Delayed Invasion for 24 Hours

11,000 Allied Planes Thrown Against Nazis

Petain Urges Aid to Nazis

Where Allied Invaders Struck

10. HAVE YOU HEARD THE NEWS?

Brig. Gen. Allen Kimball is given the most important assignment of his life, and arguably the most important assignment of World War II, beginning on March 1, 1944 when he becomes Deputy Chief Quartermaster for the European Theater of Operations. He is responsible for supplying food, clothing and equipment to American troops stationed in Great Britain and fighting in France and onward, with an initial fifty huge supply depots under his direction with millions of square feet of storage space and several thousand men at his command.

Brig. Gen. Allen Kimball (WEM)

A graduate of Amsterdam High School, he receives a congressional appointment to the Military Academy at West Point, graduating in 1907. During the first World War he commands a company of infantry, and he begins a long career in the quartermaster corps with his assignment as Assistant Quartermaster at West Point in 1921, under the superintendency of Douglas MacArthur. At various times he serves as Chief Quartermaster at the academy, and at stations in Panama and the Jefferson Barracks in Missouri, and as representative for the assistant Secretary of War on the War Budget Advisory Committee, and at the Quartermaster Staff School in Philadelphia.

The long-anticipated liberation of Europe is about to begin. It is Kimball's job to keep those supplies flowing so that the operation doesn't begin and end on a beach.

Sgt. Malcolm Tomlinson's war continues. Cornwall would be their home for the next half-year, and at least they speak a form of English there. Early in 1944 both Tomlinson and his buddy Garn are selected with four others from a battalion of 600 men to attend Officers Candidate School. It takes Eisenhower himself to overrule the selection. He can't spare the veteran non-coms from what will be needed ahead.

Headquarters Company of the Second Battalion boards three landing craft in Torquay on June 3, 1944, prepared to sail on the 4th. Hardly out of the harbor, the landing is called off and they return. Early on the morning of the 5th they board again. They pass through British mine fields. They pass through cleared German mine fields (though a nearby minesweeper blows up, killing several, wounding many, and sinking fast). By nightfall they are anchored ten to fifteen miles off the coast of Normandy.

Later they watch as planes carrying paratroopers and towing gliders fly low overhead.

The last plane briefly turns on its red tail light while passing over the fleet, blinking away in Morse Code immediately recognizable to all.

DIH-DIH-DIH—DAH.

V.

Victory.

D-Day, June 6, 1944. Preparing the way into Normandy are the paratroopers and the engineers.

Pvt. Daniel Klute of Amsterdam is aboard one of those planes, waiting quietly, nervously, as they approach the coast at night. The men stand in line, the signal is given, and before he can even comprehend what is happening, he hurtles through space.

The chute opens and jerks him alert. It seems like it takes forever to land as he passes over marshes and fields.

He hits the ground with a thud, stands up, rifle in hand and finds himself face to face with a startled German soldier. He waves his rifle and addresses the German in a universal language.

"Scram!"

The German cheerfully obeys and Klute walks away in search of his unit.

Fellow paratrooper Pfc. Harold Premo is not so lucky. The Malone, NY native who had been living with his sister on Florida Avenue when inducted is Amsterdam's first Supreme Sacrifice on the Longest Day.

Eighteen-year-old Richard Dantini from the South Side heads for shore with the famous Company A of the 116[13] Inf. Regiment in the first wave to hit the worst part of Omaha Beach, Dog Green, directly in front of outposts guarding the Vierville draw and subject to flanking fire from emplacements to the west, near Pointe de la Percee.

Of the 197 men in his company, only 18 are still fighting two hours later. All of the officers are killed or wounded in the first ten minutes, and most of the sergeants as well. Seventy per cent of the casualties come in the first half hour.

"Scared? Oh my God was I scared! Everybody was. Men were praying, crying, getting sick. It was hell," he will remember vividly almost half a century later.

One of the company's six landing craft flounders while still 1,000 yards off shore. The men hit the water with their heavy packs and drown. The Germans open fire at five hundred yards. Another LCA is blown up. The four that make it through are grounded in 4-6 feet of water still 30 yards beyond the outward band of beach obstacles.

The ramp drops. Dantini is the third man out. The first, a lieutenant, takes a round in the neck and dies in the surf. Dantini fires three or four clips from his rifle, then takes cover behind a concrete obstruction in the

---

13 Bedford, Virginia, a village of some 3,200 souls in 1944, loses 19 sons in Company A on D-Day, and three more later in the Normandy campaign

water. When he finally notices the live floating mine attached to it he decides to take his chances and heads for the beach.

He only makes it twenty or thirty feet before being hit the first time, a shot to the arm. He keeps going.

Once on the beach, he bends over to help a wounded comrade. They come under machine gun fire and the friend and a medic die right there, while Dantini is hit in the right leg.

The longest hour and a half in his life has passed since exiting the landing craft. The tide is coming in, and the Germans are shooting at any object that moves, and quite a few that don't.

"I started to crawl-- I tried to get up, but I couldn't. And then I got hit for the third time – the worst – it was in my left leg."

His body resembling bloody swiss cheese, he manages to creep behind a rock at the edge of his sector before losing consciousness. The next day, after the fighting has moved inland, a crew assigned to recover the bodies of the dead finds him alive, barely.

After thirteen months of recovery in military hospitals, he makes it home and resumes the life of a neighborhood grocer.

Being Gen. Eisenhower's barber doesn't exempt Nick Fratangelo from service on D-Day, and his future competitor Arthur Iannuzzi is there as well.

The son of an American citizen, Iannuzzi's father had brought him to America from his native Italy on the last boat the Mussolini regime allowed to leave for the United States before they declared war on us. He was sixteen. Two years later, having safely avoided the Italian draft, he receives his greetings from President Roosevelt.

He is part of a cannon platoon. Their orders are to remain off-shore until the beach has been cleared. As it happens, that takes three days. Stranded on a small launch, artillery fire lands all around them. "When you have the big guns, it's very easy to get hit, so they don't send you in until near the end. When we got there, though, there were a lot of wounded and dead soldiers. The beach was covered with them. I was scared and thinking, 'I don't want to die.'"

Others didn't see the sunset on June 6.

Pvt. John J. Schilling, 19, of Tribes Hill, a 1942 graduate of Wilbur H. Lynch High School has his rendezvous with death storming the beaches as a member of an anti-aircraft machine gun unit.

Tech. Sgt. Nicholas Foti, 23, has been in the Infantry since 1939, and wounded in North Africa. He had returned to action in time to take part in the decisive push on Troina in Sicily.

D-Day is his last day.

Garn and Tomlinson are attached to the 4th Infantry Division, whose Assistant Commander, Brig. Gen. Theodore Roosevelt, Jr., lands with the first wave on Utah Beach. In the current and smoke they have drifted a mile south of their target and form the far right flank of the D-Day invasion. Roosevelt personally scouts the area and throws away the plans. "We'll start the war from here," he says.

Wave after wave follow. The first of Malcolm Tomlinson's Headquarters Company to die takes a bullet to the forehead while still in the landing craft.

They land at low tide, just as the tide begins to turn (there's a twenty foot difference between low and high tide at Utah Beach) giving the engineers a window of opportunity to clear the obstructions and secure the beach exits while the infantry rounds up the enemy. The Higgins Boats soon reload with prisoners of war, and the combination of effective naval and aerial bombardment and airborne troops securing the inland routes results in remarkably low casualties at Utah. The sounds from Omaha Beach are not as encouraging.

Tomlinson and Garn are in a defensive platoon setting up 57mm guns. From behind the beach they are able to look out to the English Channel and see an armada such as the world has never seen, more than five thousand vessels extending from horizon to horizon: landing craft, destroyers, cruisers, battleships. Shells fly over their heads toward inland targets, the noise deafening. They follow a road running lateral to the beach about a thousand yards. Garn's squad digs in, and Tomlinson's passes by with a bulldozer hauling their big gun. A few moments later the dozer hits a land mine and the driver flies through the air landing 25 feet from the machine. Other men are wounded and a medic from Garn's squad rushes to assist, steps on a mine and gets blown in half. They all hit the deck. Garn then realizes his hand has come to rest only inches away from another mine.

News of the D-Day invasion begins trickling into Amsterdam about 6 a.m. on June 6, 1944. Bulletins from the *Recorder* are posted around town. The churches open, and at the direction of Bishop Gibbons every Catholic church in the Diocese of Albany has exposition of the Blessed Sacrament.

At Wilbur H. Lynch Senior High School, a program is quickly put together and 18 year old Senior Class President Walter Tatara addresses his schoolmates:

> Today has been set aside as a day for prayers, for mercy and grace. Throughout the land many hearts are heavy because D-Day has finally arrived and with it will come the horrible news of tragedies of war. Right now, someone very dear to us may be lying wounded or bleeding on a battlefield. We have got to prepare ourselves for whatever news is to come. Will our enemy's zeal for the cause of anti-God overcome our indifference to God?
>
> In times of peace, prosperity, good times, how easy it is to ignore God, but as soon as we are subjected to pain, suffering, confusion, turmoil, we immediately turn to our Almighty Father and pray reverently for aid. Right now we need God's intercession in this struggle. We should be united as never before, and we should all lift our hearts in prayers, whether we be Protestant, Jewish or Catholic. Let our prayers be sincere, simple, and uttered from the bottoms of our hearts. In that way we will become more powerful than any weapons used in this war. Our boys will be comforted in knowing that we, here at home, are praying for them to have strength and courage so that they may walk hand in hand with God, unafraid and prepared for whatever may befall them.
>
> Students, do we take this war seriously? Do we hope for a better world after this war? Some of us do because we realize that this world in the next fifty years will be what we make it. It won't be better unless we ourselves make it better. We must have

strength in character, a purpose in life, and above all, faith in God. We, in the United States, are fortunate because we are a Christian nation and we can speak our thoughts without being afraid of a dictator shutting us up.

Let us hope and pray it will always remain that way.

Thank God for America.

The program continued as follows:

Flag Salute
"Star Spangled Banner"
    Entire School
Solo—"The Lord's Prayer"
    Albert Sochin[14]
Song—"America the Beautiful"
    Entire School
Reading—"Recessional" -Rudyard Kipling
    Evelyn Moyer
Song—"Onward Christian Soldiers"
    Entire School

Later, when he has time to reflect, Guy Murdoch writes to his Dutch Hill boys around the globe in the June issue of the *Uniteds PX*:

Tuesday, June 6th, 1944 will go down in history as D-Day. Owing to the five hour difference in our time from Greenwich time, we here in Amsterdam learned of the invasion of Normandy about six a.m. that morning. On the way to work we noticed that some of our neighbors had already put their flags up, and on arrival at the

---

14 Contemporaries remark about what a good singing voice Albert Sochin has in high school. After serving in the war, he takes up a musical career, and, under the name Albert DaCosta (his mother's maiden name), performs for seven seasons with the Metropolitan Opera. He then stars with several companies in Europe, where he dies in a car accident in 1967 at the age of 40.

office everyone asked the same question, "Have you heard the news?"

A few minutes later I learned that a small radio was in operation in one of the large near-by offices. Little attention was being given to the regular business as reports were continuously given of the progress of the landings on the beaches. The size and strength of the naval armada, the landing craft, the opposition, the terrific bombardment of the defenses, the details of the beaches and the difficulty to be overcome and the excited tones of the commentators all created an atmosphere of awe and wonder that nothing else on earth could have done. The girls around the radio stood tense and hopeful, drinking in every word; serious and awe-stricken, and all had the same question in their minds, "Is he in it?"

Husbands and brothers of some were in it, but no one knew it then. About an hour of this and then to work. The radio was turned down but the girl at that particular desk turned it up when official announcements were made. The invasion was on, D-Day at last, long expected and waited for, the day we longed to hear about yet dreaded.

You people really know about D-Day, we do not, for many of you have known other D-days although they were not designated as such. In New Guinea at Port Moresby, Buna, Lae and Salamana in the Solomons, at Guadalcanal and Bougainville, in New Britain at Rabaul and Cape Gloucester, in the Gilbert Islands at Makin and Tarawa, and in the Marshalls at Kwajalein and Eniwetok, there were days that were D-days to many of you. In North Africa, Casablanca, Rabat, Algiers, Oran, Bougie, Phillipville, Bizerte, and Cape Bon had many days which to those of you who were there did not have any distinctive letter that was known to the world.

Then Sicily saw certain days at Cape Passero, Comiso, Mazzarine, Palermo and Messina and many other places. Then on to Italy one day to Salerno, Naples, Oassino, Anzio, Rome and on to Florence and Pisa. And in India you were going over the Big Hump of the Himalayas to China, every trip designated by a question mark. And so the days go on, marked by some code or other, but each one by itself THE DAY.

What about D-day in Amsterdam? Just a job to do, maybe a loom to fix, or some weaving to do, or finishing, or maybe just looking at things and saying yes, you get 'em or no, they're not good enough. Through our factories here examining cotton and duck, miles of it, in the plant in Rockton. At the lower mill, more duck and as we were headed over the tracks to the place where the processing plant is located we were halted. Long freight trains, carrying strange cargoes, some things covered up, others not, but it gave me a thrill to see them thunder past for they were going out to you. These were the things that helped to bring about D-day, and we felt like saluting as they hurried on.

To the processing department down by the river to see that tarpaulin cloth is waterproofed and fireproofed. And down the river came a fleet of LSTs and we wished we could deliver them to their destination. From there to Harrowers and the blanket mill where things really happen to help keep you comfortable. Then back to the tarpaulin department where they are completed and shipped. Sometimes we think we do a deal of traveling but we carry no pack and we are not disturbed. Amsterdam used to be a quiet and peaceful place engaged mainly in making carpets and rugs. It is still peaceful, but has many new engagements with you fellows out there. More radio news and reports are very encouraging, truly it is a great team.

On the way home I noticed, as I have often done, a little gray house on a corner. In the window there's a service flag with four stars. Three sons and a son-in-law from that one house. August 7th, 1942, was the first D-day for that particular home when Jack went ashore on Guadalcanal with the Marines and he has had many similar days in other places and is still out there. He must have used up all the letters in the alphabet by this time.

Then Dicky had his D-day on June 6th in Normandy and so did the little gray house on the corner. Bucky is still on this side and is ready. The son-in-law is also here. A quiet little house of gray on the corner and the number is 435 Locust Ave. The lady of the house is Mrs. Geib, God bless her, and the music from the radio on the evening of D-day as I heard it was "Goodnight, wherever you are."

This was D-day in Amsterdam; tomorrow will be D plus one.

Tomlinson and Garn are not privy, of course, to the overall success of the operation, but as the day grows longer and night falls they become more and more encouraged by the sounds of war fading farther and farther into the distance. That night, in fact, dug into foxholes next to their guns, they sleep better than they have in days. Their only annoyance comes from a lone German plane that nightly, around midnight, drops a single bomb and goes on his way.

On the morning of the third day Malcolm Tomlinson begins to move his squad for a destination further inland, walking along the road. Gen. Theodore Roosevelt's jeep, *sans* general, comes by and strikes a mine on the road's edge. The driver is killed, the jeep destroyed.

Tomlinson loses his good eardrum and once again has his faced ripped apart, this time by flying debris.

They give him an oak leaf cluster for his Purple Heart.

Pvt. Lewis Harrower goes ashore with the combat engineers on D-Day and continues inland for several more days until he finds a chance to snuggle up in a Normandy foxhole and write home to his mother in Hagaman. D-Day was "some experience," he tells her. But right now he's not reliving the battle. He's simply dreaming of a warm bath and clean clothes to replace the ones that are growing on him, and maybe a little peace.

And he's thankful for God's peace. Like Father Whelly on the other side of the world, he hasn't run into a foxhole atheist yet, and he makes sure to tell that to his mother. He doesn't know a man who isn't thanking God for bringing him safely through that landing.

* * *

V...-Mail

Francis J. Going, SK 2/c
Navy 168 c/o Fleet PO
New York, N.Y.
June 19, 1944

Dear Mom,

I'm sorry that I haven't written you sooner but I honestly haven't been able to. This is the first letter I've been allowed to write and will probably be the only one for a time so please be patient and don't worry.

I'm safe and well so there is no cause for worry. We received our first mail in some time yesterday and yours of June 6 was among them. I also received the first copy of the newspaper but no packages. As yet I have only received your last package. I remembered the baby's birthday and was thinking of her yesterday but unfortunately I was in no position to send greetings of any sort. Please tell sis that I didn't forget anyhow. I'll make it up to the kid some day. Have been attending Mass and receiving Communion daily as we have the Catholic Chaplain with us. I thank God for that opportunity. It's a great help at a time like this. My love to all and regards to Des. Please continue to write and be patient until you hear from me.

All my love
Bud

[June 19 is the day he leaves England for Normandy. But don't worry.]

A fair number of the Bigelow-Sanford Uniteds take part one way or another in the D-Day invasion and subsequent campaign.

UPX, July-August 1944, from Milt Yates in European waters: *I'm ok after taking part in the invasion of France on D-Day. We really were there to see the excitement and it was plenty exciting. I wouldn't have missed it.*

From Carl Hartig in Normandy: Landed D-Day and we've been sort of busy for the past month and a half. . . . [K]ept going until Cherbourg fell; hope the rest of the Huns give up so we can get back home.

From Bruno Petruccione, somewhere in France: The place looks like anyplace else. . . . Still in France looking over the situation. All I have to do is pick up a newspaper to see how the war is going. Guess this can't be the part of France that everyone raves about because I can't see anything very wonderful around here.

From Harold "Peanuts" Brown, in France: Well, here I am over in war torn Normandy. Just got here a while ago and am getting along OK. The only trouble is trying to talk to those French people. I have to use the sign language on them. Some understand and some don't. One thing sure, you can get all the cider you want. Anyway, they call it cider. All I can say is, it sure has a lot of kick to it for cider. Also this cognac they have here. They call it bottled lightning. I'm a little bit afraid to take any. They say it will make your toe nails bend over. Maybe so.

From James Jasper, somewhere in Italy: after reading your description of D-Day which was very good, I started to think of where we were when we heard the news. Yes, we were up around 21,000 feet and had just come off an important target in the Balkans which at that time was on the receiving end of a bombing mission. We were all congratulating our Ball Turret Gunner on his 200 and some odd gun salute he had received for his birthday. Our Ball Turret Gunner was answering us over tinter-phone saying "Well fellows I didn't ask for that many guns" and just then someone tuned in and said, "Turn to Liaison" and we all did and they were announcing the first reports of the invasion. So you see we were flying high when we heard the Great News of D-Day.

Meanwhile, on the other side of the globe:

From Johnny Campbell in Saipan: *Just a few lines from Saipan and a toast to the taking of Tojo's front porch. The fighting has been darn tough these past few weeks and I'm ready to come home for a rest now. Seventeen months over here and seven to go before I am eligible for leave. I'll be skin and bone if I have another one like this. I went down to 163 pounds. Occasional snipers and small groups bother heck out of us and we go chasing then through the hills. They run like scared rabbits with our boys after them. I've lost quite a bit of my running ability, but the Japs still can't out-run me. It is actually comical sometimes when they scatter and take off for a cave somewhere. It's just like skeet shooting. This is rather short, but I haven't much time. Knock on wood and I believe I'll come through this in one piece.*

11. SAIPAN RENDEZVOUS

I have a rendezvous with Death
At some disputed barricade,
When Spring comes back with rustling shade
And apple-blossoms fill the air-
I have a rendezvous with Death
When Spring brings back blue days and fair . . .
  -Alan Seeger

Nearly three years and nine months have passed since the Boys of Company G marched out of the New York State Armory in Amsterdam. Trips home had become rare events after December 7, 1941 and from the Spring of 1942 when they settle into the Territory of Hawaii they have been training continuously for the Pacific offensive, wherever that might take them. Trouble is, the 27th Division of the United States Army is something of an odd-man-out. Some of them, like Company M's Lt. John Campbell, take part in the Makin invasion, but for the most part their days consist of exercise after exercise preparing for they know not what.[15]

Nor do their commanders. Even after boarding ships for the upcoming engagement it is an open question whether they will be in support of the operations for Tinian or Guam or simply held in general reserve. Twenty or so different contingencies are presented, and operational logistics need to be put in place for each. Each involves coordination among the Army, Navy and Marine Corps. In the end the options narrow to one destination, but even then, where or how or who await decisions made in the fog of battle.

---

15 The principal source of information in this chapter is Love, Edmund, *The 27th Infantry Division in World War II*, Infantry Journal Press, 1949.

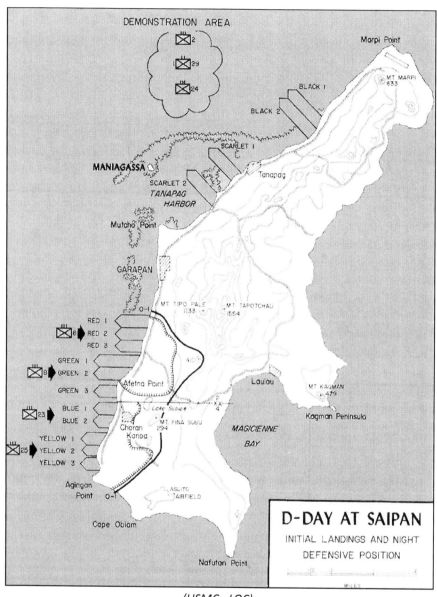

(USMC - LOC)

Much has changed since their National Guard days. Their captain, Peter Rogers, had been promoted and retired. Some of the other old-timers are gone as well. Charles DeGroff, a first lieutenant in the Big Parade, serves for a time as the new captain of Company G, then receives a promotion to Major, serving as Executive Officer of the 3rd Battalion of the 105th, while Clinton Smith emerges as captain of E Company, composed mostly of Schenectady boys. Boles Knapik, the inspiring First Sergeant when the boys move out (and Best Man at the Freer/Pileckas wedding), receives an officer's commission, as do his two successors, Frank Betinger and Lewis Dilello (climbing up from private), all three getting new assignments in the European theater.

And the company expands, of course, from its original complement of 83, as war needs grow. But the core group otherwise remains pretty much intact, and their captain now is a most resourceful Amsterdamian, Frank Olander.

While they await their orders, the Marines go to work.

The very same day that Operation Overlord takes off for Normandy, a similar armada in the Pacific leaves Pearl Harbor for the Marianas Islands. Forces aboard include the 2nd Marine Division, 4th Marine Division and 27th Infantry Division. The naval forces include fifteen battleships, eight of them Pearl Harbor survivors, along with numerous cruisers, destroyers and smaller craft.

Five miles wide and eighteen miles long, Saipan is shaped something like a pistol with the barrel facing north and the handle covering the southern third.

Naval bombardment commences on June 13th. Eight thousand Marines land beginning at 0700 on June 15th, and casualties are heavy. Amsterdam Marine Pfc. Ralph Downs, 20, goes ashore at 0845. Artillery and mortars have already taken out enough of our amphibian tractors that are supposed to transport them ashore that his company is forced to wade through the surf. They get off the beach right away, heading for a ridge where the first waves have begun to dig in. His immediate job is to help mop up pockets of Japanese soldiers that have been bypassed in the thrust forward.

His squad of seven runs into a squad of fifteen enemy. The Japs drop their rifles and run, taking only a light machine gun. The Marines eliminate all of them.

Crossing fairly level ground, they reach the railroad that parallels the shore and take cover, under heavy fire. Moving forward they reach the ridge, where they are again pinned down, and dig in for the night. Morning comes, and they form a skirmish line to meet a Japanese counter-attack that never happens. A shell lands on his squad. Three men are killed and Downs and two others wounded.

Barely a full day ashore and Downs is evacuated to a ship for medical treatment.

Pfc. Gabriel Vertucci of Fort Johnson, with the 4th Marine Division, is moving forward when suddenly a Jap appears and aims at his head from eight feet away.

He has no time to react.

The bullet hits him square in the helmet, then rolls around inside and drops out the back, giving him just the moment he needs to kill his attacker.

In a subsequent counterattack, shrapnel from a hand grenade pierces his arm. His first Purple Heart.

Later, a Japanese soldier shoots him in the pocket. The bullet is deflected by an ammo clip, but drives into his hip on the ricochet, his second Purple Heart.

Adm. Spruance learns of Japanese fleet movements and makes the decision to pull the American support fleet back on the morning of the 17th, which ultimately causes some interruption in the unloading of supplies to the beachhead.

Given the fierce defense of the island by the Japanese, the 27th Division, heretofore held in reserve, is committed to Saipan and artillery units and the 165th Regiment (the old "Fighting 69th") land immediately, with the 106th afloat in reserve. The 165th goes into action the following morning, strikes inland and takes the Aslito airfield virtually intact, and pushes east with two battalions of the 105th. Hospital ships arrive on the 18th and take aboard 1,099 injured men.

And on June 19, 1944 the Battle of the Philippine Sea guarantees that there will be no relief for the Japanese garrison on Saipan. In one of the most lop-sided engagements of the war, 402 of 542 Japanese planes employed are destroyed. The Americans lose 26 planes, with minor damage to five ships. It becomes known to history as "The Great Marianas Turkey Shoot."

But the naval conflict means that Company G and the rest of the Second Battalion of the 105th regiment go ashore with few of their supplies. That left behind includes critical communications equipment. They are forced to borrow or make do until the fleet returns.

27th Division comes ashore on Saipan (USA-LOC)

Meanwhile, the 165th Regiment has made strong advances toward their objective of securing the southern third of the island, which consists of a flat region leading to terraced ridges to high cliffs, dominated by Nafutan Ridge and Nafutan Mountain. Beginning on the morning of June 21, the Second Battalion of the 105th (which includes Company G) will receive their baptism by fire, replacing the Second Battalion of the 165th in line. Goal: take Mt. Nafutan and proceed forward.

It may be he shall take my hand
And lead me into his dark land
And close my eyes and quench my breath-
It may be I shall pass him still.
I have a rendezvous with Death
On some scarred slope of battered hill . . .

Nafutan peninsula. (USA-LOC)

Things don't always go according to plan.

The scheduled artillery bombardment of thirty minutes is delayed by twenty minutes due to the calling back of American troops too far in front. The subsequent ten minutes accomplish little, especially in the front of the Second Battalion, where only two shells fall on the nose of Mt. Nafutan, and none in the surrounding area. Company F and Company G (under Capt. Frank Olander) face the nose across a wide-open sugar cane-stubbled field. Company G sets out at 0930, two platoons abreast, moving quickly to hug the base of the cliff. They advance only about 25 yards when fierce enemy fire breaks out: rifles, machine guns, mortars. Two men are killed and three wounded immediately, the rest seeking cover wherever possible.

Sgt. Michael Makarowsky grabs a litter and dashes into the cane field to rescue one of the wounded, with the help of another man. Together they bring him back across the field to a waiting ambulance, which then itself comes under fire. Makarowsky throws the wounded man on his back and finally gets him to safety behind a stone wall, from which he is brought to the battalion aid station. The action earns Makarowsky a Silver Star. He will not live long enough to receive it.

Olander orders the men to advance again, this time individually, in short bounds. Fifty more yards are covered, three more men dead and more wounded. By this time Olander has located a source of machine gun fire in a shack on the north end of some woods (the objective of the right platoon) and orders everyone not moving to fire at the shack. After ten minutes the whole line moves forward on a dead run. Another man killed, but the rest reach cover.

The 1st Platoon, on the left, under Lt. Donald F. Lee, Jr., spots a machine gun on top of the nose, commanding all the open ground. He orders Tech. Sgt. John F. Polikowski to take the rest of the platoon under the lip of the bluff and lay down covering fire, while he takes a squad to scale the cliff and neutralize the gun. Staff Sgt. Joseph Ochal executes the scaling operation, with Lee along, and his men kill the soldier manning the machine gun. Dense undergrowth and the lay of the land prevent them from advancing farther, and they withdraw.

Meanwhile the 2nd Platoon, on the right, has reached the shack and the woods. The Japs inside are dead, the gun out of commission.

But one squad has become separated from the rest, with a clearing between them of 50-100 yards. Lt. Arthur Hansen crawls to the edge of the clearing and orders the missing squad to infiltrate to the other side. Three men killed, one wounded, two don't even try. Hansen then sends Tech. Sgt Max Tracz to find out what happened. Tracz calls out.

No answer.

He starts across and is shot four times in quick succession and drops to the ground. Hansen and Pfc. Harry Pritchard run unchallenged across the clearing to another wounded man. The remaining two men from the missing squad join them and the four together pick up the wounded man. A machine gun atop the mountain opens fire and the wounded man is cut in two, and Pritchard and another man wounded. All four rescuers manage to emerge otherwise safely on the platoon side, along with the quadruply-wounded Max Tracz, who somehow crawls out on his own.

The crappy radio equipment they had commandeered prevents Hansen from contacting Capt. Olander, who is otherwise busy moving the 3rd Platoon into the gap that has opened up between the 1st and 2nd.

But that operation is less than successful, as they end up to the left of the 1st Platoon at a cost of three more men killed and two wounded. They are promptly pinned down east of the nose and yet another man is wounded. Olander calls the Battalion Commander, Lt. Col. Leslie Jensen, for help evacuating fifteen seriously wounded men (some later died). Finally, at noon, a medical jeep arrives over the hill to the rear and is immediately hit. An aid man is wounded, the driver jumps out, and there is no medical help for Company G.

Now, ammunition is running low and once again the radio equipment fails. Capt. Olander strikes off personally to the Battalion Command Post, running full-out across the open field through intense fire.

Lt. Lee, not having made any contact with the 3rd Platoon, which is supposed to be on his right, moves his men along the right face of the cliff, then over open space to the woods and Lt. Hansen's 2nd Platoon. One killed, two wounded. They set up a perimeter defense, still without radio contact with Olander, who by this time has made contact with Lt. Col. Jensen and outlined the terrain for him.

Olander sends forward two self-propelled guns loaded with medical supplies, water, rations and ammunition. They reach Hansen, Lee and the 3rd Platoon within half an hour. Using the radios aboard the SP's, the lieutenants are finally able to receive orders from Olander. Debate and discussion ensues. Dig in? Withdraw? It seems no further advance can be made until the nose of Mt. Nafutan is cleared, and the artillery can't fire with Company G so far out front. Olander objects that withdrawal will only mean more casualties. The decision is made: the wounded are evacuated with the SP's and Company G withdraws under protective artillery fire.

Company F on the extreme left digs in facing the nose while the bone-weary men of Company G are told to dig in on the near side of the hill facing the cane field and the nose. It is impossible to dig in the coral-studded ground, so they improvise crude rock shelters instead of foxholes.

Rugged coral-based terrain offers no shelter for the 105th. (USA-LOC)

God knows 'twere better to be deep
Pillowed in silk and scented down,
Where love throbs out in blissful sleep,
Pulse nigh to pulse, and breath to breath,
Where hushed awakenings are dear...

For Sgt. Melrose Freer, it is the longest night of his life. He hears the sounds through the darkness, and he knows what they mean. The enemy soldiers are now reforming their lines, bringing more and more firepower to their front.

He hugs the ground, sinking as low as he can behind his rude shelter. There is no sleep, and little rest. His thoughts turn to home. He has seen all too little of his wife since their wedding in early 1942. And now, he has seen friends die.

Lying on the rough coral with Death just a few bushes away, he vows that if he gets out of this alive he will return to Nell and produce a dozen kids.

By early morning both captains request to withdraw beyond the rim of the saucer, so that their men won't be sitting ducks at dawn's early light.

Again, Olander's radio fails.

Again, he strikes off through outpost lines, in the dark, to Battalion Command Post. Jensen gives him permission to withdraw.

But it is too late.

The blast of fire at dawn hitting from machine guns, mortars and a company-strength of Japanese riflemen, hits all three platoons of Company G and Company Headquarters.

Six killed or mortally wounded, 21 other casualties. The enemy, as Olander had suspected, had spent the night preparing to sweep away Company G.

Olander moves three SP's forward to lay fire on the nose, enough to permit the orderly withdrawal of his men. Company E, under Amsterdam's Capt. Clinton Smith, moves up to replace them on the line.

In his first 24 hours of combat, Frank Olander has lost half his men and gained not an inch of ground.

By 0945 on June 22, Olander reports his men ready and they are sent in to relieve the 3rd Battalion of 165th Regiment, which they effectively do by 1025. With only four officers and 72 men, Olander takes over a frontage previously held by two rifle companies at full strength, 400 yards behind their farthest advance. Cooks and supply sergeants are on line, and they call for the ship's party of 22 men to join them.

The lines are far too thin, so Company E moves over between F and G and at 1300 Company K is ordered to the extreme left. With lousy communications, the better part of the day is spent just straightening out the lines.

The previous day, an enemy ammo dump had been found and ordered destroyed. No one bothers to convey this information to the Second Battalion, so at 1520 they are caught unawares by the giant explosion. The Battalion Command Post is decimated, more radios wrecked, vehicles destroyed and the Company G ship's party of 22 men, just arriving at the CP, suffers six wounded. And if that isn't enough, fire from a US Navy destroyer aiming for Mt. Nafutan hits the same Command Post instead. Eight killed, 32 wounded.

Inter-service politics rears its ugly head the next morning. Lt. Gen. Holland Smith of the USMC, in overall command of the ground operations on Saipan, is not at all pleased with the progress of the 105th Regiment and so notifies Maj. Gen. Ralph Smith, commander of the 27th Army Division. Although estimates of enemy strength vary widely, the Marine Corps believes there are no more than 300 enemy left in the Nafutan area, maybe only 90. The Army is more than sure given their experience at the front, that there are closer to 1,500. Holland Smith orders the withdrawal of all but one battalion. Ralph Smith believes that such a drastic removal will put the Aslito airfield at risk.

The Second Battalion is all that is left, along with one platoon of light tanks. They are ordered to continue offensive operations at daylight on June 23. They are to cover a frontage of three thousand yards where four battalions had failed to advance the day before, and without artillery support, and only one platoon of SP howitzers.

Company E's Capt. Clinton Smith is sent to the right to relieve a battalion with three platoons. Company G faces Ridge 300, the core of the Japanese defenses. Already down one mortar and one machine gun, Olander makes riflemen out of his weapons platoon and sends half his men straight up as a diversion while the other half circle around the west bluff. Company F is given two days of supplies to attempt to outflank Mt. Nafutan.

By 1500 Company G reaches the farthest advance made by the 165th three days earlier. The intrepid Sgt. Ochal leads a squad that stumbles on a Japanese machine gun position and liquidates its five personnel within moments.

Fire breaks out from everywhere.

Company G's one mortar attacks four heavy machine gun nests, while being constantly under fire themselves. Over the next hour, three different Japanese attacks are beaten back. Pfc. Michael Lane is killed.

Three light tanks are immobilized by the terrain and of no assistance to the front lines.

By 1730 Company G is dug in on the base of the North slope of Ridge 300, joined by Company F.

Capt. Smith, meanwhile, commanding a thousand yard frontage with Company E on the right flank, is facing a farm plateau with Ridge 300 on his left and a coral jungle dropping on his right to the Saipan Channel. The clothing of the platoon sent to clear the coral jungle is soon ripped to shreds, while another platoon clears the slopes of Ridge 300. Those men, well in advance of Company G on their left and the rest of Company E, face pitched battles all night long.

Operations resume on June 24, with Company G using an attack built around the tanks (which continue to have difficulty moving ahead), their one mortar and one machine gun. They are pinned down after 50 yards. Sgt. Ochal spots a Jap machine gun and conveys the information to Capt. Olander, who crawls into a self-propelled gun and personally supervises the firing, scoring a direct hit with one round.

Silence.

Olander orders his men forward and firing immediately recommences. He orders the SP's and the machine gun to open up on the whole front. Fighting rages for two hours near the crest of Ridge 300. Three Japanese counter-attacks are driven back, forces ranging up to company strength. The SP guns and automatic weapons are now nearly on the front lines. Three men are wounded in Olander's vehicle. They destroy four Japanese machine guns, one by one. Olander shouts to Sgt. Polikowski to rush a line of rocks with eight men and fixed bayonets. As they dive into the enemy positions, one Jap tosses a grenade, seriously wounding two men, including Sgt. Ochal. Polikowski works behind the lines while the rest of Company G surges over the rocks, ending all Japanese resistance.

Though it is nearly dark, Olander moves forward to attempt a flanking movement on part of the same line of Japanese holding off Company F on the east slope of Ridge 300. Within twenty yards they take fifty Japs by surprise. Lt. Hansen is wounded in the shoulder by a tossed grenade. Fighting rages for ten minutes, some hand-to-hand. Japanese running into Company G ranks are bayoneted. By the time the last Jap is killed it is dark and the company disorganized, with the wounded Lt. Hansen in unexpected command.

The SP carrying Capt. Olander has retreated halfway down the ridge before Olander can get out.

Company G then withdraws to the area of the previous night and organizes the night defenses.

Company G men move forward on Ridge 300. (USA-LOC)

On June 25 the offense is augmented with two batteries of the 751st AAA Gun Battalion with their 90 mm guns and four 40 mm AA guns.

Company G renews the flank attack, but the Japanese have prepared a circular defense, which is finally reduced by Company F shortly after 1500. After advancing another hundred yards, both companies withdraw in favor of the artillery and dig in atop Ridge 300 at 1700. In seizing the ridge, the Second Battalion had faced twenty mutually-supporting machine guns, fifty mortars and ten 5 inch dual purpose guns. They will later learn that on June 25 the Japanese commander had lost all his remaining heavy and automatic weapons and that they are short of ammo, food and water. About three hundred bodies of dead Japanese are found in the Nafutan Valley and Ridge 300. Many more have been removed to caves in the Japanese rear.

The next few days involve mopping up over rugged terrain, with the Japanese fighting almost to the last man, and one more Company G death. The Nafutan peninsula is in American hands.

With the rear now secured, the American forces continue their advance northward, with the 4th Marine Division covering the east coast, the 2nd Marine Division hugging the west, and the 27th Army Division slugging straight up the middle, across rugged terrain that soon earns such romantic nicknames as Purple Heart Ridge and Death Valley. Numerous caves and outcrops provide the defenders strong positions from which to rain death and destruction on their foes. Their willingness to fight to the death increases their effectiveness, a determination born with the realization that there is no hope for relief or victory.

At Lt. Gen. Yoshitsugu Saito's side stands an unusual guest, or perhaps co-commander: Vice Adm. Chuichi Nagumo. Nagumo had led the Japanese carrier fleet that had successfully launched the surprise attack on Pearl Harbor, making him a national hero. Months later, in the same command, he had been the big loser of the Battle of Midway when his carrier fleet was effectively removed from the war.

He has come ashore on Saipan to die, appropriately coming face to face with the resurrected ghost ships of Pearl Harbor and Spruance of Midway.

As the American forces advance, Saito moves his headquarters several times, ultimately to an area in the northern sector that the Americans call Paradise Valley. There he makes his final plans for his troops and himself.

Company G awaits move into coconut grove, July 6, 1944 (USA-LOC)

By July 5, the American battle plan has caused the army units to pivot northward (rather than follow the natural axis of the island north-easterly) to the western shore, cutting off the Second Marine Division. The 2nd Battalion of the 105th, back in action, moves along the beach. Coming under heavy fire, they hold their positions for the night, preparing to advance the next morning. Company G has been attached temporarily to the 3rd Battalion, farther inland, tied up in a coconut grove. On July 6, Army tanks "in search of a mission" take care of a couple of machine guns and the troops move forward.

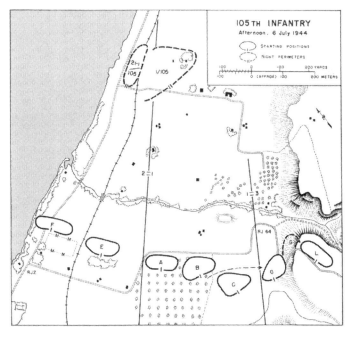

(USA-LOC)

Approaching the cliffs of Hara Kari Gulch, a more or less east-west pass near the front lines, Company K is faced with the sight of Japanese troops rushing down the cliffs toward them. They apparently blunder into one of their own mine fields, and the exploding of one sets off a chain reaction sending Japanese body parts hurtling through the air in every direction, horrifying the Americans.

Capt. Olander moves Company G forward to replace K Company. Simultaneously with the Japanese they notice a machine gun from M Company unattended on a hilltop. Company K moves back to the Battalion Command Post as Company G takes the hill and the gun, but not without opposition.

Olander's mission now is to block the mouth of Hara Kari Gulch, bottling up any Japanese inside the gulch and protecting the right flank of the troops advancing up the coastal plain. Taking two men, including a radioman (their radios have finally arrived), he personally sets out to scout the terrain, following a road that ascends along hairpin turns into the hills of the gulch. Moving along the eastern leg of a hairpin he comes across a burned-out tank tipped over in a ditch about twenty yards in front of him. On his left between the road and the west leg of the hairpin lies thirty yards of dense brush five feet lower than the road, more or less.

Olander moves alone along the deep ditch on his right as far as the tank and calls back to the radioman to move the 1st Platoon forward. Before they reach half-way to the tank, the brush on the left erupts with fire from rifles and machine guns, and from a nose on their right front. Two men are hit, and the platoon is pinned down. Olander is forward of the fire from the left and behind the fire from the right.

He calmly radios for the 2nd Platoon to advance on high ground and for the 3rd Platoon to move below the hairpin in support of the advance of the 1st.

Capt. Olander himself begins poking through the brush in search of enemy troops. It is already 1800 and darkness is approaching.

Staff Sgt. Edward Wojcicki brings his 3rd Platoon forward, moving along the lower ditch. Halfway to where the captain is beating the bushes, Olander orders them to halt and then to come through the brush toward him.

Wojcicki steps right onto the backs of Japanese soldiers. They are in the middle of a well-hidden Japanese outpost.

Machine guns open fire, grenades are tossed, men are running in all directions. Olander fires his carbine, then uses it as a club until he breaks it, then picks up a Japanese saber and uses it well.

Members of Wojcicki's platoon are wrestling and kicking and shooting and bayoneting. Two men are killed and Sgt. Benjamin Drenzek wounded four different times. Three times Japs try to carry Drenzek off, three times Wojcicki's men kill the captors.

Olander orders a retreat to their kick-off point and reevaluates.

Recognizing that he does not have the manpower to seal the mouth of the gulch, he nonetheless determines that it can be effectively controlled from a nose of ground which he quickly secures. They set up their defensive perimeter under machine gun fire from a cave on the opposite wall of the gulch. Olander personally spots it, and Pvt. Joseph Kinyone volunteers to fire a bazooka round at the target. He is hit by a bullet and killed.

Their bird's-eye seat will give Company G a spectacular view of one of the most amazing charges of the Pacific War, even as it turns toward them.

Vice Adm. Nagumo joins Gen. Saito on the evening of July 5 for a ceremonial farewell dinner of canned crab meat and *sake*. Saito prepares a message to be delivered to all his remaining officers the following morning, July 6:

> I am addressing the officers and men of the Imperial Army on Saipan. For more than twenty days since the American Devils attacked, the officers, men and civilians employees of the Imperial Army and Navy on this island have fought well and bravely. Everywhere they have demonstrated the honor and glory of the Imperial forces. I expected that every man would do his duty.
>
> Heaven has not given us an opportunity. We have not been able to utilize fully the terrain. We have fought in unison up to the present time, but now we have no materials with which to fight and our artillery for attack has been completely destroyed. Our comrades have fallen one after another. Despite the bitterness of defeat we pledge "seven lives to repay our country."
>
> The barbarous attack of the enemy is being continued. Even though the enemy has occupied only a corner of Saipan, we are

dying without avail under the violent shelling and bombing. Whether we attack, or whether we stay where we are, there is only death. However, in death there is life. We must utilize this opportunity to exalt true Japanese manhood. I will advance with those who remain to deliver still another blow to the American Devils and leave my bones on Saipan as a bulwark of the Pacific.

As it says in the *Senjikun*, "I will never suffer the disgrace of being taken alive" and "I will offer up the courage of my soul and calmly rejoice in living by the eternal principle."

Here I pray with you for the eternal life of the Emperor and the welfare of the country and I advance to seek out the enemy. Follow me!

With the message go orders for all to assemble at 1800 on July 6, with the attack to begin at 2200.

Two hours after the orders are read, at 1000 on July 6, Saito sits on a rock and faces east and shouts "*Tenno Heika! Banzai!*" in praise of his Emperor and cuts an artery with his sword, while an aide shoots him in the head.

In a cave nearby, Nagumo, the victor of Pearl Harbor and vanquished of Midway, does the same.

The forward lines on the night of July 6 have the 2nd Battalion of the 105th (minus Company G) on the left (beach side), with the 1st Battalion, called up that afternoon, to their right, with railroad tracks between them, about twelve hundred yards south of the village of Makunsha. Four hundred yards behind lies the 105th Command Post and northeast of them, just behind the front lines, the 3rd Battalion of the 10th Marines, an artillery unit.

A wide gap separates the 1st Battalion from Company G of the 2nd and the 3rd Battalion. There does not seem to be any practical way to close those lines as darkness falls, though military historians will continue to debate the issue. In any event, the last request for reinforcements is denied at 2150.

Members of the 105th Regiment face their Saipan Rendezvous.

> *. . . But I've a rendezvous with Death*
> *At midnight in some flaming town,*
> *When Spring trips north again this year,*
> *And I to my pledged word am true,*
> *I shall not fail that rendezvous.*

The Japanese attack is delayed, presumably for logistical reasons. What *sake* is available is distributed among the men. Any wounded who can walk are ordered into line. The rest are ordered to commit suicide or are killed.

There are insufficient weapons left, so men approach the line of battle with hand guns, swords, bayonets, sharpened sticks, rocks and themselves. At 0400 they run down both sides of the tracks and twenty-five yards on either side. A third line comes down the base of a cliff on the edge of the plain exploiting the gap between Company G and the 1st Battalion.

Company E's Capt. Clinton Smith, one of the veterans of Company G who had marched away with them in 1940, meets the challenge at the head of his men. He is among the first to fall, wounded in both legs, facing the enemy. Some dozen of his men surround him as thousands of Japanese race toward them. Smith orders them to fall back and leave him behind. He does not survive.[16]

The 1st and 2nd Battalions are overwhelmed in minutes, with all organization broken down and every man for himself. Fighting is hand-to-hand. Major Edward McCarthy of the 2nd Battalion later reports:

> It was like the movie stampede staged in the Wild West movies. We were the cameramen. Those Japs just kept coming and coming and didn't stop. It didn't make any difference if you shot one; five more would take his place.

As the light rises, Company G watches with amazement. Says Tech. Sgt. John Polikowski:

> Did you ever see the outside of a circus tent about the time the evening show is over? That's just the way it was. It reminded me of circus grounds, or maybe it was the Yankee Stadium. The crowd just milled on the field, pushing and shoving and yelling and shouting. There were so many of them you could just shut your eyes and pull the trigger on your rifle and you'd be bound to hit three or four with one shot.

---

16 Pfc. Alfred Peters writes Smith's widow in Amsterdam: "If ever a man was idolized by any group or groups of men, Clinton Smith was, and his memory will always live in the hearts of his men, to say nothing of what the entire battalion and his regiment think of him as an officer and leader of men."

Some of the men in the 2nd Battalion flee into the surf and swim to a reef where they are later rescued.

Exploiting the gap, the Japs get behind the 1st Battalion and attack from the rear.

Major McCarthy reorganizes the men into a second perimeter and they fight on for four more hours before again falling back. Meanwhile Lt. Col. William O'Brien re-establishes the 1st Battalion at the front. He inspires his men with a pistol firing from each hand until a shoulder wound limits the use of one arm. He leaps into a jeep and operates its .50-caliber machine gun, mowing down the Japs trying to take it away from him until he runs out of ammo. Grabbing a saber from one, he swings away until he himself is finally cut to pieces. Next to his body lie thirty dead Japanese. He is posthumously awarded one of three Congressional Medals of Honor earned that day by the 105th.

The 1st Battalion's Sgt. Thomas Baker remains on the front lines, even with part of his foot blown off. He uses his empty weapon as a club until another soldier picks him up to carry him away. The rescuer then is himself wounded, and a second continues the rescue until he is wounded as well. Baker will not allow anyone else to move him, ordering his men to prop him up against a pole with a pistol containing eight bullets, and a cigarette. They find his body later, with an empty pistol and eight dead Japs. The other hand holds a partially burned cigarette. The 105th's second Medal of Honor.

Capt. Ben Salomon is by profession a dentist, from Los Angeles, serving as a regimental surgeon for the 2nd Battalion. Soon after the battle begins he has thirty wounded men crowded into his aid tent. The Japanese begin to overrun his position, and he sees one bayoneting a patient. Dr. Salomon squats and kills him. Two more appear at the tent entrance. They are dispatched. Four more crawl under the tent wall. Salomon kicks the knife out of one's hand, shoots another and bayonets a third, then butts the fourth in the stomach while a wounded man shoots him. Salomon orders the wounded to evacuate as best they can to the regimental aid station, while he fights a rear-guard action to protect his patients' retreat. He then grabs a rifle from one of the wounded and joins the battle, taking control of a machine gun after four American operators are killed. As the dead pile up, he has to move the gun four times to maintain a field of vision. There are 98 dead Japs in front of his body. The third Medal of Honor.

Meanwhile, on the little nose at the mouth of Hara Kari Gulch, the boys of Company G are no longer casual observers. Though exposed on three sides, they also have excellent fields of fire. They will need them.

A light machine gun on the nose covers the mouth of the gulch while another across the road and to the left prevents any movement along the base of the escarpment. The latter, with a squad of riflemen, lies outside the company perimeter.

They can hear the sound like a cattle herd and when darkness lifts shortly after 0500 they can see the advancing Japs. And an initial group of about three hundred are heading toward them.

Capt. Olander orders firing to commence immediately, and at first no enemy is able to advance within three hundred yards of their position. Most are killed or scattered in minutes. But the enemy is constantly reinforced and the duel continues for another hour.

Between 0700 and 0800 (there is little opportunity to check their watches for the benefit of the historians) small raiding parties begin to hit the left flank, seeking to knock out the light machine gun outside the perimeter. They get close enough to toss grenades. Sgt. Nicholas Graziano requests permission to bring the LMG within the company perimeter, but it is hit before he can move.

Tech. Sgt. Polikowski, in charge of the platoon lowest on the hill, orders his men back ten yards, and they gain ten feet in height, but lose a man. Graziano loses his gunner and another man.

The Company G men are firing fast and furious. A sniper kills two of them, and wounds a third.

It is now 0800 and Olander is running short of ammo. It becomes "the old whites of their eyes stuff," as one man later puts it. Japs take cover behind the overturned tank from the previous day and begin tossing grenades.

And now begins a deadly game of catch, with each side tossing the grenades back toward the other. By 0830 casualties are heavy. Five Company G men are seriously wounded. One of them is their captain.

Olander has his arm nearly blown off. He calmly applies a tourniquet above the break and continues directing the defense for the next three hours. Between 1100 and 1130 there is silence, and then a rain of knee-mortar shells hits them. Frank Olander collapses at last from the loss of blood and is evacuated, while the company Executive Officer, Lt. George O'Donnell, assumes command. What's left of Company G withdraws 75-100 yards to the rear and digs in with Company L.

But the Battle for Saipan is essentially over. The suicide charge faces increasingly stiff opposition until it reaches Battalion Headquarters of the 105th where it ends with guns blazing. Two days later the island is declared secured.

Hara Kiri Gulch, the next day. (USA - LOC)

There had been 1,107 men in the 105th's 1st and 2nd Battalions. Over four hundred are killed and another five hundred wounded in that battle. Of the enemy, an actual count of 4,311 are buried between the farthest advance of the 1st and 2nd and the farthest advance of the Japanese. Of those, 2,295 are found in the combat area of the 1st and 2nd Battalion,

105th, 2,016 in the areas of the 106th infantry, the 3rd Battalion 10th Marines and the 3rd Battalion 105th (including Company G of the 2nd Battalion).

The horror, though, has not quite ended.

The 27th Army Division has no part in the mopping up operations and prepares for the occupation. Melrose Freer has, rather miraculously, survived his first combat campaign intact. He probably doesn't even know that his brother-in-law, Hank Pileckas, is serving in the Second Marine Division heading for the northern tip of the island.

Hank makes it through alright, too, but is soon to witness one of the most gruesome scenes in world history as hundreds of Japanese civilians hurl themselves, their wives and their children over cliffs to their death, rather than be taken prisoner. Others gather together in small groups and explode grenades among them. Others slaughter their children.

The Americans try desperately to stop them, employing loud speakers (one operated by Amsterdamian Lt. W. Morris Brown, nick-named "The Talking Jeep").

In the battle and its aftermath, some twenty-two thousand Japanese civilians die, and nearly all of their thirty thousand servicemen stationed there.

What the boys of Company G and the 105th Regiment and the whole 27th Division do not know at the time is that the Commander of the operation, Marine Gen. Holland "Howlin' Mad" Smith, has described them to his superiors as "the worst division I've ever seen."

More than that, "They're yellow. They are not aggressive. They've just held up the battle and caused my Marines casualties."

He tells Adm. Spruance that the *banzai* attack of July 7 had been undertaken by "300 enemy supported by two or three tanks."

This preposterous claim does not make it into Spruance's final report, which is based on the factual evidence of the battlefield. But Smith has a secret weapon in his public relations battle with the Army: *TIME* magazine correspondent Robert Sherrod, embedded with the Marines on Saipan. The version of the Battle of Saipan that the folks back home get to read about is this one, published in the September 18, 1944 issue of *TIME*:

By the eighth day of the Saipan battle the Second and Fourth Marine Divisions had advanced rapidly on each side of the island. Then they had to wait, because two regiments of the 27th Army Division—with battalions faced in three directions, unable even to form a line—were hopelessly bogged down in the center. The third regiment of the 27th meanwhile had failed dismally to clean out a pocket of Japs in the southeast corner of the island.

Although terrific artillery barrages were laid down in front of them, Ralph Smith's men froze in their foxholes. For days these men, who lacked confidence in their officers, were held up by handfuls of Japs in caves. When it began to look as if what had been gained might be lost, Fourth Marine Division troops even moved in front of a sector of the 27th's line to save it. From the Marine point of view, Gen. Ralph Smith's chief fault was that he had long ago failed to get tough enough to remove incompetent subordinate officers.

On the ninth day Ralph Smith was relieved (technically, for disobeying an order to attack), and Major Gen. Sanderford Jarman, who had come along as Saipan's post-battle commander, took over the 27th temporarily, fired several officers, including a regimental colonel. Thereafter, the 27th performed fairly well until its greenest regiment broke and let some 3,000 Japs through in a suicide charge which a Marine artillery battalion finally stopped, at great cost to itself.

Behind the scenes efforts are made to publicly correct the account. Adm. Chester Nimitz himself even offers to do so. But the War Department decides that ultimately it is better not to reopen the inter-service conflict when there are so many real battles yet to be fought.

No Marine general will ever again command Army troops for the duration of the war, and "Howlin' Mad" Smith will never again command troops in combat.

But the boys of Company G, after all that they have sacrificed and endured, have now been branded cowards.

And then come the telegrams.

Staff Sgt. Peter J. Sanzen, 26, 216 Florida Avenue, a member of Company G, who had not been home in the nearly four years since they marched out of the Armory, killed in action, Saipan.

Pvt. First Class Paul P. Sierota of Amsterdam RD 5, Company G, an employee of Mohawk Carpet Mills, killed in action, Saipan.

Sgt. Edward R. Golenbiewski, 2 Wren Street, Company G, one of the guests at the wedding of Melrose Freer and Nell Pileckas, killed in action, Saipan.

Pvt. First Class Daniel F. Slusarz, 46 Milton Avenue, formerly in Company G but later transferred to an anti-tank company, killed in action, Saipan.

Capt. Clinton F. Smith, 32, 5 First Avenue, commanding officer of Schenectady's Company E, 105th Infantry, having transferred from Company G on his promotion to captain in 1943, killed in action, Saipan.

Sgt. Michael Makarowsky, 45 Grand Street, Company G, a Ukrainian Folk Dancer, another guest at the wedding of Melrose Freer and Nell Pileckas, killed in action, Saipan. He had taken command of his platoon when their lieutenant had been killed and led them in defiance of all enemy opposition.

Pvt. First Class Stanli Soltys, USMCR, 24, Amsterdam RD 5, who never came home after joining the Marines in November of 1942, recipient of a Purple Heart for wounds received in the Battle of Tarawa in November, 1943, veteran of the machine shop in the Shuttleworth Division of Mohawk Carpet Mills, killed in action, Saipan.

Cpl. Victor Fondacaro, USMCR, born in Amsterdam the day the last war ended, November 11, 1918, and so named for the victory (and peace) achieved that day. His brother Samuel had been in Company G when they left town, but later transferred to the Airborne Division in the Pacific. Another brother, Joseph, had been wounded in battle in the Normandy invasion on June 8. Killed in action, Central Pacific.

And the wounded, among them these veterans of the old Company G:

> Pfc. Robert Miller, Pvt. Ralph Litchfield, Pfc. Dominick Lamori, Pfc. Thomas J. Mantagnino, Tech. Sgt. Max Tracz, Pfc. Louis Aldi, Pfc. John Lang, Tech. Sgt. Henry Gawlak, Sgt. Earl Smith, Pfc. Joseph LoBalbo, Staff Sgt. Joseph Ochal, Sgt. Benjamin Drenzek, Capt. Frank Olander, Staff Sgt. Edwin Luck.

> And the Marines: Pfc. Ralph Downs, Pfc. Gabriel Vertucci, Sgt. Archie Gatto.

Pharmacist's Mate First Class Calvin Robitaille of Cohoes cares for many of the wounded of the 105th Infantry and tells of the grim reality of the battle for Saipan:

> They might have been men from my own home town, but I didn't have time to ask. They were a spunky lot. They wanted to get back on shore. Most of all they wanted to get some of those Jap soldiers who had armed the kids, knowing that we protect civilians.
>
> Well, I guess that the people around here know now that Saipan was a tough fight. There's got to be battles like that to win the war. You can all be proud that our fellows were picked to fight on Saipan. It does something to the folks at home to have to face casualties like that, but don't forget that it does something to us, too.

Company G is no longer just an Amsterdam group but has been expanded and augmented by other troops to bring them up to regulation strength. The expanded Company G casualty list includes 31 enlisted personnel killed, 69 wounded and one officer killed and two wounded. After the *banzai* attack of July 7, the sector in front of Company G contains the bodies of 438 Japanese.

Cowards.

Yellow.

The valiant never taste of death but once.

12. THE FINE AND MANLY ARTS

Amsterdam sends its share of musicians and thespians into the war. Louis Vorse plays in the Army Air Force Band, Dean D'Allesandro (later a local fixture with his "Dean Dale Trio") plays in the Army Band, Chester Szypula for the Navy. But two guys get the biggest music gig of World War II.

Irving Berlin does his part by throwing together an All-Army musical show, *This Is The Army*, which not only tours the country and plays for President Roosevelt, but also becomes a major Technicolor motion picture starring Ronald Reagan, George Murphy and the original cast. The orchestra for the show comes mostly from fellows who have played with the big bands, including Amsterdam's Ronald "Bunny" Snyder on trumpet and Abe "Al" Siegel on bass violin. Both appear on camera in the film.

Lt. Vernon Ehle, a veteran of the Butch Robertshaw orchestra, throws together a 23-piece all-black marching band in ten days in 1943, and Sgt. Dominick Peters puts together an entertainment band in Hawaii.

The success of *This Is The Army* spawns many imitators, like *Private Maxie Reporting*, staged in Savannah, featuring song and dance man Pfc. Cecil Hage as a captain. Meanwhile, in Fort Lewis, Washington, Pvt. Edward Ruman, lately President of the Amsterdam Little Theater, provides the scenic and lighting effects for the big Army musical *Sound Off*.

Some guys play just for the heck of it, like popular piano-player Petty Officer Third Class Eugene R. Greco, who entertains his comrades in the local canteens.[17] Back home he had played with the Guy Reynolds Orchestra and Butch Robertshaw's orchestra, even before graduating from Wilbur H. Lynch High School in 1942. On June 5, 1943 his plane goes down over the Atlantic. The body is never recovered. He is eighteen.

In London, Cpl. Murray Sitzer appears in the all-Army Maxwell Anderson drama *Eve of St. Mark*. Sitzer, an efficiency expert for a firm of

---

17 He is the brother of Marine Pfc. Albert Greco, mentioned in the Guadalcanal chapter

dry cleaners before the war, had once been a chorus boy, back in 1933, appearing with Milton Berle in *The Mickey Mouse Follies.*

Malcolm Atterbury is a name that might sound only vaguely familiar, if at all, but you've probably seen his face hundreds of times as one of the most prolific movie and television character actors in the 50's and 60's. Arguably his most famous scene gets him no screen billing at all, in Alfred Hitchcock's *North By Northwest*. He's the guy standing at the bus stop next to Cary Grant in the middle of nowhere who casually observes, "That's funny; that plane's dustin' crops where there ain't no crops."

Born Malcolm Macleod, Jr. in 1907, he is later adopted by his mother's husband, William Wallace Atterbury, a brigadier general in the first World War and later the president of the Pennsylvania Railroad. Malcolm has no interest in running railroads and instead goes into acting, running a small radio station, then some vaudeville and the legitimate stage.

He becomes an Amsterdamian by his marriage to Ellen Hardies, and together they form their own summer-stock troupe in 1938, the Tamarack Players. Later they have a "winter-stock" company in Albany as well. Some of their up-and-comers include Karl Malden, Cliff Robertson, Grace Kelly, Tom Bosley, Barbara Cook and a kid from Amsterdam named Izzy Demsky. Atterbury renames him.

They would present a new show every week at the playhouse in Lake Pleasant in the lower Adirondacks some sixty miles north of Amsterdam. On Mondays they would bring the whole show into Amsterdam's Junior High School auditorium. This goes on for several years until the war intervenes.

Malcolm Atterbury is also the most over-qualified theater reviewer in the history of the *Amsterdam Evening Recorder*. He and his wife go to New York several times a year and bring the locals up to date on all the new shows opening and closing. Even today, they are interesting and informative. Here's an example, from November 22, 1941:

> On Thursday afternoon I saw Grace George in "Spring Again," a really delightful play that anyone would enjoy. It's a story you won't remember long, but Miss George's performance you will

find difficult to forget. Kirk Douglas, from Amsterdam, who spent two summers with the Tamarack Playhouse, marks his debut in this show. He has one very short scene with Miss George which is quite funny and, as the second act curtain falls, the audience is in gales of laughter. Now that Kirk has made his start, I hope to see more of him in Broadway shows.

Too young for World War I, too old for World War II, Atterbury decides to do his part by putting together, on his own dime, a roving cast of players to bring legitimate theater to the USO circuit. At the request of the home-town paper, he reinvigorates his old column, "ON STAGE," which, though heavily censored, presents a rare glimpse of life on the road and in the camps. By the time the column begins, in April of 1943, they have been on the road for three months, in some sixty different locations, under all kinds of circumstances. They have dinner with the men in the mess halls and chat with them in the recreation rooms.

The company consists of Velma Royton, Sara Floyd, Barbara Barton and myself, oh yes and two small dogs. Did you ever hear of a theatrical troupe without pets? Those of you who have seen the plays at Tamarack will remember each of the above players.

Back to the dogs, we use one of them in the show. Her name is Miss Scarlet O'Hara. The other one is an understudy. We don't carry an extra actor, we just play regardless of how we feel. We make quite an impressive entrance at each camp. You know the soldiers love dogs and each camp has at least 25 mongrels. So when we arrive they all immediately gather around to have a look at the civilian dogs, barking and yelling. There's generally one fight, sometimes two before they all become acquainted. I mean the dogs.

One night they play before 450 colored troops,[18] most of whom have never seen a stage play of any kind.

> When we were ready to begin, the officer went before the curtain and talked to the boys. He explained that they were going to see something like a movie, except instead of the people being on the screen they would be right there in person. He told them several stories, got them laughing. Then I stepped out and before I started the show, I asked them how many had ever seen a play. Four of them raised their hands. That meant we were the first actors the other 446 had ever seen. Five minutes after the show had started you could sense how interested they all were. They grasped the situation right away and laughed whenever they wanted. Many of you have heard one colored man really laugh, well imagine 450 of them laughing. Sometimes the laughs were so long that we on the stage had to wait minutes before we could go on with the next line. That to an actor is a great thrill.
>
> During the intermissions we gave out over a thousand cigarettes. At the final curtain we had five minutes of applause. I finally got the boys to stop and said: "Boys, your courteous, enthusiastic reception of our play has been something each member of the cast will long remember. We've enjoyed playing to you more than you will ever know. Now there is just one thing you can do for us. For 20 minutes or so, you put on a show for us."
>
> We went and sat in the front row and in a few seconds we were entertained by a quartet, some dancers, a boy with a harmonica. They danced and sang and for half an hour we had a wonderful time.
>
> When it was over one of the colored fellows came to me and said, "Mr. Atterbury, it's nearly the end of the month and none of us has much money left, but we raised enough among ourselves to buy seven candy bars, one for each member of your group. Will

---

18 Throughout this book I have employed the terminology of the era with no attempt to scrub it. Thus, you will find Japs, Nips, Krauts, Chinks and "colored boys." It is what it was.

you accept it as a small token of our great appreciation for the fun and entertainment you have given tonight."

I tried to thank the boy but I just couldn't find the words. I took the candy, shook hands with him and did manage to say "thanks." I turned to the cast gave them each a candy bar and,well, perhaps you can sense how deeply touched we all were. You see why it was a night that we will all remember.

There are many more adventures recorded, sharing a "stage" with a pool table, and another with a working pay phone that keeps interrupting the dialog, and crammed sets where the audiences share the "stage" with them. Atterbury saves the most poignant entry for last.

June 18, 1943

We arrived at the main gate of this Army camp on our tour at 6:30 o'clock one evening. I had telephoned earlier in the day and was told to be there at that time.

A sergeant greeted us and took me into the office, where my papers were very carefully examined. In about half an hour we were back in the car again ready to drive on to the place where we would play. The sergeant came with us. He told us it was a half hour drive to the theatre. He had left there at 5:30 and the boys were all looking forward to the show. It was the first one they had had in two months. Of course they had movies several times a week, but a stage show was something new and they were all very anxious to see it. I asked him about how many we would have in the audience.

"The theatre," he replied, "seats about 750, and I'm sure every seat will be taken. Would you be willing to do a second performance if necessary?"

"Of course we will be glad to do a second show. Just let us know if you want it," I said.

Our drive through the camp was very interesting, and our escort kept us well amused with stories. We came to a crossroad and he told me to turn left. As we did I looked down the road, and as far as I could see there were soldiers lined up on both sides. They were standing at attention and seemed to have their full equipment with them. I stopped the car and an officer came up and told me to drive on slowly.

It was very impressive driving through the double line of men at attention. Finally we came to the theatre. The sergeant told us to wait a moment in the car and he would find out what was going on.

He came back In a few minutes and said very quietly: "I'm afraid you won't have much of an audience. After I left to go to the gate to meet you the order came through to prepare for a hike, and the boys will be starting out now in a few minutes."

"Won't any of them be left here?" I asked.

"Yes, maybe a hundred or so," he replied.

"Well, we will do the show for them."

While we had been sitting there in the car I had noticed that some of the boys were giving a few of the soldiers who were evidently not going on the hike slips of papers. Some were still hastily writing. I asked the sergeant what they were doing.

"Probably sending a letter home. You see, it will be quite awhile before their parents get another letter."

"You mean," I said, "that they won't be coming back here?"

"That's right," he said. "We call it a hike, and the order always comes just about an hour before the boys leave. No one has time to write home, and these messages won't be sent for at least two or three weeks. By that time the boys will all have arrived safely on the other side."

We got out and were told we could talk to some of the fellows who were leaving. We spent a half hour doing that. Some of them were gay and excited, others were very quiet. It was an experience that I shall never forget, one that I could not describe to you in words. After the men left we set up the show and about 8:30 started the performance. We had about 120 In the audience, and they were very quiet and depressed. Along about the middle of the first act they began to forget and got into the swing of the play. They cheered up and laughed and were one of the best audiences we played to on the whole tour.

After the show practically all of them came back stage and thanked us so much. They all had just one regret, and that was that their buddies hadn't had a chance to see the show before they left on the "hike".

Atterbury is not the only Amsterdamian with the USO. Joining popular Boston area radio stars "Hum & Strum" on their overseas tour is veteran performer Raymond Kretser, who had previously traveled the country with the Major Bowes circuit, demonstrating his fan-favorite barnyard imitations. Kretser bumps into quite a few guys from home on his trip through Italy and Sardinia.

Edward Peckenpaugh (Class of 1935) trod the same Wilbur H. Lynch Senior High School stage as his contemporary Isadore Demsky (Class of 1934). Like "Kirk Douglas," he adopts a stage name, "Edward Barry" when appearing with the Tamarack Players. Like Douglas, he has studied at the New York Academy of Dramatic Arts. He is serious about his acting career.

And he is serious about being a Marine, rising to the rank of sergeant. Assigned to the Second Marine Division, he fights on Guadalcanal in 1942, and Tarawa in 1943, where he is wounded. He writes to his parents (relocated in Cocoa Beach, Florida) on December 10 of that year:

I know that you will think it ages since I last wrote you, and if you have been reading your papers, you've probably guessed the reason for the long delay. I have to be very vague as to . . . what has been going on. Some of it is censorable, and a good deal of it I would not tell you anyhow. This last jamboree made Guadalcanal seem like a strawberry festival, and I consider myself pretty lucky to get out as lightly as I did . . . . I am writing this from a naval hospital, but I can't tell you where. . . . It's a beautiful and perfectly equipped one, and I am expecting to be discharged any day now. . . . Then I imagine I will be sent back to I company, so do not attempt to address me here . . . use the old address . . . . I'll be glad to get back, in a way. I have not seen them since the morning of the assault, and I am anxious to learn how they made out. From what I hear, they did not get out without quite a few casualties. You see I got separated from the company in the confusion of landing, and our boat took us into a spot where there was no beachhead established. I was K.O.'d by a big one that exploded nearby, and I had to stay put for quite a while to keep from drawing fire, until it got dark enough to move.

There is no sense in writing you a lot of gibberish that will probably be cut out anyway, but the upshot of the whole business was that in trying to rush a Nip machine-gun I got second place in a race with a couple of hand grenades and absorbed some fragments in the region of the left eye and a few in my back, left arm and leg. . . . Before you light any candles, Mom, let me assure you that I am perfectly Okay, and won't even have a glamorous scar to exhibit.

I was finally evacuated early on the third day, and there is no reason for my being in the hospital now, except as an example of the wonderful medical care we've had. I have received a couple of thorough examinations and have been pronounced "fit as the proverbial fiddle." So don't waste any alarm over me. . . . When I look at some of the boys around me and think of the ones who were left on the beach, I realize that I am a very lucky guy.

I just had another examination, a brief one and my last one, I hope. The doctor again pronounced me O.K. And said, I quote, "We'll make some disposition of you very shortly." That could mean anything, so I won't make any guesses . . . probably back to my outfit . . . they are not so very far away.

By the way, you may have noticed that my fountain pen is conspicuous by its absence. I had it in my pack with my toilet gear, and it was smashed all to h--- by a slug that hit the pack. I didn't know the pack had been hit until the following morning. Close enough, heh?

I am not sure about Willie, but I think he is O.K. One of the boys here remembers seeing him shortly before they left, and says he was all right then. Other good reasons for getting back, I should have a good stack of mail . . . none since November 1st*. I know this will not get there in time, but Merry Christmas anyhow. Don't worry about me, darlings, take good care of yourselves. I miss you both more than ever.*

He returns to his outfit and fights through the Battle of Saipan. Once Saipan has been secured, the Second Marine Division attacks the nearby island of Tinian, which soon becomes a base for long-range bombers to attack the Japanese home islands. It is from Tinian that the atomic bombs will be launched that end the war.

And it is on Tinian that Sgt. Edward Peckenpaugh gives his life in service of his country.

There is something just a little spooky about the yearbook page of the Wilbur H. Lynch High School Class of 1934 featuring the ragman's son who will become Kirk Douglas. Isadore Demsky's list of accomplishments is so long that it completely overruns the space allotted to the guy above him, Walter Degutis. There's Izzy Demsky, the Senior Class Treasurer, Business Manager of the school newspaper and the Yearbook, Best Actor of 1934, Junior Public Speaking prize winner, cheerleader, prize-winning essayist, etc. etc., the spunky photograph with the famous grin and the dimpled chin, with a quote chosen by his peers, *"Not to know him argues yourself unknown."*

Walter Degutis is listed simply as "Red Cross Alternate." Later a gunner in a B-17 Flying Fortress bomber that goes down over Germany on June 29, 1944, his class quote reads, *"Safe in the hallowed quiet of the past."*

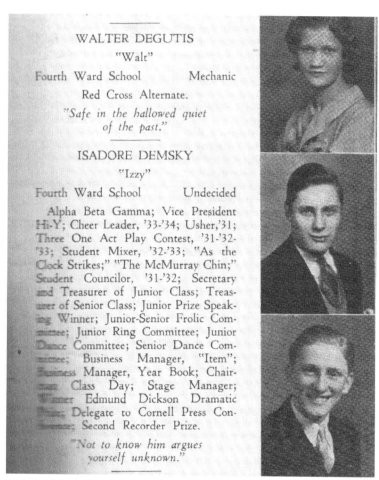

WALTER DEGUTIS

"Walt"

Fourth Ward School   Mechanic

Red Cross Alternate.

*"Safe in the hallowed quiet
of the past."*

ISADORE DEMSKY

"Izzy"

Fourth Ward School   Undecided

Alpha Beta Gamma; Vice President Hi-Y; Cheer Leader, '33-'34; Usher,'31; Three One Act Play Contest, '31-'32-'33; Student Mixer, '32-'33; "As the Clock Strikes;" "The McMurray Chin;" Student Councilor, '31-'32; Secretary and Treasurer of Junior Class; Treasurer of Senior Class; Junior Prize Speaking Winner; Junior-Senior Frolic Committee; Junior Ring Committee; Junior Dance Committee; Senior Dance Committee; Business Manager, "Item"; Business Manager, Year Book; Chairman Class Day; Stage Manager; Winner Edmund Dickson Dramatic Prize; Delegate to Cornell Press Conference; Second Recorder Prize.

*"Not to know him argues
yourself unknown."*

1934 Wilbur H. Lynch Yearbook (WEM)

The glory days of high school do not by any means guarantee future success for Izzy Demsky.[19] Scraping pennies every which way possible from the time he was a small boy, he has managed to put aside a tidy nest egg for his college education before he has even entered high school, but he loans it all to his father who manages to squander it on a get rich quick scheme worthy of Ralph Kramden. As his friends go off to college, Izzy

---

19 The wartime adventures of Kirk Douglas are largely derived from his autobiography *The Ragman's Son,* Simon and Schuster, New York:1988.

takes a job as a clerk in Lurie's Department store in menswear and contemplates someday being manager of the division.

He does a little local amateur theater and after a long, lonely year saves up just enough money to maybe get himself into college. So he hitches a ride, along with his friend Pete Riccio, on a manure truck headed in the direction of St. Lawrence University. There he prospers both as an actor and an athlete (a champion wrestler). He is even elected student body president. Summers he joins up with the Tamarack Players: first as a stage hand, later as a member of the stock company. By the time World War II has broken out he has played that minor part on Broadway and a pathway to success has opened up. He has, somewhat bitterly, left his home town behind him.

Malcolm Atterbury had given him the stage name "Kirk Douglas" and by and by the thespian formerly known as Isadore Demsky has a judge change it permanently.

Getting into the war does not happen as easily. He flunks the vision test. Not to be deterred, he discovers some exercises designed to improve eyesight, and practices them daily for a month. Next time he passes.

In short time comes Officer's Training School at Notre Dame, marriage, and a ship assignment in New Orleans. As the communications officer, Ens. Douglas is not in any way responsible for the inauspicious debut of *PC 1139* which manages to slam into the dock both bow and stern, crash into (and partially sink) the ship behind it and rip a lifeboat off the ship in front of it before finally making it to open water in the Mississippi. Before even hitting the Gulf of Mexico, Douglas is seasick.

Nor does the fate of the Patrol Craft change much. Various incidents at sea, including nicking a Russian destroyer, keep them in and out of dry dock in Miami for a month and a half. Finally, they set off for the Panama Canal and the Pacific. After some anti-submarine training in the Galapagos Islands, in the spring of 1944 they receive their first real assignment: escorting a cargo ship to Hawaii. From there they are to continue West, sweeping the Pacific Ocean of Japanese subs. To conserve fuel, however, for the first part of the voyage the cargo ship actually tows the PC, much to the merriment of the merchant mariners and the chagrin of the Navy.

When at last they break out on their own, the *ping-ping* of the ship's sonar reveals what appears to them to be an enemy submarine. Springing into action, the crew releases small bombs into the water. There is an explosion, which means they might have hit something. The play acting of all the training exercises is over.

Douglas is the gunnery officer astern. The captain orders the release of a depth charge marker, to establish with green dye a target on the surface of the vast ocean.

A sudden explosion rocks the ship right out of the water. Men begin yelling, "Torpedo! Torpedo!"

But there is no torpedo.

A nervous green crew member has released a depth *charge* instead of a depth charge *marker*. They have attacked their own ship, chewing up the steering gear. In the tossing about, Douglas slams into the depth charge rack and receives severe abdominal bruising. Did they sink the sub? Had there really been a sub? They will never know.

Orders are changed. They reverse course for Mexico. Before long Kirk Douglas finds himself in a Navy Hospital in San Diego suffering from amoebic dysentery, probably from a bug picked up in Panama. It ends his Navy career at about the same time he finds out that his wife is pregnant.

The man who will later play many a valiant officer on the screen is honorably discharged in June of 1944.

Not every local with the acting bug gets to join the Tamarack Players. For the amateurs, there exists a pretty solid company, Ed Ruman's *Amsterdam Little Theater.* Michael E. Kleopfel, Jr., who had knocked them dead playing the male lead in *Pride and Prejudice*, the senior play of 1938 at Lynch High (the year he is voted by his classmates *Boy Most Likely to Succeed)*, becomes a regular with the Little Theater troupe, until called to the Army Air Force. Says Malcolm Atterbury of him, in a review of 1941's "No Boots in Bed," directed by Marv Robinson:

> One of the really pleasant surprises of the evening was the performance given by Michael Kleopfel. I have seen this young man in several shows before and the way he has progressed in his

acting is a tribute to the group, the director, and to himself. A fine voice, a good appearance and a boyish charm are some of his assets which he used to great advantage.

(Also in the cast of that show, though not quite so favorably reviewed, is future Cpl. Robert E. Denton, who, on October 16, 1944, at the age of 23, dies when a heavy bomber he is training in crashes into a mountain in Vermont.)

Michael Kleopfel's father, who used as his ring name Mike Clifford, had been a colorful local character, purported to have come down on the wrong side of the law in some prohibition matters, something about using a gym as a front for a speakeasy, which had landed him in jail at a time when his son was approaching puberty. According to his obituary he had been "a prominent figure in local athletic circles and for a long time was popular as a boxing referee" and was "an instructor in physical culture." According to family legend, he took under his wing young teenager Izzy Demsky and taught him to, at very least, defend himself, serving almost as a surrogate father at a time when the future Hollywood legend had become estranged from his own father.

After a little over a year at the University of Michigan, Kleopfel, Jr. returns to Amsterdam to care for his dying mother. While acting with the Little Theater he plays opposite Mary York of Albany. When, during rehearsal, he approaches a kissing scene with her somewhat awkwardly, the director takes York aside and urges her to put the shy fellow at ease. She does. And becomes Mrs. Michael Kleopfel.

He joins the Army Air Force and proceeds to England, the birth country of his mother, there to carry out bombing raids over the native land of his Bavarian-born grandfather.

First Lt. Michael E. Kleopfel, Jr. pilots a Havoc fighter-bomber with a three man crew that is shot down over Germany on May 20, 1944. The other crew members survive and are taken prisoner, thus delaying this letter to the widow until July of 1945:

Dear Mrs Kleopfel

I am not much of a hand at writing letters but I will try to write a few lines to let you know about your husband, Lt. Kleopfel.

He was killed in the line of duty doing his job. He was a mighty nice boy, well-liked by Shaw and myself as well as by the ground crew of our ship. He always had a smile for everybody. I know it is hard to give him up, but to win, some of the boys had to go and you can always be sure he went like a man. We were bombing an airfield that morning on the 20th of May and had just dropped our bombs and were leaving the target when we started to get the anti-aircraft fire from the ground. We were flying right on the rear of the formation which is a bad spot and they got us and another plane with a few shots. Within two or three minutes Lt. Kleopfel gave the order for Shaw and me to bail out. He didn't say anything about being hit, but he never got out of the plane.

Well, Mrs. Kleopfel, if there is any other detail or anything you would like to know about it, just let me know. I will be glad to tell you if I can. You probably heard everything from the War Department, but I know how short and cool some of their messages are.

S/Sgt. Ray Bankston Jr.

Michael Kleopfel , Jr. (center) with Bankston and Shaw (Kleopfel Family)

Mary Kleopfel is pregnant when her husband is killed, and gives birth five months later to a son, whom she names Michael.

When, on September 25, 1944, Mr. and Mrs. Kirk Douglas have their first child, Mrs. Douglas suggests that he be named Kirk Douglas, Jr.

The former ensign demurs. It is not in the Jewish tradition to name a son after someone still living, he tells her.

No, Kirk Douglas, Jr. will not do.

They name him Michael.

For many years the top student drama honors at Wilbur H. Lynch High School are named the Michael E. Kleopfel, Jr. Award and the Kirk Douglas Award.

The Conti brothers fudge the line between entertainment and athletics, forming a family tumbling act that ultimately plays under the big top of the Ringling Brothers, Barnum and Bailey Circus. Sons of former performers from Brooklyn, the Conti family moves to Amsterdam when the older boys are still young. From the age of five their father begins their training high in the Adirondacks, tumbling onto hard, frozen ground, running, calisthenics. Their mother feeds them meat, eggs, milk and vegetables. They grow strong and agile, practicing every day after school until they reach perfection. John, the oldest, helps develop and encourage the younger brothers.

One problem they have, though, is putting together a pyramid. The Conti boys are all a good size, such that whichever one of them they try on top, the pyramid collapses. So they talk their light-weight friend Francis DeJulius into joining the act. While still a teenager, DeJulius loses his family in a fire, so Mr. and Mrs. Thomas Conti take him in. What's another kid when you already have nine?

They begin performing locally, in the High School auditorium, the YMCA and the Rialto Theater's vaudeville stage, eventually working into coast-to-coast tours and Ringling Brothers.

Jimmy and Tony even bring their skills to Hollywood, as movie stunt men. And when they aren't acrobating they are taking up boxing in their spare time, under the guidance of "Measles" Raco and Jo-Jo Zeno. Tony becomes middleweight champ of Amsterdam with a legendary victory over Matt Syzdek in 1938 at the Columbian Hall on East Main Street.

Even before World War II comes, the act breaks up in October of 1940 when John Conti joins the Navy (later serving in North Africa, Salerno and Anzio, among other places) and with Jimmy, Tom and Tony, along with Francis DeJulius, joining the Marines. Later in the war, Joe becomes a Leatherneck as well. And eventually Ernie, the baby, enters the Army as a medic. With all seven in the service, the Contis tie the Bubniaks for most members of one family from Amsterdam serving in World War II.

And serve they do. Cpl. Tom and Cpl. Tony, along with Pvt. DeJulius, take part in the First Marine Division assault on Guadalcanal, where Tony earns a Purple Heart. Dashing across open ground, he is shot twice in the leg, then dives into a foxhole with brother Tom, who renders first aid and then carries him to a medic. Assigned to guard Henderson Field, they come under Japanese fire on several occasions. Once the two brothers jump into 55 gallon drums as planes approach. Tony's is nice and clean. Tom's is the garbage can.

During another air attack, a bomb uproots a palm tree that lands on Tom Conti and pins him to the ground for two hours before he can be rescued. Told he is entitled to a Purple Heart, he declines. "Some day I may have kids, and I don't want to have to tell them that I got a medal for being attacked by a tree."

And Tom Conti also receives a reprimand for shooting down a Japanese airplane. He instinctively grabs an anti-tank gun and fires away at the low-flying craft, nailing it in the tail. Regulations called for the use of a different weapon.

Three times he narrowly escapes death. A bullet hits his helmet straight on and drops harmlessly down his back. Coming across a fellow Marine building a cooking fire, improvising a grill with scrap pipes, Conti offers to make breakfast, but is instructed to gather wood instead. One of the scrap pipes contains explosives and the cook enters the next world shortly thereafter. The third time, sick with malaria, he is too weak to climb onto the medical evacuation truck, so is told to wait for the next one. The first truck hits a land mine.

Malaria strikes both brothers on Guadalcanal and effectively takes them out of the war, facing years of treatment. In Australia Tony takes a wife and Tom's records get misplaced. After months in the hospital he is startled to learn that he's been carried on the books as AWOL.

Cpl. Joe will fight on Iwo Jima with the Sixth Marine Division, and later Okinawa.

Cpl. Jimmy takes part in the invasion of Tarawa with the Second Marine Division, and the Saipan campaign, where he takes shrapnel, badly injuring one leg. Ultimately he undergoes twenty-two operations. (Decades afterwards, a gall-bladder surgery will produce even more souvenirs from the war). Eight months later, he begins to learn to walk again, rehabbing in a naval hospital in St. Albans, New York, where he bumps into two familiar faces, brothers Tom and Tony (undergoing voluntary malaria experiments). Hospitalized for a year and a half,

Cpl. James Conti (Conti Family)

Jimmy eventually makes it home with a Purple Heart and Bronze Star, as well as a division boxing championship. Tony earns the Navy/Marine Caribbean middleweight crown while stationed in Cuba early in the war.

And Francis DeJulius gives his life in service to his country and the United States Marine Corps on Iwo Jima, March 2, 1945.

They have enough war injuries (and death) among them that the Conti Brothers never tumble, or box, again.

As impressive as the achievements of the Conti brothers in the ring are (Tony 34-1 with 25 KOs, Jimmy 26-2, 7 KOs), they are but a small corner of an incredible stable of Amsterdam boxers in the late 20's, 30's and early 40's. Brought along initially by Mike Hamill and Mike Clifford (Kleopfel), they train at the Sons of Italy and the Carbonelli halls on Bridge Street, the upper floor of the John E. Larrabee hardware store on Market Street and the gym over O'Shaugnessy's Grill on East Main Street. Fights are held at the State Armory and the Pythian Temple. Later Jimmy Pepe and his brother Sam get in the game, organizing their fighters in the Amsterdam

Athletic Club in the basement of the Our Lady of Mt. Carmel Church on the South Side. The Pepes later joined forces with Jo-Jo Zeno's Ringside Athletic Club on East Main Street.

Charles C. "Cliff" Gaskins, starts out as a bantamweight, and moves up the scale, competing as a featherweight in the national Diamond Belt championships in Boston. In November, 1940 he volunteers for the draft and is chosen as the "enforcer" for the first group of draftees to leave town. Later, he battles to become the Welterweight Champ of Fort Dix.

In January of 1942 an Army truck he is driving in Rocky Mount, North Carolina, flips over and Gaskins dies not long after.

John W. "Buddy" Lenahan, former district Golden Gloves and Diamond Belt champ, joins the Marines. Says the *Recorder* of him:

> A skillful ringman, Lenahan combined punching and poise. He had a blow that struck sharper than a rattlesnake. The fights for which he will be best remembered here are those with Joe DeMeo of Schenectady and Les Brown of Albany. The time he decisioned DeMeo was one of the toughest scraps ever seen in Amsterdam. It was what boxing men like Ben Becker called a "civil war."

On April 3, 1942, enroute home for Easter, Sgt. Lenahan and three of his Marine companions are killed when their car slams into a tree. Lenahan is 19.

One of the best of the "older" fighters is Carmen "Shorty" Persico. Though he had already done time in the Army, when war looms Shorty re-enlists. On Patriot's Day, April 19, 1942, he manages to get home on a short furlough to attend the South Side Bowling League banquet, where patriotic keglers chip in from their cash prizes to purchase a carton of cigarettes for each of their members in the service.

According to *Recorder* sports editor Jack Minnoch:

> When "Shorty" Persico got up to speak the rafters at Luigi Lanzi's big banquet hall literally rattled, so loud was the ovation he got.

And it wasn't so much what "Shorty" said as the way he said it that got him the big hand he received at the finish. The one-time boxer who fought Lou Ambers to a standstill as an amateur spoke the same as he once socked – straight from the shoulder, and with no punch pulling. If the boys don't remember another thing he said, they'll never forget that last line: "We're in this fight to win. And there's only one way to win: that's fight!"

Lou Ambers, "The Herkimer Hurricane," went on in his professional career to become Lightweight Champion of the World in 1936, a title he held off and on until May of 1940.

That's how good Shorty is in his day.

Shorty goes on to the Pacific, serving in Saipan, after the battle, among other places.

When Delor "Buddy" Benoit is being screened by the Navy for aptitude and placement, they ask him whether he has ever boxed. "A little," he says. In his career that "little" amounts to 120 amateur and 76 professional fights. A middleweight, he turns pro at the age of twenty in 1940 while still in college, going by the ring name of Buddy O'Dell. Jimmy McDaniels, a solid fighter who after the war will take on Sugar Ray Robinson in Madison Square Garden, fights Benoit twice in 1941, the first a draw, and the second a McDaniels victory by decision, after Benoit fights much of the match with a broken hand.

The Amsterdamian's most noted pre-service fight is a split-decision loss to Jake LaMotta, "The Raging Bull," on April 21, 1942. LaMotta will go on to become Middleweight Champ of the World in 1949, and along the way becomes the first to beat Sugar Ray Robinson. That's how good Buddy Benoit is in his day.

In August of '42 Benoit begins his naval career and later serves aboard the *USS Princeton*, a light carrier, along with his friend from Amsterdam Jack Peretz. During peaceful cruises, he organizes boxing instruction and exhibitions aboard the ship, and develops a team to challenge other Navy crews. The *Princeton* punchers go undefeated in inter-ship competition.

In 1944 the *Princeton* fights in just about every action in the Western Pacific, including Saipan, Guam,Tinian and the Battle of the Philippine Sea. She takes part in the invasion of the Philippines in October of 1944 leading up to the Battle of Leyte Gulf. Shortly before 1000 on October 24, a Japanese dive-bomber drops a lone bomb on the ship, which crashes through several decks and explodes below. That single bomb sets off a chain reaction with ship-board ordnance.

USS Princeton ablaze. (LOC)

Buddy Benoit assumes his battle station on the bridge. The sailor standing right next to him dies instantly when one of the explosions crushes his head.

On hearing the order to abandon ship, Benoit goes over the side into the waters of the Pacific. That is the first moment that he has the time to be scared, more scared, he says later, than he had ever been stepping into the ring.

His only injury is a strained shoulder, but still he spends an hour in the shark-infested waters before being rescued by the crew of a near-by destroyer. He loses everything in the sinking of the *Princeton*, save for the dungarees and jacket he is wearing.

In the confusion, he is initially thought to be among the 108 crew members who die that day and so he remains in the official record for 48 hours. Fortunately, the telegram announcing his death does not go out.

QM3c John Peretz survives as well, though it is more than two weeks before his family, who know the *Princeton* has sunk, receive word that he is safe.

Frankie Marcellino wins a lot of fights in his day, as does his brother Tony. But maybe Frankie's best day in the ring is against Carl Palombo, a split decision witnessed by 4,000 fans, including heavyweight contender Bob Pastor, in an event sponsored by the Amsterdam Recreation Commission on August 27, 1941. Frankie comes out at the short end of that split, but, hey, this is against Amsterdam's mighty Carl Palombo.

While brother Tony ships off with the Marines to Panama, where he continues to box successfully with his corner-man being Lou Riccio (one of the six Riccio brothers of Amsterdam to serve in the war), Frankie joins up with the Navy and becomes part of the amphibious corps, where in July of 1943 he helps shuttle Army troops ashore from North Africa to Gela, Sicily.

After a short visit home the Navy transfers him to the Pacific and the battle for Tarawa, where Betio, an island in the Tarawa atoll half the size of New York's Central Park, holds up the Marines for 76 hours of some of the toughest fighting of the war. In the initial landings, planners misjudge the tides and so the Higgins Boats landing craft mostly run aground on offshore coral reefs where they become targets for the Japanese defenders, as do the Marines they are forced to unload in chest-deep water. And of the 125 LVT's employed (tracked landing vehicles, designed to hold 18 fully equipped men or 4,500 pounds of equipment, which are capable of passing over the reefs), only 35 survive the first day. Some of the hung-up landing craft are even overtaken by the enemy on the first night, and the guns turned on our own men, forcing the Navy to blow up our own boats.

Frankie Marcellino survives Tarawa.

As do 17 of the Japanese defenders, of the 3,636 who garrison the island.

Carl Palombo just might be the best of them all. Son of an Italian immigrant shoemaker, he fights under the moniker "Carl the Cobbler." By the time he wins the Allied Forces Featherweight championship in Algiers in the winter of 1943/44, he has gained everyone's attention. Shortly afterward he returns to his infantry unit to carry on the war against the Germans, but *Ring* magazine takes notice of him in their November, 1944 issue (released in late September):

> Carl Palombo, a fighting member of the Fifth Army, is a former National Golden Gloves champion in the featherweight class. Palombo has fought 45 fights overseas, of which he has won 44 and lost only one. He defeated Jimmy Cass of the Fifth Army for the Allied Championship in Algiers. He also fought in North Africa, Sicily and Italy and holds the P.B.S. Featherweight title.
>
> Palombo has seen action in Sicily, Anzio and Rome. Great fighters who are now overseas and have seen Palombo predict a coming featherweight world champion in him. Joe Louis, Jack Sharkey, Fidel LaBarba, Johnny Hanlon and Frankie Nelson have heaped praise on him.
>
> While in the States, Palombo held the All-Eastern Diamond Belt championship, won the Adirondack Golden Gloves tournament for three successive years, held the Diamond Belt Championship and the Eastern States title for two years.
>
> Palombo started boxing when he was a kid of 13. During his boxing career of 220 fights in seven years of boxing, he has won 183 fights and lost 37.

That's how good Carl Palombo is in his day.

A couple of weeks after that story hits the news stands of America, while serving with the 179th Infantry, 45th Division in Granville, France, a German mortar shell rips through Carl Palombo's right arm and left leg. Although a brief news article at the time indicates his boxing career is over, Carl refuses to give up. After multiple surgeries, he returns home to Amsterdam and begins training in earnest with Jo-Jo Zeno's stable of fighters.

But it is not to be.

For a while he works for the city's Recreation Department as a boxing instructor, later taking bar-tending jobs. In 1955 he moves to the west coast, where, fifteen years after taking a hit for his country, Carl Palombo loses his leg from continuing complications of his war injuries.

13. SHADES OF SAIPAN

By the time Robert Sherrod's critique of the 27th Division in *TIME* magazine hits the stands, the remaining men of the division have settled on *Espiritu Santo* island for rest, rehabilitation, reorganization (many new recruits to fill the huge holes left in the companies) and training for their next mission.

Already haunted by the horror of Saipan, the magazine article both infuriates and demoralizes them.

"Somewhere in South Pacific"
October 20, 1944
To the Editor of The Amsterdam Recorder:

Dear Sir:
I take the liberty and responsibility of contacting you with the hope that you will print this letter in behalf of the men of Amsterdam who fought and died on Saipan Island in the Marianas.

Time Magazine issue of September18 carried an article on the inefficiency of the 27th Infantry Division in that battle and I know that there must be some doubt in the minds of our people back home as to the particulars concerning the same.

This article dragged us through the mud, showing no mercy. But—did it mention that the 105th Infantry, our own sectional representative, was the sole unit in the front line sector that received the full force of the enemy counterattack during the overwhelming enemy attack on July 7th? No it did not! And did it mention that these men of Amsterdam, Schenectady, Albany, Troy, Saratoga and many other points in Central New York State, piled up 3,200 enemy dead before reinforcements reached them? No it didn't!

And did it mention that the reinforcements that came to our assistance initially was the 106th Infantry Regiment of the 27th Infantry Division? I guess not.

It slammed and falsely accused our men of breaking ranks and permitting the enemy to penetrate our lines. Were they there? I guess not, but I was! I saw the men with whom I played sports in Amsterdam stand there and tangle with the enemy and disorganize and rout the counterattack. I saw my friends wounded and perform deeds that could never be written up in history because words could not be found to relate the incidents. They would sound fantastic to the public.

I am not belittling the Marines. They are American men, the same as we are, and I have fought in two operations now with them. In my estimation—they are wonderful fighting men and should be proud of their Corps, but I have always given credit where credit is due and I assure you that the article I refer to is the most untrue statement that anyone with common sense could write. It is a direct miscarriage of justice for the men who made the supreme sacrifice in defending our country and an insult to them personally. In me—it leaves the same hurt feeling that would come to a ballplayer who has poked one into the stands, fair by all means, and the umpire blindly calls it a foul ball.

It is not my privilege to berate a man for his statements and beliefs. I am not doing that by any means. But I am doing this—I am giving you the true facts concerning that battle. That battle— one in which the enemy threw all it had against men, who, although outnumbered, took a toll of enemy dead that was never equaled before in 24 hours of fighting in this Pacific war. Articles like this are just the thing that makes a man wonder what all those sacrifices are worth. Men who died and were wounded on July 7th have been berated and deprived of the honor they earned and deserve. I only hope that these men receive their due credit and the one responsible for this injustice is forced to retract his pack of untruths.

I thank you for your kind attention and may it be God's will that all this nonsense cease and competent men be the only ones permitted to pass on the efficiency of that I have clarified some points our American fighting men. I hope that may have been a matter of discussion on the home front. Let's fight this damn war together and forget about minor discrepancies that may cause dissension in the ranks. We aren't perfect but I defy anyone to show me where I am wrong in the statements I have made in this letter concerning the part we played at Saipan.

Sincerely
JOHN J. CAMPBELL,
1st Lt, 105th Infantry

Back home, of course, the folks become numbed with the steady onslaught of casualty reports in the local paper, with Saipan imposed on top of the campaign for Normandy and France. And word of Saipan reaches a special bunch of men, men who have lived with and suffered with and trained with the shades of Saipan: the alumni of Company G.

Many doctors of the mind will tell you that there is such a thing as "survivor's guilt," and that it affects different people in different ways. Whether true or not, there can be no question that the men who didn't go to Saipan with their friends go on to make names for themselves in battles around the globe.

Boleslaw Knapik had been First Sergeant of Company G from before they marched out of Amsterdam until they prepared to ship out to Hawaii in early 1942. Not long after he serves as Best Man for Melrose Freer he leaves his men to attend Officers Candidate School. Commissioned a second lieutenant in July of 1942, by November 27, 1943 he has already advanced to captain. Though he has been in the regular Army since October of 1940, he doesn't get shipped overseas until September of 1944.

Frank C. Betinger succeeds Knapik as First Sergeant for about four months, then he, too, goes to OCS, commissioned in January of 1943. He serves as an Infantry Instructor for a time, then as a Company Executive Officer. He, too, departs for Europe in September of 1944 as a first lieutenant.

Betinger in turn is succeeded by Lewis Dilello as First Sergeant. Dilello had been the private caught in a kissing sandwich in a photograph in the *Recorder* as they departed town in 1940, with the caption, "Oh, Boy! Ain't It Great To Be a Soldier!" Also sent to OCS, he arrives in France in August of 1944 as a second lieutenant, fresh with the news of the Saipan casualties.

Dilello finds himself in another Company G, this one in the 11th Infantry Regiment, commanding the third platoon. Sent to attack an entrance to German-held Fort Driant in northern France on October 4, 1944, his men come under intense artillery and small arms fire.

He orders his men to withdraw, and covers their retreat single-handedly with a Browning Automatic Rifle. He stands his ground until his troops reach safety. They survive, he does not, cut down by an enemy hand grenade.

Initially awarded a Bronze Star for valor, on further review 2nd Lt. Lewis S. Dilello is posthumously granted the Distinguished Service Cross, the country's second-highest award for bravery in battle.

Exactly one month later, on November 4, 1944, 1st Lt. Frank C. Betinger is killed in action leading troops in Holland, as part of a broader campaign to secure Antwerp.

Betinger is survived by his parents and two brothers, including one then serving in the Navy in the Pacific.

Boles Knapik, serving with the 405th Infantry Regiment, writes to a friend in Amsterdam of his determination to give his best in the cause of his country.

He does.

On November 22, 1944, he leads his company against a strongly defended German town. Pinned down by heavy enemy artillery, mortar and machine gun and sniper fire, Knapik personally maintains contact with his platoons, crossing open ground, in order to keep the attack moving, thus exposing himself to fire.

He moves his company some eight hundred yards forward, despite the stiff defense.

And then he is caught by German machine gun fire. Boles Knapik is dead.

The Army awards him a posthumous Silver Star for gallantry in action.

Capt. Boleslaw Knapik is survived by his wife and year-old son, his parents, two sisters and four brothers. One of the brothers, Pfc. Frank Knapik, has served in Company M of the 105th Infantry (John Campbell's company) on Makin and in the Saipan campaign. Frank has two Purple Hearts and a Bronze Star.

Pvt. Anthony Kubas had served his time in Company G, and been honorably discharged in 1941. But the country calls him back in April of 1942 and assigns him to the infantry. He is seriously wounded in action in France in August of 1944.

Capt. William Wilde, formerly a junior officer of Company G, had been long-since transferred to the Quartermaster Corps, with the 3619th Quartermaster Trucking Company, bringing supplies to the front.

On December 19, 1944, he personally commands a convoy moving a portion of the 101st Airborne Division and several thousand tons of supplies, including four days' rations and thousands of rounds of artillery shells, to Bastogne, in the Ardennes region of southern Belgium, to help the American forces push back against a counterattack by German forces that would become the Battle of the Bulge.

Wilde expects a quick drop-off and return to headquarters, but thirty minutes after they arrive the Germans complete their encirclement of Bastogne (where seven major roads crucial to the German advance intersect) and there is no escape. The famous seven day siege begins.

Officers, clerks, drivers and laborers of the Quartermaster Trucking Company, most of whom haven't fired a shot since boot camp, are handed rifles and become part of a heroic defense that stymies the invaders.

Capt. Wilde quickly and effectively adapts his men to a situation for which they have no training, and the 3619th will ultimately receive a unit citation from the Commanding General of the 101st Airborne Division, General Maxwell Taylor. They suffer four casualties, with five vehicles destroyed or damaged.

Pfc. Paul S. Romeo leaves Company G while still in Alabama and transfers to the Military Police, later returning to the infantry. His mother is informed that he has been "slightly wounded" near the right eye in action in France on January 29, 1945. The rest of his slight wound is described in a letter he writes home:

February 18, 1945
Dear Mom,
I hope you haven't been worrying about me but I had the operation done a week ago. They had to take my right eye out. Today is the first day I've been up. I had what the doctors call a tough operation. Everything is fine now and I'm feeling well. …. I got a wonderful doctor working with me and he is always taking good care of me. In a few weeks I'll be all healed up and you'll never

Paul Romeo and Mom, Oct. 23, 1940 (Romeo Family)

know the difference when you see me. …. Keep your chin up. God bless you Mom. Love and kisses, Son Paul
  PS Please answer soon.

Radioman Third Class Michael Polikowski has two brothers serving in Company G during the battle for Saipan, Staff Sgts. John and Stephen Polikowski. He serves aboard the submarine *U.S.S. Shark*, which goes down somewhere between Hainan island and the Bashi Channel in the Pacific on or about October 24, 1944.

According to his Wilbur H. Lynch High School Class of 1940 yearbook, Polikowski was "A regular fellow," with a nickname of "Bookie."

MICHAEL POLIKOWSKI
"Bookie"
Milton Avenue School   Textiles
Academy Street School
"A regular fellow."

Did you know Michael Polikowski, Uncle Sy?
Sure. We used to walk to school together every day.
Why did they call him "Bookie?"
Because he used to book numbers in school. Why else?

The *U.S.S. Shark* has never been found.

John Curran had been a postal clerk in Amsterdam for twenty-three years, the guy who sold you the stamps over the counter. Before that he had served in the old Company H at the armory and had fought with the 27th Division in France during the first World War. As president of Post 4, 27th Division Association, he had proudly marched as part of an Honor Guard for the Boys of Company G as they marched away in 1940.

When war comes again, he needs to do more. One of several Amsterdam World War I vets to re-up for their country, he employs his skills as Chief Mailman for a Navy SeaBee unit. By strange coincidence he finds himself stationed in Saipan in early 1945, and there he locates the 27th Division Cemetery.

A photograph of Chief Curran looking down at the crosses bearing the names of Clinton Smith and Paul Sanzen and Daniel Slusarz goes out over the wires.

These are his boys.

They are lying in coral sand, thousands and thousands of miles from home.

But only 1,500 miles from Tokyo.

14. HERE IS WHERE I BELONG

Probably not a great many American servicemen receive decorations for valor from the Germans during the war, but Capt. Rev. Anthony Sidoti does not have an ordinary bone in his body. A 1930 graduate of St. Mary's Institute, Father Sidoti does his preliminary studies first at the University of Notre Dame, then at Niagara University, where he becomes captain of the boxing team, right tackle on the varsity football team, and plays basketball as well. Following his 1936 graduation he studies for the priesthood in Rome, and then spends a year in Louvain, Belgium studying philosophy and theology, until the situation in Europe necessitates bringing him home to Our Lady of Angels seminary to complete his preparation. He is ordained a Roman Catholic priest on May 18, 1940 by Bishop Edmund Gibbons of the Diocese of Albany, and his first assignment comes a month later to Our Lady of Mt. Carmel parish in Gloversville.

The grim future of the world greets the young priest immediately. On the same page as the testimonial dinner welcoming him to the priesthood is an article about Marshal Petain being appointed to head the French defense against the German onslaught. On the dais sits the Italian Consul assigned to Albany. Father Walsh of St. Mary's calls Sidoti a "soldier of God."

And when the war comes he quickly volunteers for the Chaplain Corps. Granted leave by his bishop, he is commissioned on October 13, 1942. Thirteen months later he receives a brevet promotion to captain, and following some stateside duties where he engages in such important activities as requisitioning phonographs for rec halls, he ships off to England in February, 1944 as Chaplain for the 32nd Evacuation Hospital, then assigned to the Third Army.

Shortly after D-Day Father Sidoti serves with the EVAC hospital at the front (temporarily attached to 1st Army until reverting to Third Army in August when Gen. George S. Patton joins the action), and then in

September he receives orders reassigning him to serve as Chaplain for the Third Battalion of the 358th Infantry Regiment with the 90th Division (Third Army).

Third Army sweeps across France, but stalls near the German border when the long supply lines and the needs of Operation Market Garden cut off their fuel. By November they face the twin obstacles of the Moselle River and the Maginot Line fortresses on the ridge beyond. While originally designed to keep the Germans out, by 1944 they serve equally well pointing in the other direction. In order to re-start the forward thrust, Patton's generals put together a plan for a giant pincer movement to isolate and reduce the primary fortress at Metz. This requires a dangerous crossing of the Moselle at night, with the 90th Division leading the charge on the left, with battalions of the 359th and 358th Regiments up front.

To preserve the element of surprise, the troops move to the assembly area over several nights of cold, driving rain. The plan calls for the operation to commence at the latest on the night of November 8/9, and the rain necessitates delay to the last. The closest the heavy assault boats can get is 400 swampy yards from the 350-foot wide Moselle River. From there the men carry the boats and supplies by hand.

At 0330 the Third Battalion of the 358th hits the water and makes the first crossing. K company's commander, Capt. Max Short, is the first to land on the far shore. At his side, Capt. Anthony Sidoti. The troops advance, and Father Sidoti sets up an aid station a thousand yards inland in an old cement factory. But even before the first wave of troops has crossed, the Germans find their target and begin shelling the west bank assembly areas, and waiting troops and engineers begin to drop before even entering battle.

And now the river itself becomes the enemy. The days of incessant rain begin to catch up with the Moselle basin, and what had been a 350 foot crossing now expands to 400 then 600 then 800 *yards*. It is the worst flood in the history of the river. Engineers who had hoped to swiftly build bridges to bring across armor and supplies, now find themselves stymied. The swift flow of the river makes the assault boats unstable, and so they lighten the loads, even as many of the boats are swept downstream. No longer launching from marshy river banks, the boats are loaded up in the center of now flooded villages, and run over fields where unplanned obstacles such as farm fences cripple propellers.

And yet, the 90th Division makes do. Patrols run down the river banks, retrieving as many lost boats as possible. On the far shore, deprived of the support they need, men fight with raw courage and hand-held weapons assaulting and reducing German defenses. When supplies dwindle, low-flying aircraft, at great risk, drop more.

Casualties mount. Father Sidoti personally directs the evacuation of the wounded. For 36 hours straight he assists their removal across the swollen river, making trip after trip under heavy fire. He moves from foxhole to foxhole giving aid and encouragement and spiritual relief to the men.

His boys prevail, the hill forts are taken, the bombardment ceases, the bridges, after several days, are built, armor and supplies cross the river and the fight moves on.

Chaplain Sidoti's actions do not go unnoticed.

He earns his first Silver Star.

Metz falls, and the 358th turns east, to Germany's Saar Valley. Wherever the front lies, Father Sidoti ministers. On November 24, they fight on German soil for the first time, in the area of Tettingen. Capt. Short's Company K takes Butzdorf, to the north, but loses contact and communication with the rest of the battalion. Enemy armor comes in and fires at point-blank range. Every officer becomes a casualty. Thirty-five survivors, low on ammunition, fight all night until finally relieved the next day.

Later, Father Sidoti writes to his friend's widow:

> *My dear Mrs. Short,*
> *I am Chaplain Anthony R. Sidoti, the Catholic chaplain of the regiment which your husband made so famous. Needless to say, Max and I were buddies but this is nothing unusual as everyone who knew Max were friends of his. His personality, aggressiveness, intelligence and his general make-up seemed to be an attraction which none could resist. Consequently, he had many friends.*

As a fighting man, his reputation is tops and always will be. In fact, he is to our minds one of the real heroes of this war. The men who fought with him and under him have nothing but the highest praise for him as a leader, courageous, thinking nothing of self but always putting the welfare and safety of his men foremost in his mind at all times. The night of the crossing of the Moselle River, November 9th, 3:30 a.m., Max and I were together in the first boat to hit the other side of the river. It was our boast that we were the first to hit the enemy in that difficult operation. As you probably know, Max's company, Co K, was known as the Kraut Killers. That name was not merely a newspaper appellation. It was really a hard earned and deserving designation of one of the best units of World War II ever produced. Its reputation and success was due to a very great measure to your husband's efforts and courageous spirit.

On behalf of the officers and men of this unit, I want you to know the high regard and esteem we all had for him. Tragic as his death may seem, we are sure it was not in vain. For it is because of men such as him that the final victory was ours. We are all proud to have known him and privileged to have had him in our unit.

Some day I hope that I shall have the honor of meeting you personally and tell you many more stories concerning Max. There are some things which cannot be written and have to be spoken. Believe me, Mrs. Short, although Max was not of my faith, I count him among my very best friends and one whom I shall always remember. It was a privilege and an honor to have worked with him and to have known him. If, at any time, there is anything that we can do for you, please let me know.

May God bless you.

> *Sincerely yours,*
> *Anthony R. Sidoti*
> *Chaplain, Third Battalion, 358th Infantry*

On November 25, 1944, still on the job, Father Sidoti becomes an unsuccessful target for a German sniper, rescues a few men, and gets hit himself.

> *We had been in Germany awhile and our progress had been satisfactory. However, on November 25 we were attacking a town in Germany and, as I usually did, I went with my boys. The going was a bit tough, and as some of the kids were wounded I picked them up and brought them into a safer place, bandaged them, and then went back to find more. I did this for a few hours and finally the town was cleared and I got my jeep and brought it up to evacuate the kids to the aid station. I cleared them out and went back to pick up the last two. As I did, I spotted a sniper in one of the houses. I called for some riflemen and went on with my work. He tried to get me twice, but all he did was put some holes in my jacket. I finally got my boys out and back to safety.*
>
> *As I walked back German artillery started. I was busy looking to make sure all my boys had been taken out. As I turned to go back to the aid station, one of the shells hit just over my head and a small piece of the shrapnel hit me in the shoulder. I didn't realize for a few seconds what had happened. But when I did I bandaged my arm myself and walked back a mile and a half to the aid station. The jeep was gone, because I was worried about my driver exposing himself and sent him back.*
>
> *The rest of the story is very simple. They shipped me back to England. Now I am all set. My arm is as good as new and I am feeling swell.*

"Slightly wounded" is how they classify him in the nomenclature of the day. So slightly wounded that he is not able to write the above letter to his mother until February 11. He spends nearly four months recuperating in that hospital in England.

And then, on March 13, 1945, he goes back.

The only child of a widowed mother, he does his best to explain it to her.

Mother, I pray to God that you are well and happy, happy as possible under the existing circumstances. I realize that you miss me very much and all that. I miss you people very much also, but that will be remedied as soon as God wills it. Let His Will be done. As a priest, I feel that my job is here and not at home. So, Mother, please try to understand. I have left everything in His hands.

Father Sidoti later describes his joyful reunion with the boys.

Here I am, back again and happy as a lark. You should have seen them welcome me. They yelled all along the streets and roads. You see, Mother, here is where I belong, where I am needed.

This afternoon I said Mass for them in a German church. It was crowded to overflowing. There were Protestants, Jews and Catholics. When I turned around to talk to them there was a lump in my throat. They looked so good to me, so faithful. The colonel was very kind to me and thanked me very profusely for coming back. He never got a replacement for me.

Well, Mom, time is short, but my love and longing for all of you at home is eternal. However, my duty to God and my country is, and justly so, greater and very obvious. Please try to understand. I know and feel that you do. You are the world's best soldier.

Four days later he picks up an Oak Leaf Cluster for his Silver Star. The citation speaks for itself:

For gallantry in action on 17 March 1945 in the vicinity of Ehr, Germany. During an attack, a company sustained many casualties, including the company commander, and became disorganized by the intense mortar, machine gun and small arms fire directed upon it. Learning of a seriously wounded man lying in an exposed position, Chaplain Sidoti unhesitatingly advanced through the fire, reached the casualty, and carried him to a litter squad. He then carried the dead body of another soldier to a place of cover. The men of the company, inspired by his courageous and selfless actions, reorganized themselves and completed the mission successfully and without further casualties. The gallantry of Chaplain Sidoti was in accordance with high military tradition.

Nor does his indomitable spirit go unnoticed by the other side. A flag of truce goes up, and a German general requests the service of the Catholic chaplain to minister the sacraments to his men. Father Sidoti crosses the lines and celebrates Mass. The general is so moved by his courage and humanity that he removes a Silver Cross from his own uniform and pins it on his enemy.[20]

---

20 While I do not doubt for a moment the veracity of this anecdote, I have been unable to pin it down as to time and place from any written records I have reviewed. Logic would seem to suggest that it wouldn't have taken place until the cessation of hostilities, and yet, with Father Sidoti, as with his Boss, all things are possible.

15. WE DIDN'T KNOW ENOUGH TO BE SCARED

Before the war, Pvt. William Bylina has a tailor shop on Hibbard Street. He somehow convinces the army to let him take his combination workbench/sewing machine overseas with him. One of those big foot-pedal models. He serves in the 36th "Texas" Infantry Division and carts his tailor shop through North Africa, Italy and France while participating in the Salerno and Riviera invasions, servicing over 500 customers a month, from privates to generals. "There is no rank distinction in this shop. To me, a hole in a pair of pants is simply a hole in a pair of pants. Personally, I don't care who wears the pants!"

Besides altering uniforms and patching holes, he receives an order from his regimental commander for 300 white camouflage suits. "Camouflage By Bylina," he proudly notes when he sees a picture of two GI's wearing his apparel on the front page of the paper.

Tech. Sgt. Sam Belardi, a teacher at Wilbur H. Lynch High School and an accomplished violinist before the war, fiddles with a few other things as well with his DC Air Force Service Squadron.

North American Aircraft Corporation's P-51 Mustang, a long-range fighter-bomber, revolutionizes the air war by providing cover for the bombers dumping on Germany and effectively eliminating the Luftwaffe as a significant force in the weeks leading up to D-Day. In the course of the war, P-51 pilots shoot down 4,950 enemy aircraft. It has one flaw, however. It is impossible to install a camera in its tail for reconnaissance work. The manufacturer says so. The Wright Field aeronautical engineers say so.

Sam Belardi wants a crack at it, and the commanding general of the Ninth Air Force fighter command gives him and his squad a green light. Under difficult field conditions, they solve the problem and install the camera in one week.

In less than three months they similarly equip sixty more Mustangs, greatly enhancing the efficiency of the air war in both theaters.

Eagle Scout 1st Lt. W. Howard English participates in more than 60

bombing missions over enemy territory in North Africa, Sicily and Italy, risking his life day after day. Finally they send him home, where on January 2, 1944 he enthralls the local Rotary Club with tales of his experiences, describing anti-aircraft fire bursting "so close that you can smell it." He says, "When I'm in the air I know: that is what I want to do."

Piloting a B-26 toward a railroad bridge target near Sapri on the western coast of Italy, English is part of a squadron led by Major Jack Sims, 24, a veteran of the Doolittle raid over Tokyo. It is noon before they reach Italy. They face no opposition until they approach their target and open the bomb bay doors.

The flak from the anti-aircraft guns is so close that at first they think they are under machine gun attack and the gunners swing around looking for targets. The next burst is three feet to their left. Fifty or more bursts follow, some pattering against the plane like summer rain on a tin roof.

The five hundred pound bombs are released and as he leans over the Plexiglas to admire his work, the bombardier nearly loses his face as a large piece of shrapnel comes flying at him. Another burst and the skin of the aircraft is pierced and fragments fly within an inch or two of Lt. English's head.

"I could read my name on it," he says afterwards, "but they spelled it wrong."

Thirty minutes later he's back at his base, planning the next one, and another follows, and more until finally he completes his required number of missions and gets to go home.

After a month's r&r in Amsterdam, Lt. English is reassigned as a flying instructor state-side.

Having survived the worst of battle, he is killed in an airplane accident over Lovettesville, Virginia on September 21, 1944. He is 27.

UPX, June, 1944 From George Hughes: After reading the letters of the different fellows the world is only a small place after all and for us fellows from Amsterdam, Amsterdam is still the place where all of us long to be. We are well-represented all over the face of the world and that is an indication that the best wishes of the folks back home are being carried to all parts of the world.

From Lins Johnston: These Italian people tell me a lot about Brooklyn. I get quite a kick out of them, they all have relatives in that wonderful city. They are very friendly toward us, much more than the French in N. Africa. The only trouble here in this part of the country is, they haven't much Vino. I guess the old Tedeschi drank it all before we got here. I had the good fortune to visit the capital of this country for a few days and I must say I certainly enjoyed myself . I went and seen all the Roman ruins and the rest of the historical places. I wish you could all see the stadium the Romans used for feeding the Christians to the Lions. It's quite a place. I understand they, I mean the American architects, copied its style for some of the football bowls back home. It looks almost like one, only on a smaller scale. Too bad Bruno isn't headed this way, as he would do alright by these Italian signorinas; they are very pretty and dress in the same style as the girls back home. . . . I don't know how the Germans can last much longer over here, the way they are losing their equipment. It's just scattered all over, and they sure did retreat in a hurry on the drive that was made over here. I guess they took all the vehicles they could lay their hands on from taxis to big civilian buses, but they didn't get far with them before our planes caught up with them. We found them all along the highway, burned all to L, as we came along.

UPX, September, 1944 from Johnny Campbell from the South Pacific: I'm having a wonderful rest at the present. Good food, nurses and no Japs floating around. Of course, the beverage situation is drastic – none whatsoever. Well, I don't miss it too much, but a drink now and then would tend to keep the hair off my feet. I wore out two pairs of G.I. shoes in the last four months, yet they say that this modern army is streamlined. Let them come down and tell us that.

* **From Harry DeGroff, somewhere in Italy:** After reading Lins Johnston's letter I would say he has covered the situation over here very well, at least along the path which we both seem to be following. Through correspondence recently, Lins and I have decided that we have been quite close to each other at times, and at present the chances of our meeting up should be very good, providing we don't get going in different directions, which is very possible with our gypsy movements. I too enjoyed the many places of interest which the City of Rome has to offer, and it sort of brought back to mind my history studies of these surroundings while at school. The news of the additional landings of late along the coast of France was received with much joy by all the boys over here and it sure begins to look as though the end is in sight. Jerry is as tenacious as ever in these parts in contesting each yard of ground, but just as long as he insists on going down the hard way I am sure the boys are willing to oblige.*

* **From Paul Sykes in New Guinea:** Had a swell surprise yesterday (outside of the P.X.) I got a few packages from my honey. Yep, my camera and film arrived okay along with some good eats, etc. Now I will get busy and take some snaps of this God-forsaken country. We do have lots of beautiful terrain – mostly jungle. But I can now take pictures of the natives, etc. to keep for my post-war scrapbook. Right now I have a couple pictures to send you, not of me but of some native pin-up girls. Aren't they "beauts" – if you know what I mean? Nothing like giving the boys an eyeful, eh? I should say handful, shouldn't I? . . . Guess all the Japs are out of New Guinea – and out of this world. War news in Europe is darn good and it looks like the end of the axis soon. Then we can concentrate on Tojo's boys. In general I look forward to coming*

home for good by August of '45, and am I right, fellows? Another year will end it, eh?

__From Arnie Eckelman:__ I'm inclined to agree with "Soup" Campbell on putting these so-called wonder boys in athletics out where they can do a little fighting. One of these days I may be lucky and run into Jack Geib as I think I am in or around the same area. Sure would like to see Jack. Regards to you, Jack. We have done a little moving and I think from all aspects that I will see plenty of more action out here.

__From Don Campbell:__ If the original orders I am under had been followed, this letter would have been written in France, but as you see, they weren't. We packed and got on the train to Ft. Meade, but instead of going to New York we ended up here in western Pennsylvania.

__From Jim Jasper, somewhere in Italy:__ Congratulations Lt. John J. Campbell on being awarded the Bronze Star and I guess the Japs won't tangle with any more of the Blues. Well, if all goes well I might be seeing you soon, Guy. I just completed my fifty missions over here and waiting my turn to go home.

__From Dick Hayden:__ I'm sorry I didn't write sooner, but for the past couple of months I've been pretty busy helping to push Tojo's boys off Saipan and Tinian. I'm now in a Naval hospital recuperating from a broken leg that I received in one of the actions.

Now promoted to captain, David Shuttleworth continues his aerial exploits, leading a flight of P-47 Thunderbolts in the Mediterranean. On his 136th mission piloting a fighter-bomber, he scores his second kill, downing a German ME-109.

When he sees his squadron challenged by a dozen German fighters, he orders his men to jettison their bombs and prepare for combat, climbing to meet the threat. One of his pilots shoots down an enemy plane moving in on Shuttleworth's tail.

> Then I saw another ME-109 on the tail of one of our pilots. I closed in to give a burst from 300 yards. He started in a climbing right turn and I got in a fast burst at 150 yards and saw strikes on the wings and about canopy and black smoke started to pour from both wings.

The German plane snaps and goes down.

It is a rough year for the Dargush family. Peter Charles Urban, the husband of the former Ann Dargush, is killed in Normandy on June 8. Her twin brother, Pfc. Anthony V. Dargush, 23, 9 John Street, Wilbur H. Lynch Class of 1939, is killed in action in France on August 18. Nearly simultaneously with that telegram comes another that a different brother, Lieutenant Vincent B. Dargush, has been wounded.

Vincent Dargush has already seen his share of the war. He's been to Anzio and Rome and the southern France landings on August 15, 1944, where he is in the first wave ashore.

He's with a 3rd Division tank-destroyer crew. The Germans are pretty much in full retreat as the division pushes north when his crew spots a line of enemy vehicles from their hill-top vantage point. Says Dargush:

> We waited until they got within good gun range and then let go, and I have never seen such confusion in my life. Germans were flying every way, ammunition was going off and flares lit the place up like the Fourth of July back home. We had three T-D's going full blast at them.
>
> I'll never forget the sight when one of our shells smacked right into a speeding German reconnaissance car. It rolled that vehicle over and over like a ten-pin in a bowling alley. The Germans inside never knew what hit them.
>
> When they sought to escape us, the Krauts ran down hill – right into the arms of 3rd Division infantry who cut them to ribbons.

Almost every Jerry in the 20-vehicle convoy was killed or injured. I never will forget that sight if I live to be a million.

By September 10 they are already pushing to cross the Moselle River when they are struck by an artillery barrage. A red hot piece of a shell rips through his upper right leg and shreds the bone. He lies in a ditch with an aid man for three hours at night while the attack continues. It is his 25th birthday.

After seventh months of hospitalization, he finally makes it home on leave, a steel brace wrapped around his leg, supporting his 240 pound frame. It seems like a million years from his days as a basketball star for one of the best teams Amsterdam High ever produced, back in 1937 and '38. His brother Tony, a rather talented hoopster himself, had played with the team, too.

Vince had come across him one day, sitting by the road in France.

Fenton Brown: One Man Army. You look at his picture and you think maybe Wally Cox as Mr. Peepers. Mild mannered, go along, get along. Uniform seems like it might be a little too big for him.

In fact, there isn't a uniform made big enough for Fenton Brown.

He and his twin brother Forbes Brown grow up mostly in Fulton County, but move to Amsterdam with their mother when their father dies, and when orphaned continue to live with their aunt and uncle on Orange Street. Both excel in athletics at Wilbur H. Lynch High School in football and track. Together they go on to Cornell University where both are varsity wrestlers. Forbes majors in zoology, which comes in handy when, as a first lieutenant, he confronts and dispatches a boa constrictor in a supply room in Panama. He later rises to captain.

Despite his native athleticism, the Army rejects Fenton Brown when he is drafted, but when his twin decides to sign up in August of 1942, he goes along and this time is accepted.

He could have stayed home.

They enter the service together, but soon head in different directions. Staff Sgt. Fenton Brown lands with the 36th "Texas" Division in Italy below Salerno on September 9, 1943 and is wounded in action on October 3 during the battle for Naples. On that occasion he crawls out of his foxhole and drags a wounded comrade, who has been shot in both legs, to safety while rendering first aid under fire. He earns a Bronze Star for valor in that day's work.

He continues to fight with the 36th through Italy and later in France as well, battle after battle.

In late August of 1944, the German Army is retreating north in France after our Mediterranean landings. It is the job of the 36th Division to trap and destroy that army. Our artillery sets up a 16 mile gauntlet the Germans have to run. On August 26, Sgt. Brown's battalion itself becomes trapped in a German tank attack near the town of San Martin, and when his lieutenant is wounded, Brown finds himself in temporary command of a 35-man light machine gun platoon assigned to cover the battalion's retreat. In addition to organizing his men strategically, he personally kills or wounds twenty-five Germans with his machine gun, then picks up his M-1 rifle and shoots two more attempting to infiltrate the American lines. After safely evacuating his men, he organizes a counter-attack and regains the ground previously won and lost.

For that day's work he earns a Silver Star.

On October 5, 1944, at the Belford Gap, a sniper gets him. He is 26.

At a ceremony in Panama his twin brother accepts the Bronze and Silver Stars awarded posthumously. After the war, Forbes Brown returns to Cornell to complete his education, alone.

According to the 1938 Wilbur H. Lynch High School yearbook, Fenton Brown had hoped to be a football hero.

He goes way past that.

Steve Rutkowski does not get killed in battle, but certainly not for lack of opportunity. One of three brothers in the war, and one of eight children of a widowed mother on Voorhees Street, he wades ashore on Omaha Beach on July 5, 1944 as a 1st Lieutenant in the 35th Infantry Division, and almost immediately they are called into front line action. The mission is to advance seven miles and capture St. Lo, a city of 12,000 during normal times, and a key to the breakout needed to sweep across France into Germany.

The 35th is placed in the center of the line between the 29th and 30th Divisions as part of a 5,000 yard front. The advance begins on the morning of July 11. It takes eight days of hard fighting to cover the seven miles, field by field, hedgerow by hedgerow. Rutkowski's platoon is under near-constant fire during each step forward.

According to the division historian, Maj. Norman C. Carey:

> The entire line had jumped off on time but nobody got very far, as we all ran into a German main line of resistance with 75mm, 88mm, and 150mm cannon fire, light and heavy machine guns and machine pistols, and both light and 80mm mortars. We ran into land mines, booby traps and Mauser equipped snipers and riflemen.

Rutkowski is a natural born leader and something of a philosopher, applying what he modestly calls "The Rutkowski Method" to each situation encountered. It's a simple approach. All you need to do is examine all the facts and the solution will be obvious.

For Rutkowski and his platoon, the hedgerow country means just taking one step at a time, figure out where the Germans are, and eliminate them. Then start all over again on the next field and hedgerow.

The division tallies 2,437 casualties in the Battle of the Hedgerows, some 16% of their men. There is no rest. Replacement troops are rushed to the front, some with only thirteen weeks of training and no chance for a furlough home before embarking from the states. Squads, platoons, companies, battalions, regiments, divisions all need to quickly reorganize.

The breakout begins on July 25, when 2,430 planes bomb the living bejeezus out of the German companies ahead of them. To prevent any mistakes, a line of smoke clearly marks the American lines, but as time rolls on a gentle breeze pushes the smoke back over our troops, and friendly fire devastates the 30th Division, on the right of the 35th. And yet, when the order comes to move out, every battalion gets off. American armor breaks through on the 27th, followed by the infantry.

The 35th Division fights continuously forward until August 5 when they reach the Vire River and are pinched off by the 2nd Division. They get a rest that lasts for a few hours, and then begin a circuitous 52 mile journey that brings them just a bit west of the town of Mortain. Hitler has ordered a four division Panzer counter-attack on Mortain to drive the newly-activated Third Army back to the beaches.

To meet the new offensive, the 35th is ordered to attack.

Their attack succeeds, they rescue a brave and beleaguered battalion of the 30th which had been holding back the offensive, and they are formally attached to Patton's Third Army. On August 15, with the Germans in full retreat, the 35th is trucked seventy miles to a point near LeMans. This is the same day that the American 7th Army opens a second front in France with their landings on the Mediterranean and begin their march up the Rhone Valley.

Thirty hours after assembling in the LeMans area, the 35th Division, guarding the right , southern, flank of Third Army, has already captured Orleans on the Loire River, eighty miles to the east, and secured the airfield and German supply depots there. By September 1 they are heading toward Nancy on the Moselle where the Germans have set up another strong line of defense. The only things slowing them down are the processing of prisoners and the gradually troublesome fuel shortages.

The 35th Division crosses the Muerthe River, a tributary of the Moselle, southeast of Nancy, on September 11th and 12th while the 80th Division crosses the Moselle just north of Nancy. The goal is to meet up and tighten the noose east of the city. Units of the 35th take the city on September 15.

1ˢᵗ Lt. Stephen J. Rutkowski's platoon has one mission: keep moving forward until you link up with the 80ᵗʰ Division. On September 16ᵗʰ he leads a surprise attack against a German position.

He gets wounded in the arm.

He moves the assault forward.

A mortar shell hits and wounds him in both legs.

He is unable to walk, but continues giving orders to his men.

For three more hours.

It is only when his platoon has obtained its immediate objective and set up defensive positions to hold their gains that Rutkowski allows himself to be evacuated. He loses a leg.[21] Gen. George S. Patton himself visits him as he settles in for a long recovery.

He is awarded the Silver Star and promoted to captain.

In Amsterdam, the wife of Pvt. First Class Anthony Kosiba, 35, trembles as she opens the telegram.

> *REGRET TO INFORM . . .*
> *KILLED IN ACTION . . .*
> *GERMANY . . .*
> *OCTOBER 6, 1944 . . .*

He had been employed at the Fitzgerald Bottling Works.

Word travels, friends and family call on her, the paper runs the obituary, talking about his fighting through France and Belgium. Arrangements are made for a memorial Mass at St. Stanislaus.

---

21 For the rest of his life Rutkowski wears his wooden leg with pride. He takes it off from time to time to show kids that it's nothing to be afraid of. He even amuses some by pulling up his pants leg and showing them the hole that is drilled through the calf. Nothing holds him down. In 1978 he and his wife Virginia, long-time librarian at St. Mary's Institute, dance the polka at our wedding. "The Rutkowski Method," however, is not universally appreciated and although he is twice elected alderman of Amsterdam's 4ᵗʰ Ward, the terms are fourteen years apart and neither leads to reelection.

And just as the numbness begins to wear off a week or so later, the mailman arrives, and hand delivers what she knows to be the last letter from her husband. She reads it over and over, her tears staining the paper. Finally, as she moves to put it down, she absorbs the date.

It is after October 6.

He had been left for dead, his dog tags gathered up. The burial crew detects life and he is removed to a hospital. Eventually a corrected telegram is issued and after a period of rehab, Anthony Kosiba returns home to Amsterdam, where he dies a second time, peacefully, in 2003 at the age of 93.

Pvt. Francis Lais is another one of those guys in the do-everything 36th "Texas" Division, the group that had fought at Cassino in Italy, Anzio, the push through Rome and then with the landings in southern France in August of 1944, subsequently fighting their way north.

On November 7, 1944 his platoon is attacked by mortar and artillery fire in a mountainous region of France. Seven men are wounded, including the aid man. Lais himself is wounded in the leg. Though the platoon is pinned to the ground, he immediately makes his way to the side of the most seriously injured, a soldier whose right arm is nearly severed. He personally gives first aid to three of the wounded, and verifies the others have been treated before taking care of his own wound.

The route to the aid station is a difficult mountain path in direct sight of the enemy and subject to shell fire. Completely disregarding his own safety, Lais lends his assistance to the soldier with the destroyed arm and leads him to safety.

Tech. Sgt. Richard Marnell lands on Utah Beach on July 9, 1944 with the 5th Infantry Regiment as part of Patton's Third Army and is immediately prepared to take on not only the entire German army, but the German nation and Hitler personally and anybody else who might get in his way, for he has learned (falsely, as it turns out) that his friend from the South

Side, Richard Dantini, had been killed on D-Day. Even the subsequent news that Dantini is alive doesn't settle him down much.

After the breakout in Normandy, he takes part in the Moselle River crossing in November and his regiment faces the German fortress at Metz. On November 15 his platoon comes under direct fire from not only machine guns, but anti-aircraft guns as well.

Marnell drops face down and, under constant fire, crawls through a long ditch to within a few yards of a gun placement and takes it out with a well-placed hand grenade. Then he stands up, completely exposing himself, and fires a rifle grenade at another enemy position, eliminating it as well, and capturing seven Germans to boot.

For extraordinary heroism, Marnell is awarded the Distinguished Service Cross.

It goes along with two Bronze Stars, three Purple Hearts, five battle stars, the ETO ribbon and the Good Conduct Medal. He finishes the war as Amsterdam's most-decorated hero, and its only living recipient of the Distinguished Service Cross.[22]

> ***UPX, October, 1944 from Paul Sykes:****The Yanks down under are going to town now and it won't be long before we have the Philippines in our hands. As a matter of fact I am nine hundred miles closer to them as of today. And I'm pretty close to the boys from our National Guard and you all know where they're at. They sure did a fine job there.*
>
> ***Later:*** *[E]very move from now on means that much nearer to the Philippines. And so I hope it won't be too long before we get there. They have started to strike there already, so it shouldn't be too long before a landing is made.*
>
> ***From Arnie Eckelman:*** *Our stay at sea each time we go out gets longer. As Bruno always says, I see by the newspaper that we are*

---

22 Nearly sixty years later, a section of Bridge Street is posthumously named Marnell Square in his honor.

doing pretty good out here and no fooling that is the way we do hear about it out here.

*   **From Jack Geib:** *I must admit, now, that it was "D-Day" that prompted me to write this letter. The entire trend of thought of "D-Day" was wonderful and a tribute to all mothers, wives and sweethearts. It is, needless to say, how I feel about it. The D-Days such as I have known last for a short space of hours, while those of our loved ones will end only with Peace. It is coincidental that I should read "D-Day" at this time for September 15 was again D-Day for me. I landed on Pelelieu, one of the Palou Islands, on that day. As I look back to that day, I consider myself one of the luckiest persons alive. At the time it seemed like a series of dull, sharp and crackling sounds mixed with a confusion of thoughts. Now they are no longer bewildering; they define themselves clearly, each thought and each sound. As each action of mind becomes clearer, I wonder what prompted me to do them. I wish I could tell you about them; but as D-Days pass they become only dim memories and soon I will have forgotten all about this last one.*

*   **From Frank Cionek:** *Here I am on a stepping stone heading toward the South Pacific, God forbid, I've had enough! First it was Iceland, a year there wasn't enough, they had to keep me an even two; then it was England, this was sort of a break even though I did expect to go home; now it's France, never did I dream I would participate in the big push. This isn't enough, rumors have it that we're going to give the boys in the S. Pacific a little added strength. Oh well, who am I to make a liar out of the composer of "Three Little Sisters," only I'm the three sisters rolled up into one brother, "from Iceland to the Philippines."*

The flights "over the hump" from India to China become more interesting with the addition of the newer, larger C-54 Super Cargo Carrier in October of 1944, and the regular pilots squabble over who will be the first to fly one. Eight men vie for the short straw, including Amsterdam's Capt. John B. Igoe.

A ten month veteran of the Air Transport Command in the China-Burma-India theater, he triumphantly displays the winning straw.

"I go!" shouts Igoe.

Pvt. Leon W. Kline, Jr. is a former duck and axminster weaver for Mohawk

Carpet Mills, assigned to the Seventh Infantry of the Third Division as a medic. His father had been a combat veteran of World War I, seeing action in the Argonne, Bellau Woods and St. Mihiel with the 82nd Division.

The Army Public Relations Office releases this story:

All the heroic action of the Third Division is not being done by the troops who fire the weapons. Plenty is being done by the men who man the bandages—the company aid men. A perfect case in point is the work of Private Leon W. Kline, Jr., who dared the Germans to do their worst as he saved the life of an American soldier.

The platoon to which Kline was attached prepared to attack a strong Kraut position. Just as they were ready to jump off, a machine gun slug wounded a rifleman in his foxhole, 100 yards from where the aid man crouched.

Bullets and mortar fragments struck within inches of Kline as he crawled across the 100 yards of open ground to the wounded man's foxhole. Once there, Kline reached down into the hole, lifted the soldier out, threw him across his back and ran back to the platoon CP behind a farm building, where he administered first aid.

Then he ran 400 bullet-spattered yards to the company CP where he secured a litter squad to evacuate the wounded soldier, action that meant life or death for the casualty.

"Somehow or other you don't notice the bullets so much, because you're concentrating entirely on the job you have to do,"' remarked Private Kline.

On another occasion, with tanks and small arms firing from only 300 yards away, Kline works his way up a hill to treat eight wounded *German* soldiers. He patches up one, brings him back to the American aid station, then, with some help from German prisoners, goes back for the others. One is an officer who has now been wounded on both fronts. He's had enough.

On October 20, 1944 Private Leon W. Kline, Jr., 23, of 292 East Main Street, a "Cotton Baler" soldier, while his unit is attacking a fortified enemy position in France, takes a rifle bullet to the chest and is killed instantly.

One of six siblings participating in World War II, Sylvester Foltman is in the Navy a year when assigned to his first and only ship, the *USS Marcus Island*, a brand-new escort carrier, in January of 1944. These small carriers are nothing more than Liberty ships with a flight deck, carrying virtually no armor plate and but a handful of anti-aircraft guns. They are designed to provide close air support for amphibious troops and the *Marcus Island* participates in four distinct battles: at Peleliu, Leyte Gulf, Mindoro and Okinawa. Sy is in charge of part of the flight deck crew, seeing the planes get off safely and return safely. The pilots are no older than he is.

On the 25th of October, 1944, while providing coverage for the landings on Leyte, the better part of the Japanese Imperial Navy suddenly approaches them from the northwest. Due to a communication mix-up, there is no advance warning and Adm. Halsey has taken all our heavy ships north to chase a part of the Japanese fleet that has been deliberately set up as a decoy. The navy CE groups known as Taffy 1, 2 and 3 are hopelessly out-powered. The Japanese approach with battleships, heavy and light cruisers and large destroyers while the American 7th Fleet has only destroyers, destroyer escorts and escort carriers, all lightly armored or not armored at all.

From the flight deck Foltman sees a very much faster enemy cruiser appear on the horizon.

Shells from its big guns begin splashing all around them.

The men of the *Marcus Island,* flag ship of Taffy 2, know they are in trouble. They are sitting ducks. The only thing standing between them and utter disaster is the indomitable courage of the men who fight the Battle of Leyte Gulf.

From before sun-up to sundown, CPO Foltman helps launch wave after wave of light planes: fighters and dive bombers mostly, some armed only with machine guns.

It will be many years before he learns what feats he does that day, but the end result is that the courageous attacks convince the Japanese admiral that he faces a much larger force and withdraws.

It is one of the greatest moments in America's storied naval history.

Several weeks later, back in the Philippines, the *Marcus Island* comes under attack from Japanese bombers and *kamikaze* planes. All are shot down by her anti-aircraft guns and fighter pilots, but two land close enough to cause damage to the ship, one on each side, and several injuries to the crew.

Kamikaze attack on USS Marcus Island, as seen from the flight deck.

"Weren't you scared, Uncle Sy?" asks one of our kids when he tells that story.

"We were 21, 22 years old. We didn't know enough to be scared."

Five days after the Leyte landings, the Red Cross flies in Chuckie Huntington, a top Amsterdam basketball and baseball player in the 20's. Two days later he's got his machines hooked up and he's right behind the lines serving fresh coffee and home-made doughnuts to the GI's and liberated natives. The doughnuts become so popular that he is soon kicking out 1,400 a day. When his batter runs out he improvises with a mixture of flour, spices, baking powder and a half margarine/half cheese spread that they use in the jungle areas as a substitute for butter.

At one point, Japanese paratroopers infiltrate their lines and they are cut off from the main body of troops, much to the delight of Tokyo Rose, who reports to the world that they have been exterminated, which they find amusing. In fairness to Rose, she takes it back the next day:

> I wish to correct my statement that American troops have been exterminated on Leyte. A few survivors have been found, but their supplies are so low that the American Red Cross is feeding them on doughnuts and cookies.

That brings the house down in the Leyte jungle, and the well-fed, doughnut-enhanced GI's make quick work of dispatching the Japanese counter-attackers.

Cpl. Ralph Marotta is with the 32nd Infantry Division on Leyte, as a medical aid man. While two rifle companies are trying to dislodge Japanese defenders from a stretch of high ground, several are wounded by machine gun fire. Marotta crawls to one man, bandages him up, then, with enemy fire hitting all around him he pulls a second man to safety behind a log and takes care of him. Then he goes back for more, ultimately treating seven men under fire before the skirmish ends.

Marotta is one of the original Company G men who left Amsterdam in October of 1940.

One of the early *kamikaze* attacks takes place on November 1, 1944 off of Leyte. Not only does the plane run into the destroyer *USS Abner Read*, but it drops a bomb down one of the stacks just before crashing. The bomb drops straight to the engine room and blows the ship apart. Twenty-two men are killed, but Torpedoman 2c Vito Greco of 8 Gardiner Street survives.

> **UPX, November, 1944 from Bill Leonard:** *Give Harold Gotobed a hello for me and congratulations to Jimmy Jasper on his completions of missions with the 15th AAF. Your missions are familiar with me and I know what memories they left. I sure would like to see you, Jimmy, but you will be home before I get to the U.S.A. I finished up in good shape and expect to see a White Christmas in good old Amsterdam. Your experience with fighters and flak is a familiar one. One of our roughest missions carried us down the heart of Vienna, Austria (or as you would say, Jim, down main street). To top it off I was left broke from a poker game! – We were in that flak nineteen minutes which seemed a year. We caught one burst below our bomb bays and one below the waist. A few pieces of flak landed near my radio table which I now have in my possession. We were darn lucky and thanked the Lord we made it back "O.K." Now that's all in the past and I look forward to seeing a home town which several times during our raids seemed a life time away from me. Well, enough of the chatter, thanks again for the issue. By the way, tell Jimmy to save some Cold Beer for me! God bless the gang wherever they may be.*

Guy Murdoch paints a word picture for the boys, describing East Main Street as Christmas, 1944 approaches.

PRE-XMAS NOTES

The same old Xmas decorations downtown but they always look new, and the regular neon signs, mostly red and blue seem to become a part of the scheme. Salvation Army booth outside the 10 cent store with the attendant in a shelter like a sentry box. The crowds in Kresge's dollar store looking for the little things that complete all Xmas plans. Everybody looking for small gifts for some grab bag. A little red-headed boy, about five, buying War Stamps in the First National Bank, on his snow suit the Asiatic-Pacific Theater ribbon. Cigarettes, one package to a customer, and not always available, are a popular topic of conversation. Brands that we had never heard of are for sale. Ramesis, Chelseas, Wings, etc. Beautiful young girl at the woolen counter in Kresge's buying angora wool for a baby bonnet. On her coat lapel is the Army Good Conduct Ribbon, and it is quite evident that the bonnet will soon have an owner. All over the store a buzz of activity, but above it all the recorded voice of Bing Crosby singing in reverent rhythm, "Silent Night, Holy Night" as only Bing can sing it, softens the scene and breaks down the commercialism. God Bless you all, and again a Merry Christmas.

No one seemed to know quite what to do with the 531st. They are restructured, reordered, renamed, reassigned and reassigned again and eventually wander up to Belgium, off the front lines. There will be no more beach landings in Europe, but somehow the Army can't get around to just admitting, "We don't really need you fellows any more."

Cpl. Garn is still in Headquarters Company for their battalion, so he gets the news first and in December of 1944 the news is that certain guys are getting furloughed home to the States, provided that they've been twice decorated. Garn quickly realizes that Malcolm Tomlinson fits the category with his two Purple Hearts and, with a bunch of other friends, goes looking for him in Company C where he's been lodging since being transferred to a line company. On arriving at Company C they learn that his platoon has been temporarily detached from the company, then they find his platoon and his squad is detached from the platoon. So they traipse all over Flanders before finally locating him, holed up in a private home. Says Garn:

> We dropped the good news on Doc.
>
> "Soldier, you won't believe this but you're going home," I said.
>
> "You got to be kidding. Don't fool around with me," was the reply from the astonished soldier.
>
> We told him we were deadly serious and explained how we knew. Doc pointed out very carefully to us that the army would never be successful in getting him back to the European theater once he reached his home in upstate New York. We said goodbye to Doc and left him in his billet feverishly packing up his gear.

He doesn't quite make it home for Christmas, but arrives just after the first of the year, the first time he has seen Amsterdam in thirty months. The celebratory article in the *Recorder* on January 17, 1945 notes that he is one of only 1,368 soldiers granted a 30 day furlough from Europe. He doesn't bring up his four D-Day landings or his two Purple Hearts or his eight battle stars or his *Croix de Guerre avec Palm,* simply explaining to the reporter that he is just a "lucky guy."

Coxswain Edward Bablin shifts uncomfortably from the leg injury that has landed him in the naval hospital in Cherbourg. He looks over at the guy in the next bed and a startled look comes across his face.

"What's that you're reading?"

The sailor looks up. "My hometown paper. My mother sends it to me."

"Isn't that the *Amsterdam Recorder*?"

"It is."

"Hell, I'm from Amsterdam, too! Who are you?"

"Frank Going."

Thus begins a life-long friendship of two men from the same town who had never heard of each other.

Turns out that hospital stay is not the only experience they share.

On Christmas Eve, 1944, the *SS Leopoldville*, a Belgian vessel converted as a troop carrier, collides with a German torpedo just off of the harbor at

Cherbourg. The ship carries 2,235 American soldiers being rushed to the front during the Battle of the Bulge. Below decks panic ensues after the explosion, until one soldier begins singing *Silent Night.* Others join in as they calmly make their way to the open air, where they watch the Belgian crew escape in a life boat. Soldiers try to launch the remaining lifeboats, but no one aboard has the skills or training and the ropes become hopelessly entangled. A destroyer escorting them takes off in pursuit of the German U-boat that had launched the attack, not realizing the Leopoldville has been hit, nor that it carries troops.

By the time the word reaches Cherbourg and every available craft responds, including fishing boats, it is too late.

The sinking ship takes 515 men down with it. Another 248 do not survive the icy waters. Ed Bablin's assignment is to pull the frozen bodies from the English Channel.

Frank Going, an inventory and supplies petty officer, wanders the port and sees the trembling survivors being brought to warmth and safety.

And then he watches as the bodies wash into the harbor, and pile up on the docks, one after another after another after another after another after . . . .

.

16. INTO EACH LIFE SOME RAIN MUST FALL

O n November 28, 1944 James A. "Jake" Blanchfield is attending to his regular duties as Circulation Manager of the *Amsterdam Evening Recorder* at their Railroad Street headquarters in downtown Amsterdam near the train depot and across the street from the Central Hotel. His is the first station as you enter the offices through the revolving door which keeps the cold out and the opinions in. Everybody knows Jake, and everyone knows where to find him. He knows every current paperboy in town by name, and plenty of the ones who came before them. Some have already made the city's Honor Roll, and he makes sure that the news reporters mention that the dead heroes are part of the *Recorder* family.

The kid from Western Union goes straight to the circulation counter.

Jake turns pale and rushes home to find his wife at the kitchen stove.

"Tess. It's Jack. He's missing in action."

She spills a pot of boiling water on her legs.

Jack Blanchfield is a 17 year old Freshman at Niagara University, waiting at a bus stop with four college buddies in front of a Walgreen's in downtown Niagara Falls on December 7, 1941 when they hear the news. The bus trip back to campus is silent; the same at their Sunday supper of cold cuts, salads, cookies and milk.

Over the next few days, upperclassmen ROTC officers leave school to enlist, as do professors, priests and laymen. Blanchfield turns 18 in March of 1942 and immediately attempts to enlist in the Army Air Force.

He is rejected. An irregular heart beat and a recent bout of appendicitis nixes him.

And so, he continues in college, including ROTC training, has his appendix removed in August, and returns for his second year. In December of 1942 he successfully signs up for the Enlisted Reserve Corps of the Army, finishes his school year and reports for duty on May 23, 1943.

It takes the Army five days to find a uniform to fit his 5'4", 115 pound frame (he is one of the taller of the five Blanchfield brothers). Soon he finds himself in the midst of thirteen weeks of basic infantry training at Fort McClellan, Alabama. With his 148 IQ, and ROTC and college backgrounds, he has no trouble getting into the Army Specialized Training Program, and soon is back in the classroom, at North Carolina State in Raleigh, courtesy of Uncle Sam. They even put him into a pre-med course.

But the Army needs men, and, after two crammed semesters, in March of 1944 he joins Company C, 346th Infantry, 87th Division at Fort Jackson, South Carolina, still a private, and ready for action.

Right after D-Day they board the *Mauritania*, a seven day trip to Liverpool without convoy in a hammock on D-Deck with exactly one half hour a day of fresh air. In less than a week they board the *Nieuw Amsterdam* for the trip across the channel, from whence they scramble down ropes into LCI's for the short hop to Omaha Beach.

He stumbles in the high tide under his full field pack and might well have drowned but for the GI behind him who grabs him by his pack and tells him to keep walking.

They reach the beach and climb a rise and immediately come face to face with thousands of white crosses and stars of David. He finds the one bearing the name of Pfc. Thomas E. Cronin and pauses long enough to say a quick prayer for his classmate at St. Mary's Institute. Cronin had been killed in action in Normandy on June 26, 1944.

These are the replacement troops, sent to fill the gaps in fighting units worn thin by D-Day and the fierce Normandy campaign. Pfc. Blanchfield becomes a member of Gen. George Patton's Third Army, assigned to Company C, 11th Regiment, 5th Division, armed with grenades, two bandoleers of ammo and a 60mm mortar shell, with a red diamond stenciled to his helmet, which he stuffs with extra toilet paper. Armed with a light pack, raincoat, shovel, half a shelter, a dry pair of socks, K rations and a spoon, he is ready for anything that comes.

Except for the German 88 shell which roars over his head.

He grabs his helmet, freezes and prays.

They move out behind tanks, heading east, and meet no Germans until two days later when they are stopped by machine gun fire in a small village. Pfc. Blanchfield lies protected behind a small hill.

"Fire, damn it!' he hears his sergeant shout.

"Who, me?"

"Yes, you!"

He opens fire on the remains of a two story stone building.

He is a veteran.

By next morning the Germans have fled and the 5th Division advances to the Moselle River. The troops ride tanks and trucks or just walk. The German Panzers and their 88's inflict many casualties in an attempt to stop the crossing, but once the troops to his south make it over, the Panzers flee.

And then it rains. A cold, driving rain. Jack and the other men sleep in slit trenches with just a raincoat, their M-1's and water. They move forward a few miles, near the old Maginot line, and dig in. And there they stay for weeks, while Patton begs for fuel to keep his army going.

Jack Blanchfield's fox hole becomes a small apartment. A valley separates the two armies and occasionally a wandering cow strolls through the middle and becomes target practice for both sides. Pfc. Blanchfield leads frequent patrols to check out Fort Driant, the prime target in Patton's stalled offensive near Metz, and gets fired upon for his curiosity.

The days and the nights grow colder as 1944 ebbs away. They add long underwear, gloves, wool caps and field jackets. In mid-October they are rotated to a rest area for a couple of weeks, and then back to the dirt apartment.

On November 4, 1944, his sergeant informs him that he is being temporarily assigned to A Company. He makes a brief farewell to his buddies, expecting to be back shortly.

His assignment: an outpost a few hundred yards in front of the main line. Two foxholes, two men each. His partner is a guy named Couch from

Vermont whom he is meeting for the first time. Later, Blanchfield remembers his meal vividly: pork chops and boiled potatoes and bread.

Beyond that, they have a telephone. The plan is to spend two hours on and two hours off through the night, so that one of the guys will be awake at all times. Jack has just fallen asleep after midnight when Couch nudges him.

"We have company."

They fire, throw grenades. So do the other two men.

He tries the phone.

The line is cut.

He knows what this means. The Germans are in their rear.

The fire fight is brief. Couch falls forward dead, mowed down by machine gun fire. A voice comes from behind Blanchfield.

"Hands up!"

He is the only survivor. No one from the American side comes to help. Much, much later he learns that a patrol is sent out the next day and, naturally, finds no trace of him.

Pfc. Blanchfield, hands over his head, is in the custody of SS troops from the 1st German Division.

They taunt him.

"What do you think of the war now?"

There are cat-calls and boos and what he presumes are barnyard epithets and such in German.

They take his cigarettes and his D Bar.

But not his rosary. That he had sewn into his clothing.

Just in case.

The Germans lead him finally into a stone building and a room full of maps, phones, telegraphs and SS.

The interrogation begins. Election Day in the USA is only a couple of days away, and the Nazis want to know everything that Pfc. Blanchfield knows about the massive attack which surely must be in the works, timed to insure Roosevelt's re-election over Republican Tom Dewey.

"Blanchfield, John J., private first class, Serial # 12216536."

The record is not clear as to whether he actually says out loud what he is thinking, that neither Ike nor Blood and Guts Patton has yet consulted with him as to their specific war strategy. Regardless, his obstinacy gets him a bayonet jab in the rear. Finally, near dawn, they lock him in a small room and give him some bread and what he will recall as "ersatz tea."

He sits there tired, scared and very, very alone.

Around noon they take him away, hands tied behind his back, two guards with skull and cross-bone insignia on their uniforms who throw him in the back of their version of a jeep. They head east.

Stopping for the night in a farm complex, they lock him in a barn, where eventually he is joined by a French-speaking Yugoslavian prisoner, or so he claims. Jack knows enough conversational French to get along, but he has his suspicions, and when the Yugoslav is gone in the morning he feels his suspicions mostly confirmed. A German medic treats an elbow wound with stitches and crepe paper, and they are on their way again.

Next stop is a village jail where he finally meets up with an American, greeting him from an adjoining cell, a downed fighter pilot from Chicago named Green, who had parachuted to safety and capture a few days before. They chat for a while before getting some shut-eye.

The next morning the guards take Green from his cell and lead him outdoors. Pfc. Blanchfield hears a ruckus and looks out the small barred window of his cell.

There is Green, surrounded by civilians with shovels and pitchforks.

The guards walk away.

As they beat him to death, Green lets out blood-curdling screams until he can scream no more.

The twenty-year-old son of the Circulation Manager of the *Amsterdam Evening Recorder* watches it all.

And then he locks it away for a long, long time in that small corner of the human brain where nightmares are born.

They move him a couple of days later to another local jail in Forbush and after a couple of more days he is brought before a young German Luftwaffe officer, who tells Blanchfield that he will allow him to make a radio broadcast, to let the world know his name and home address and that he is a Prisoner of War and okay.

And all they want in return is a little bit about his background. Where and when, what he knows of his outfit, the ships he has traveled on, that's all.

"Blanchfield, John J., private first class, Serial # 12216536."

He refuses a radio broadcast and answers no questions.

No notification of his prisoner status is released to international agencies, directly or indirectly.

And they take his nearly empty wallet, which contains only two things: a hand-written note which his brother Pat had sent him when Pat was eight years old, and a poem written for him by his Grandmother Blanchfield.

They load him on a boxcar with about twenty GI's for a two-day ride with no food and no water to Stalag XII-A in Limburg, a hell-hole of discomfort, disease and deprivation. Because it serves primarily as a way-station to other camps for troops captured on the Western Front, there is little opportunity for the POWs to organize their own system of sanitation.

Pfc. Blanchfield is housed for three days in a barn-like building with broken windows and straw floors to sleep on. Meals consist of a cup of "ersatz tea" for breakfast, boiled potato in water at noon and two slices of black bread in the evening.

And here he discovers the joys of lice for the first time.

One morning about forty of them are herded out to the showers, after which they are doused in anti-lice powder. Most of their clothes, including Blanchfield's helmet, are missing. In their place are piles of old clothes and wooden shoes. The uniforms, it would develop, will be used later by German troops in the Battle of the Bulge as part of their efforts to sow confusion and chaos.

But Jack Blanchfield is lucky. He is so short that none of the camp Germans fit into his uniform, so he gets to keep his.

From here he is issued a straw mat, a piece of blanket and a wooden slab to sleep on. Now they are placed in a barracks with, for the first time, a toilet and cold running water. They take his official POW photo holding his ID number 078-069.

The war continues, of course, and allied planes fly over the camp daily, at which time the troops dutifully file into cement trenches.[23]

The black bread, "tea" and potato or cabbage "soup" diet continues. Men grow desperate from hunger. One day a GI has somehow come into possession of some white bread and Blanchfield gladly trades him an extra pair of socks for a couple of slices. He eats one and hides the other in his mattress. Next morning it is gone.

Seventeen days after his capture, the POW is handed two pieces of paper and told he can write twenty words home. Words like, "I'm okay, a POW, don't worry, love."

And then he is jammed into a boxcar with 44 other men, for a journey of unknown length (to them) that lasts seven days. Straw on the floor. Garbage can in corner. German guard stationed in a small cubicle above them.

There are three more boxcars of GI's, and later the train picks up several others loaded with civilians.

Decades later he's pretty sure he knows what happened to them.

Winter starts early, and it is one of the coldest ever. They have only their own body heat to keep warm, and most are wearing only the old clothes handed out when their uniforms were stolen.

The garbage can has an obvious function, and is soon filled to the brim and overflows at every bump of the rails. Human waste seeps into the straw. They are hungry, thirsty, cold. Many suffer from wounds and dysentery. There is enough room for all to sit, but they soon find that half will have to stand for the others to sleep.

They grab spoons and whatever metal they can find to claw away at the floor of the boxcar to cut a hole big enough to drain away some of the biological discharge.

Occasionally the guard overhead opens a slot and lowers some bread and water.

---

23 Later, after he had moved on, the camp will be hit by American bombers on Christmas Eve with many casualties. After that the GI's paint "POW" in large letters on the roofs.

The train sometimes stops for hours on end. On one occasion they can see through the knotholes that they are in a large rail yard. A large rail yard under attack by allied planes. They are locked in and prime targets, helpless and terrified. They pray, together and alone.

When the all-clear sounds, they bump along eastward.

After five days they arrive in Danzig, now the Polish port of Gdansk. From there they head back west and two days later pull into Neubrandenburg's Stalag IIA, thirty miles north of Berlin and just south of the Baltic Sea.

Stiff, dehydrated, starved and cold, they are marched into their new home. While folks celebrate Thanksgiving back in Amsterdam, Jack Blanchfield and his colleagues feast on cabbage "soup" (cabbage in hot water) and black bread, seated on the frozen ground. Devouring the food swiftly, they pay the price internally over the next few days.

Tom "Porky" Blanchfield comes home from SMI to find his father crying, a yellow piece of paper dangling from his hand. For the first time that he can remember, Jake hugs him, then hands him the telegram and walks away.

Soon the grandparents and aunts from Schenectady arrive. The news hits the papers and the whole thing becomes somewhat overwhelming for the young teenager. Every day, people stop him and ask, "Any news of Jack?" and then he shakes his head and hears, "No news is good news!"

His younger brothers are too little to talk to, his parents too upset. Older brother Jim has dropped out of high school to join the Merchant Marine, off somewhere in the North Atlantic without even knowing about Jack. So Pork takes out his frustrations on his paper route, tightly rolling up each *Recorder*, pretending it is a hand grenade, pulling the imaginary pin, tossing it on the porch and muttering to himself, "Fuck you, Nazis!" One of his grenades breaks a window at the home of the Chief of Police. Though feeling completely guiltless (this is war, after all), he knocks on the door and offers the chief's wife two dollars to replace the glass. She refuses, kindly.

Not long before Christmas Porky pulls a usual ruse on his folks, telling them he is off to serve the Novena Mass at St. Mary's and dropping into a pool hall instead. Lining up a shot he hears a commotion at the door, and in walks brother Jim, in pea coat and Merchant Marine uniform, a white duffel slung over his shoulder. Two of the guys greeting him say, "Sorry about your brother Jack."

Never one to keep his emotions buried too deeply beneath the surface, Jim Blanchfield grabs his kid brother by the collar and asks, "What's going on with Jack?" then yanks him out of the pool room. They walk home silently, then the tearful reunion with Mom and Dad, who doubtless think, if they think about it at all, that the two boys had met up in church.

Jim only stays for a couple of days, then leaves for Brooklyn to ship off again, but not before confiding with his brother:

"I'm getting a ship to Europe, get near France, then I'm gonna jump ship and find Jack and bring him home. I swear to God, I will." Porky doesn't doubt it for a minute.[24]

They are among the first group of Americans at the camp, which segregates them from the British, Canadians and Russians. The Russians have it bad. Nearly every day he sees four Russians carrying a litter bearing a dead comrade wrapped in brown paper. They bury the bodies in the hard ground somewhere outside the barbed wire. On their way back they beg the Americans for bread, pleading with them. But there is no bread to share, the Germans still giving the Americans the bare daily sustenance of "tea", two slices of black bread, and cabbage or potato "soup."

Stalag IIA, he learns in his travels, is a very large camp. Large gates are surrounded by electrified barbed wire about twelve feet high, with periodic guard towers equipped with machine guns and search lights. About ten feet inside the main fence is another about six feet high. Between them the guards patrol with their burp guns. Inside are a series of smaller camps, each with more gates and barbed wire.

Blanchfield is lodged in a one-story wooden hut on stilts with a one foot clearance over the ground. They have a latrine with cold water. They sleep on wooden shelves, one over the other, with a piece of blanket and

---

24 Fortunately for the Nazis, Jim never gets close enough to France to try it.

straw mattresses. They are allowed out in the morning for roll call and locked in the barracks at dusk.

Rations, such as they are, arrive on hand trucks and are doled out by GIs.

They vote in their own "Camp Leader," a sergeant, who instructs them on their duties as POWs. An Escape Committee is chosen, and they elect barracks leaders.

In less than four weeks of captivity, the never very large Pfc. Blanchfield has already lost a notable amount of weight. He has grown a beard, where lice nest. He has become somber, withdrawn, pessimistic.

Depressed, with much to be depressed about.

And so he jumps at the chance when, a couple of days later, a German guard asks for volunteers for a work group. Beats lying on a straw mattress all day feeling sorry for yourself.

It being late in the war, their guards are a couple of old men and a couple of equally aged civilians. They take a civilian train to Dunnewald where they are led to a small barbed-wire enclosure containing one barrack with a stove, latrine, and outdoor cold water well. There is plenty of snow on the ground and bitter cold temperatures. They are issued razors, soap and Red Cross packages (four men to a package meant for one).

The Germans are building a new road, and the job of the Blanchfield crew is to remove the stumps from felled trees, digging around, cutting roots, lifting them out with a pump lift. The two elderly civilians are the bosses, and Jack begins to pick up some German. He had previously traded a guard some cigarettes for a German/French dictionary, and so he asks the civilians to point out the German word and uses his rudimentary high school French to figure out the rest, becoming reasonably fluent in short order.

The cold keeps the lice under control, the hard work helps build up his strength, the cleared wood gives them fuel for their stove, which gives them not only warmth but hot water for shaving and washing their clothes and themselves. And they are able to toast their black bread, which makes it go down a little more easily.

Christmas Day 1944 comes and they are marched to a rail yard where they unload a box car filled with fifty-pound bags of cement. They finish by noon and are given the rest of the day off.

Back in their barracks they decorate a small pine tree with colored paper and tinsel. (Tinsel is easy to come by: the allies drop it regularly from the sky to confound the German radar). Jack receives a present from Jim "Gooch" Adams, a tank man from Auburn, NY: a single cigarette, neatly wrapped.

A while after, when permitted to write again, Pfc. Blanchfield writes home about his first Christmas in captivity:

> January 7, 1945
> Dear Mom, Dad and Gang:
> Hope you had a nice Xmas and even if I couldn't be with you in body I was there in mind. The American Red Cross made my Xmas for me-- turkey and plum pudding. But I still missed being home with you-- for everything it always meant. I'm thankful, though, that God spared my life to observe Xmas no matter where I am. I'm working, as I must, and as usual feeling well physically. I've written to you for a package. You can check with the Red Cross as to details about shipment. I need sweets and candy more than anything else, so use your own judgment. Above all else, Mom, don't worry about me-- just keep praying that I can be home soon. Give my love and regards to all. Be good fellows – and don't worry! Love always,
> JACK

But back at 19 Trinity Place, Christmas is as sad as it can be. Fifty days have passed and nothing at all has been heard of Jack's existence.

Days, weeks, months go by without a word.

Working at the *Recorder* on January 24, 1945, Jake Blanchfield learns that two of Jack's classmates from St. Mary's Institute Class of 1941, Pvt. William Burns and Staff Sgt. William Vidulich, have each turned up as prisoners of war. If there is a flicker of hope in that news, it is tempered by the realization that with each passing hour the odds that Jack Blanchfield will ever be seen alive again grow worse and worse.

These are some of the things the Blanchfield family read about in Jake's newspaper during the holiday season that surely must have been the most horrible in the history of the City of Amsterdam:

November 23, 1944, Thanksgiving Day. Former St. Ann's Church choir boy and Mohawk Carpet Mills employee Pfc. Warren S. Johnson, overseas since September, killed in action, Germany.

November 23. Pfc. Richard Wasson, wounded in action, Belgium.

November 24. Pvt. John Blonkowski, wounded in action, Belgium.

November 25. Capt. (Rev.) Anthony Sidoti, wounded in action, Germany.

November27. Staff Sgt. George H. Coursen, an aerial gunner aboard a B-26, formerly employed at the A&P on Walnut Street, killed in action over France.

November30. Pvt. Alfred Grzelecki, wounded in action, Germany.

November30. Pfc. Joseph Billis, wounded in action, France.

December 1. Sgt. William Garwacki, St. Stanislaus Parish and School, employee of Bigelow-Sanford, killed in action in France while serving with the Armored Division of Gen. Patton's Third Army.

December 2. Pfc. Stanley Bryk, missing in action, Germany.

December 5. Pfc. Douglas Gifford, killed in action, Leyte.

December 6. Pvt. Harold Countryman, killed in action, France.

December 6. Pfc. Edwin McConnell, missing in action, Germany.

December 6. Pvt. William Richards, missing in action, Germany.

December 6. Pfc. Alfonso Provenzano, wounded in action, France.

December 6. Pvt. Ralph DiCaterino, wounded in action, Germany.

December 7. Pfc. Carl Anderson, wounded in action, France.

December 10. Pvt. Frank Nardo, wounded in action, France.

December 11. First Lt. E.A. Cooley, missing in action over Austria.

December 11. Pfc. Joseph Wozniak, wounded in action, Leyte.

December 11. Pvt. Frank Pilecki, wounded in action, Germany.

December 11. Pfc. Edward Hage, wounded in action, France.

December 12. Pfc. Frank A. Pacillo, 22, killed in action, Germany.

December 13. Lt. Alfred J. Agard, 21, Wilbur H. Lynch Class of 1940, nephew of Recorder (Police Court Judge) Francis Collins, former Amsterdam Evening Recorder paperboy, killed in a plane crash in Italy.

December 13. Navy Machinist's Mate, 3rd Class, Edward Partyka, 21, 42 Crane Street, Wilbur H. Lynch Class of 1940. Missing in Aleutian Islands,. Later declared dead.

December 13. Staff Sgt. Lawrence Pelotte, wounded in action, Germany.

December 14. Pvt. Ralph J. DiCaterino, 24, 275 Cleveland Avenue, died in France of wounds received in action in Germany on December 6.

December 15. Tech (5) Dominick Crocetti, wounded in action, Italy.

December 15. Staff Sgt. Lauren Barnett, wounded in action, Germany.

December 16. Pvt. Peter Gawron, wounded in action, Belgium.

December 16. Pfc. Mario Checca, missing in action, France.

December 16. Sgt. Joseph Niemczura, wounded in action, Leyte.

December 17. Pfc. William K. Hoppy, 19, the only child of his parents of 70 Arnold Avenue, killed in action, France while serving with Gen. Patch's Seventh Army.

December 17. Staff Sgt. Peter J. Poremba, Amsterdam RD 5, former employee of the Ford garage in Fort Plain, killed in action, Germany.

December 17. Pvt. Annunzio Greco, wounded in action, France.

December 18. Pfc. Thomas F. Engle, 19, 69 Union Street, classmate of Pfc. William Hoppy in the Wilbur H. Lynch Class of 1943, killed in action, Germany.

December 19. A.O. 2/c Thomas Rutkowski, 17 Voorhees Street, killed in the crash of a Navy plane in South America. Steve's brother.

December 20. Sgt. George McKnight, missing in action, Luxembourg.

December 20. Pvt. Frank Stachnik, missing in action, Luxembourg.

December 20. Pfc. William Tomalski, missing in action, Luxembourg.

December 21. Tech (5) Joseph Taberski, wounded in action, Belgium.

December 21. Pfc. Joseph Waveris, missing in action, Germany.

December 22. Pvt. Charles J. Ryan, 20, 51 Lincoln Avenue, killed in action, Luxembourg.

December 22. Pfc. Wallace L. "Sharkey" Siarkowski, Technical High School Class of 1942, avid bowler, killed in action in Belgium while serving with Gen. Hodges' First Army.

December 22. Pvt. First Class Anthony W. Domkowski, 33, killed in action, France after having served in the campaigns in North Africa and Italy.

December 23. Lt. Robert Gilston, wounded in action, Luxembourg.

December 23. Corp. Theodore Albers, missing in action, Belgium.

December 24. Pfc. John Salten, wounded in action, Luxembourg.

December 26. On the second day of Christmas, the feast of Stephen, Sgt. Joseph J. Colistra, 28, killed in action, Germany, while serving with the First Army in the Battle of the Bulge.

December 26. Pfc. Stephen Grzywacz, wounded in action, Belgium.

December 26. Sgt. Michael Kaminski, wounded in action, Germany.

December 29. The fifth day of Christmas. Pfc. Willard M. Austin, 21, 70 Lyon Street (formerly of Perth and Broadalbin), killed in France.

December 30. Pfc. Raymond Denton, missing in action, France.

January 2, 1945. The ninth day of Christmas. Pfc. Jacob F. Sovik dies of wounds received in battle.

January 2. Sgt. Ward Flanders, killed in action, Pacific.

January 2. Pfc. Robert Cotanche, killed in action.

January 3. The tenth day of Christmas. Fonda native Sgt. Kenneth Snyder, 26, serving with the 248th Combat Engineering Division, died of wounds received in action.

January 3. Staff Sgt. John Soodol, wounded in action, Luxembourg.

January 4. The eleventh day of Christmas. Pvt. Daniel H. Clute, our intrepid paratrooper who told a German soldier to "scram!" on D-Day, killed in action in Belgium. The Recorder notes that he had been one of their most reliable paperboys. Wilbur H. Lynch Class of 1940.

January 4. Pfc. James Melillo, wounded in action, Belgium.

January 5. The twelfth day of Christmas. Pvt. Norman F. Briskie, 19, Star Route, Hagaman, takes part with the 16th Infantry in an assault on the northern flank of the German Ardennes salient in Belgium, fighting through heavy snow and spirited resistance from the Germans to seize an important road center, which proves to be of great tactical importance. Killed by the explosion of an artillery shell.

January 5. Pfc. Frank E. Kaminski, 18, with the 223rd Infantry, overseas since November, killed in action in France. He is survived by four brothers, including twice-wounded Sgt. Michael J. Kaminski, and five sisters.

It doesn't stop there, of course. Only the holiday season stops.

One morning at roll call the German guards unexpectedly check everyone's dog tags. A fellow from Brooklyn named "Hank", who has been acting as interpreter for the POWs, is put on a truck and carted away.

Hank is Jewish.

From then on the GI's hide their dog tags.

Not everyone handles the stress of captivity. A GI named Nixon from Colorado flips out completely, wandering the barracks at night. Jack wakes once to find him hovering over him, explaining, "I am Jesus of Nazareth, King of the Jews." Other times he claims to be a spot on the wall. When he is off, he is out of control. Jack emerges from his stump hole one day only to receive an unprovoked powerful right cross to the jaw. Two days later, again in his stump hole, Nixon suddenly begins pummeling him on the back with a shovel. Nixon screams as the Germans haul him away. They never hear of him again.

The other workers cover for Jack for the several days it takes for his back to heal.

The Dunnewald stump project ends by mid-January, and the men return to Stalag IIA. To amuse them on their way, the Germans provide a camp newspaper, the *Stalag News*, filled with the glorious reports of German victories in the Battle of the Bulge.

WE HAVE TAKEN ANTWERP! THE ALLIES HAVE BEEN FORCED BACK TO THE ENGLISH CHANNEL!

By this time, of course, the Battle of the Bulge has been fought and lost, the western allies are mounting their big offensive for the sweep across Germany and the Russians are getting close to knocking on the gates of Berlin.

Once back at the camp, this all becomes clear as the GI's have gotten access to a radio picking up the BBC, and the news of Patton lifting the siege of Bastogne lifts the spirits of the POWs as well.

Another work project develops, based in large part on the rapid Russian advance heading in their direction: the erection of concrete road blocks to hinder the Soviets. This time Pfc. Jack Blanchfield is elected Interpreter and Camp Leader for the 162 men who march five miles to their new barracks, the large camp in miniature, with two buildings of four large rooms each, twenty men to a room, and a semi-private room for Jack and a medic from South Carolina named White, who had been captured in North Africa and has only his summer uniform to face the bitter cold of that winter.

The latrine consists of a no-seat ditch. The cold running water faucet is located outside, three feet from the latrine. To keep clean personally, they trade soap and cigarettes for magazines and papers to use on themselves.

Pfc. Blanchfield has each room elect a barracks chief, and together with Jack the nine of them make the camp rules and enforce them. They appoint an Escape Committee and a Communications Committee.

The men are divided into specialized work groups. Some build the wooden forms, others mix the cement and sand, still others pour the mixture into the frames.

As leader, Blanchfield advises the German unteroffizier in charge that forcing them to build this road block, a military work, is a violation of the Geneva Conventions.

He also complains about the lack of blankets, medical supplies and food. He protests the state of the latrine and the water supply being so close to it.

"You will build the road blocks regardless of Geneva, or else."

Or else.

One day in February, when the incoming mail is being sorted for delivery, Amsterdam Postmaster Deegan spots the Red Cross envelope and personally drives it straight to Trinity Place. By 10:30 Jake Blanchfield is knocking on Porky's classroom door at SMI. Porky figures he must be in his deepest trouble yet.

But the tears this time are of joy.

Jack is alive.

Later, at home, Teresa Blanchfield says to her husband, "It's Vinny's birthday."

Vincent Moriarty, a graduate of St. Augustine's High School in Brooklyn, had been Jack's roommate in his freshman year at Niagara University. Outgoing, handsome, he has the world at his feet. But before the school year ends he comes down with a fatal disease.

On his deathbed he invokes the Catholic doctrine of the Communion of Saints.

"If you ever need anything real bad, pray to me."

That short sentence keeps hope alive for the Blanchfield family. Somehow, Jake comes into possession of a ring that had belonged to Vinny Moriarty. He will wear it for the rest of his life.

By mid-February, 1945 he has been a prisoner almost four months. His legs are spindly from the loss of weight, his feet are raw, cold, blistered and sometimes bleeding. His only pair of socks (recall that he had traded an extra pair for two slices of white bread) has large holes, so he cuts them off at the feet and pulls the ankle part down and snuggles them into his boots. Everyone walks with his hands in his arm pits. The diet, despite all the hard work, remains two slices of bread, "tea" and hot water with potato or cabbage or occasionally a turnip.

Eventually Blanchfield's gums begin to bleed and his teeth start to fall out.

About every two weeks now they receive Red Cross packages, still one for every four men, loaded with powdered milk, chocolate "D Bars," soap, lard, sugar, canned meat, canned fruit and cigarettes. Some of these items prove useful in the grand art of trading with the enemy. As time goes on and the Russians get closer, the parcels arrive more frequently, and enough for everyone. It is no exaggeration to suggest that those packages from home keep them alive.

Balls and a bat arrive from the YMCA, though there is no time to use them until the war is almost over, and the Salvation Army gets them a crank-operated record player with two records. They rotate the machine from room to room. One of the records is Crosby's *White Christmas* (and on the flip side, *Let's Start the New Year Right*).

The other contains the Ink Spots, with Ella Fitzgerald. It does little to cheer them.

Into each life some rain must fall,
But too much is falling in mine.
Into each heart some tears must fall,
But someday the sun will shine.
Some folks can lose the blues in their hearts,
But when I think of you another shower starts.
Into each life some rain must fall,
But too much is falling in mine.

With songs like that, keeping morale up can be a problem.

Roll call consists simply of a morning head count. During the work day, Blanchfield is brought to the various sites, as needed, to act as interpreter, accompanied by the unteroffizier (essentially a sergeant), who fancies himself an opera singer and displays his talents regularly.

The guards, at this late stage of the war, clearly do not come from the top ranks of the German Army. One they call Peanut Head, a veteran of the Eastern Front who suffers from shell-shock. Picture the day a group he is guarding carry him unconscious back through the camp gate. One of the GI's is even carrying his rifle.

The opera-singing unteroffizier senses something is amiss.

"SHORTY!" he screams in German for the Camp Leader.

Pvt. Blanchfield conducts a quick investigation.

What he learns is that the guard had gone a little wacky and turned his rifle on the work crew, threatening to shoot them if they didn't speed up. This, naturally, upsets the half-starved and testy Americans, so they punch his lights out and take the gun away before anyone gets hurt.

Blanchfield employs his negotiating skills.

"Look, this situation is unacceptable. You really can't let this nut case roam around with a loaded rifle."

The unteroffizier can not dispute the logic of the argument. They agree to remove the firing pin from Peanut Head's weapon. Everyone but Peanut Head knows he is unarmed, the men go back to work, and peace reigns. ●

Peanut Head has always been rather casual about his rifle. Once he has one of the GI's clean it for him while Peanut Head darns the GI's socks in exchange. Unfortunately, the unteroffizier walks in on this homey scene unexpectedly and the arrangement is abruptly discontinued.

Contact with the outside world comes in several ways. Daily rations are delivered by Polish and French prisoners who are able to travel between certain places unguarded. They become the middlemen in the underground trade of chocolate and cigarettes for food and other items.

Each day a guard named Kurt Popke accompanies Blanchfield and four hand-picked GIs to the local village bakery for their ration of bread. Kurt is a young infantryman who had been wounded on the Russian front. As they walk past a wooden area one day they sense the unmistakable aroma of a wiener roast. Following their noses, the prison guard and the American POW soon find themselves in the company of three friendly German *frauleins*, with whom they spend a most sociable afternoon.

In early March, 1945 the Russians are at the Oder River and fighting for Stetten, a mere thirty miles east of them. They can hear the artillery fire. American planes fly bombing raids overhead to Berlin by day, and the RAF at night. Occasionally unspent bombs and used gas tanks are dropped in their laps.

The Camp Leader grows more bold.

One day the soup ration fails to arrive for the noon meal. The unteroffizier orders the men back to work.

Says Blanchfield, in German, "No food, no work."

Says the unteroffizier to Blanchfield, "No work, no food."

The soup arrives two hours late.

The men eat, then go back to work.

On March 10, 1945, Pfc. John J. Blanchfield, leader of 161 men, turns twenty-one years old. Finally, old enough to vote.

Alone in the compound except for the medic, he can't believe his eyes, for there, just outside the barbed wire, pecks a white chicken.

A most delicious-looking white chicken.

An accomplished high school athlete, he picks up a rock and throws a perfect strike, then grabs the chicken through the barbed wire, wrings its neck, plucks it and boils it. His hands are scraped and the chicken bloodied, but he becomes a hero to the men he shares it with.

The Escape Committee, meanwhile, is asked to approve a plan conceived by two of the men who have no American uniforms, which is good if you're trying to pass as a German, but speak no German, which can be something of a handicap. Still, they feel they can escape from their work group and head west toward the advancing allies. Blanchfield thinks the plan full of holes, but the men have a map and guts, so the committee approves and all contribute D Bars, soap and cigarettes.

Everything goes as planned. They slip away in the morning, the other men cover for them at noon, and at dusk they are brought back by three surly guards and placed in solitary for seven days with no window and only black bread (now being extended by sawdust) and water. Still, the effort revitalizes the other men, and the Germans become more skittish.

Next comes a visit of a Swiss gentleman from the International Red Cross, guardians of the Geneva Conventions. The GIs are told in advance that they will not have to work that day and also that they had best not complain of their treatment.

On the appointed day, the Swiss-man arrives in an old car with large Red Cross insignias on the top and both sides. He is middle-aged, short, mustached, wearing a suit, shirt and tie, long coat and fedora. He speaks German and English. Used to working seven days a week, this day the GI's just stroll casually around the camp.

Disregarding completely the warnings of the unteroffizier, Blanchfield presents the inspector with a list of complaints: inadequate food, no heat, no medical help or equipment, substandard latrine next to water supply.

They are delightfully surprised that day with oatmeal for breakfast, potato soup with meat, and bread with lard. Blanchfield comments to the inspector how thrilled they are with the unique meals that day.

Message conveyed.

As a result of the visit, plans are developed for a modern latrine facility with four toilets and wash basins, built by the GI's under supervision. The men nearly drool at the sight of the gleaming white necessaries.

Of course, no water or sewage connections are ever installed and they continue to use the ditch for the remainder of their stay.

The road block work goes on, speeding up with the warmer weather.

One evening at dusk an American C47 transport plane flies low overhead, unchallenged by German planes or guns. It circles over Stalag IIA. Search lights follow it as it drops medical supplies into the Stalag and flies away. The roadblock work crew receives much appreciated aspirin, bandages and iodine.

On Sunday nights the Catholics gather in one room and the Protestants in another. Jack Blanchfield's precious rosary beads are put to use, and a Bible (acquired by trade), enriches the Protestants. One evening, unannounced, a French priest arrives and says Mass, gives them general absolution and distributes communion. For Jack Blanchfield, it is his first reception of the sacraments of his Church since the rest area in October of 1944.

On another occasion a Father Sampson, Catholic chaplain of the 101st Airborne, is allowed to visit. He had been captured shortly after D-Day. He speaks to the men confidently of God and their relationship with Him, and prays for liberation and a safe journey home.

When the unteroffizier comes in and tries to hurry him along and out, Capt. Sampson loudly explains that he will remain as long as it takes to complete his mission.

The men clap. The unteroffizier leaves.

It is late in the evening in Germany when President Franklin D. Roosevelt dies of a cerebral hemorrhage in Warm Springs, Georgia and, remarkably, the news reaches the POWs, via BBC, before it reaches their captors.

The next morning the rag-tag band of half-starved prisoners gathers for roll call in the prison yard. Instead of the standard quick head count, Private First Class John J. Blanchfield barks to his men.

"ATTENTION!

"RIGHT FACE!

"PRESENT ARMS!"

The company bugler plays *TAPS*.

The unteroffizier looks on, mystified, but does not interrupt.

After Blanchfield calls the men to PARADE REST, he explains their tribute to the dead Commander in Chief.

And then, they go to work.

The Russians have broken through at Stetten and are again moving rapidly westward. Berlin now has Russian armies on three sides, and the conquest of Stetten begins the closing of the noose on Hitler's capital.

Pfc. Blanchfield and his men grow even bolder. They call a strike. The Lord God had previously ordered a day of rest in every seven, and now Blanchfield does the same.

The following Sunday they gather for roll call as usual, are counted and given their work assignments. Standing directly next to the unteroffizier, Pfc. Blanchfield then gives the unexpected order "DISMISSED!"

The GI's go back to their rooms and barricade themselves in.

The unteroffizier, at first stunned, becomes furious. He orders his men. "BRING THEM BACK!"

His men, rifles now loaded, are at a loss as to how to accomplish the order.

"What is happening?" he demands of Blanchfield.

He doesn't know the German word for "Strike" so he just carefully explains that the Russians are coming and that they do not intend to do any more work on Sundays.

Two men with rifles are ordered to escort Blanchfield to the guards' quarters where he is to sit while the unteroffizier consults by phone with the local Burgomeister and the major in charge to tell them of the strike. Not long after a weapons carrier arrives at the gate and about twenty Germans with burp guns take positions around the compound.

"You are to instruct your men that they are to line up and go to work or they will be shot."

They then escort him back to meet with his committee. He explains the possibility that the Germans would open fire. On the other hand, the

Russians are near. They talk it over and resolve that their answer is *NO*. No work on Sundays.

He returns to the guards' house with their answer. Present now are the unteroffizier, the Burgomeister of the village and the major, a short man with an intimidating Hitler mustache. After a brief discussion, a compromise is proposed.

"Work until noon, and then take the rest of the day off."

"May I convey this offer to the men?" He is given permission to return to the compound, where they talk and talk, deliberately using up valuable time. Finally he comes back and reports to the angry and confused Germans that the answer is still *NEIN*.

Noon approaches and the changing of the guard.

Back in the barracks the men hear the commotion of the military movements.

Suddenly, chillingly, they also hear a single shot ring out and echo hauntingly through the camp.

Assuming the worst, the men elect a big part-Indian from Oklahoma, Earl Cross, to replace their camp leader, and Cross dutifully presents himself to the triumvirate to convey the new message of the POWs.

The answer is still *NEIN*. Cross prepares himself to deliver the word that will almost certainly result in his own summary execution.

Instead he finds Blanchfield very much alive. With all the tension of the moment and stomping about to attention, a German rifle had accidentally discharged and a bullet sailed through the roof.

Faced with now two, and probably a hundred and sixty-two, prepared to die, the Germans blink again.

"Alright, no work today, Sunday, but work every Sunday after."

Another conference.

Another *NEIN*.

"Alright. No more working on Sundays."

They report back to the men, who rejoice, break out the YMCA athletic equipment, and play softball for the rest of the day.

Except for Jack Blanchfield, who is placed in solitary for a week on bread and water.

The following Sunday he celebrates his release and joins the others for a softball game across the street from the compound. The German guards watch the game, as do a large contingent of Polish and Russian forced labor women as they march by. It may be the largest crowd ever to watch a softball game in eastern Germany.

Finally, their job done, the day comes for the grand unveiling of the dual concrete barriers. Two German drummers lead a march of the POWs to the site where the major in charge (the little guy with the Hitler mustache), the local Burgomeister, various town-folks and a small squad of German soldiers are gathering.

After a few short speeches, the German soldiers are ordered to dismantle the wooden forms and unveil the concrete marvels, the mighty road blocks which will halt the Russian onslaught in its tracks!

One hundred and sixty-two Americans gaze triumphantly at their work.

A small crack appears near the top.

It begins to widen as it works its way downward to the road bed.

Bits of sand and cement begin trickling to the ground.

The mighty fortresses crumble.

The Germans watch with horror.

The Americans watch with mischievous delight.

Not a good idea to leave your starving enemy in charge of building your defenses.

What the heck do they know about sand and cement ratios anyway?

On Friday, April 27 after roll call the men are dismissed. Soon, they are packing up and leaving, heading for Denmark as the German Army makes a last stand. The Germans had already decided to leave the main camp, Stalag IIA, for the Russians to liberate.

By mid-afternoon they are ready. The prisoners look at the Victrola.

It just sits there, silent, and yet each one of them can still hear it playing, burned into their brains.

Some folks can lose the blues in their heart
But when I think of you another shower starts
Into each life some rain must fall,
But too much is fallin' in mine.

They take turns smashing it to smithereens.

Jack Blanchfield has the honor and pleasure of flinging the Ink Spots with Ella Fitzgerald like a Frisbee. Crosby meets a similar fate.

A small contingent of Hitler Youth (boys aged 12 to 14) arrive with youthful enthusiasm to take over the compound, eager to defend the Fatherland against the Russians, armed only with ancient rifles.

Meanwhile, thousands of Russian and Polish females in their blue and white striped dresses and wooden shoes pass by the camp on their way west. The German army had used them as their economic and sexual slaves. The ones with the most Aryan features had been chosen to mate with suitable German specimens to produce the new Master Race. The rest are simply worked to death. These are the survivors.

Near dusk, one hundred and sixty two optimistic GI's and six German guards begin their march into the sunset. After four hours they stop for the night in a large barn. The friendly German guard, Kurt Popke, spends the night in Blanchfield's company. Meanwhile, the Escape Committee works overtime.

At dawn one of his men wakes Camp Leader Blanchfield and hands him a pistol. He has seen it many times before. It had belonged to the unteroffizier.

There are now one hundred and sixty-two GI's and one German guard, the cooperative Kurt Popke.

For the other five, the war is over.

Westward they continue, a small American Army, now, in the midst of enemy territory. They meet no resistance. Only anarchy reigns as civilians and soldiers alike make a desperate rush for the American lines with the Red Army at their backs. The air is filled with U.S. and Soviet planes, but not a German fighter to be seen.

Blanchfield sends scouts ahead, and abandoned farms soon produce potatoes and cabbage and carrots. Up to this point they have been marching cross country, but after a couple of days they use their "guard" Kurt as a pretend captor and join the clogged roads with the rest of German and multinational humanity.

With their feet sore and their meager belongings getting heavier, they manage to commandeer a horse, then find a wagon. A clever GI farmer is able to rig the double harness for the single horse, and the lame prisoners and the slim worldly goods begin to ride. By the third day they find another horse, and on the fourth another team, a wagon and a pig.

Unfortunately, the horses understand no English.

Fortunately, they make the acquaintance of a free Pole ex-prisoner who takes over the reins and commands them in Polish.

A river of refugees flows west, along with the American freedom-seekers. They pass through villages with white sheets and white cloths hanging everywhere, surrendering to anyone who would receive their surrender.

On the fifth day after leaving Neubrandenberg a Russian two-man plane begins strafing the narrow highway. The Americans dive for cover and Jack finds sanctuary in a narrow culvert that he never would have fit into before his Nazi diet. He watches as the plane flies straight down the road firing its nose gun and then, as it rises, the tail gunner fires as well at the mass of people.

It is a massacre. Men, women and children, some in carriages, scream. Some are trampled as they run for shelter. Blanchfield's men spend several hours tending to the wounded, tearing apart what few clothes they have to make bandages. Not once do they inquire as to anyone's nationality.

When the time comes to move on, Kurt Popke, their "guard," remains behind to join up with a group of German soldiers making an heroic last stand against the Russians. Their defense, as it turns out, lasts all of a day and they soon catch up with the Americans and tell them all about what would turn out to be one of the last skirmishes of the war in Europe.

On the sixth day they reach the remains of the town of Teterow. One of the scouts reports that a train is about to leave Teterow heading west.

Thirteen of Blanchfield's men run to the tracks and hop into a box car, and the train begins to leave, the train to freedom and home.

A Russian plane appears, drops a bomb and blows the box car apart.

Of their thirteen men there are no survivors.

There is no time to bury them. Blanchfield takes possession of their dog tags and the rest of them keep marching.

> *SPOKEN :*
> *Into each and every life some rain has got to fall*
> *But too much of that stuff is fallin' into mine*
> *And into each heart some tears gotta fall*
> *And I know that someday that sun is bound to shine*

The next night they rest in a barn, with an entourage now including four horses, two wagons, a Polish driver, an old Latvian woman barber from Riga and a young Yugoslavian girl about twelve. The scouts report that the American Eighth Division is only a few miles away. Preparing for his return to freedom, Pfc. John J. Blanchfield treats himself to a haircut.

Daybreak comes.

One of the men had traded his shirt for a camera and begins taking their pictures.

And then, before they have even left the barn, one of the scouts returns.

Sitting on top of a Sherman tank with a big white American star.

They are being escorted to safety. Mustering all their energy, they march proudly and smartly.

Bedraggled, tired, sore, hungry.

Laughing. Crying.

Jack and Kurt lead the parade. Among those asking politely to join them now is the little German major from Neubrandenberg of the ill-fated road barrier project, now shorn of his Hitler mustache.

He leans over to Jack, speaking casually in German.

Translated into Amsterdamian, "Hitler shit!"

Pfc. Jack Blanchfield, far right, accompanied by German "guard" Kurt Popke, leads his company of POWs to freedom. (Blanchfield family)

The first real confirmation of freedom comes with the sight of two GI's sitting by the side of the road collecting German rifles and small arms and sending their new prisoners to the rear. Just behind them two machine gun squads mark the American front line. Blanchfield's men pass through the line joyfully and tearfully.

On instruction, they report to the nearest MPs with two questions: "Where do we go?" and, uh, what exactly should they do with Kurt, who, they suppose, is technically their captive.

"Keep him with you. Grab some chow, find a place to sleep, and report in once a day."

The town is Schwerin, and there is an Opera House quite suitable for Pfc. Blanchfield's company, having a roof, running water and toilet facilities. They wash up, smoke, talk, laugh, rejoice.

And think of the thirteen guys who almost made it.

Schwerin overflows with refugees. Their Polish driver gives the horses to some of them. One of the horses becomes the entrée of a great celebration feast, real meat, with wine, schnapps, music and dancing. Jack and his men join in the jubilation.

Another horse finds a different purpose.

Some Polish concentration camp survivors discover one of their guards dressed as one of them. With his hands tied behind his back they rope him to the horse, which drags him, screaming, over the cobblestones.

The screaming does not last long.

They leave his body by the side of the road for all to witness.

VE Day on May 8 is just another day of celebration. The next day they get ready to ship out, loading Kurt down with cigarettes and finally turning him over. They split up onto transfer trucks for the few mile drive to the German airfield at Hildesheim where Jack runs into some guys from the 87th and learns that two of his friends from the days at Camp Jackson had been killed at the Bulge. He also finds a classmate from Niagara who had been captured at the Bulge.

While waiting to board a C47, suddenly the air raid siren goes off and everyone scatters. By and by a German ME109 settles down on the runway. Out pops a very young pilot with hands over his head, a little late in getting the word that his country has surrendered, or maybe just getting away from the Russians.

At Namur, Belgium they are given showers, deloused and finally issued fresh uniforms, and are treated to their first sit-down hot meal in months. Jack wanders over to the PX, still not really fully believing his ordeal has ended, and has his picture taken in a photo booth. Later, he finds a scale to weigh himself.

Eighty-eight pounds.

The following day they head for Camp Lucky Strike in LeHavre, France, where they are separated alphabetically.

And that is the last he sees, ever, of his buddies from Neubrandenburg.

After a debriefing about his experiences, which does not include anything beyond how and where he had been captured and the names of other prisoners he has encountered in his travels, Private First Class Blanchfield, who for months has been in charge of enough men to be the equivalent of a captain, receives some startling news.

"You've been promoted!

"Congratulations, corporal!"

After two or three weeks they are summoned to a nearby landing field. Cpl. Blanchfield gets up close to the wing of a C47, where stands an imposing figure.

General of the Army Dwight David Eisenhower.

He presents a single question to them.

"Do you want to go home?"

The response, of course, is a thunderous roar.

Soon they are on the *SS Explorer*, one of Henry Kaiser's Liberty Ships, overflowing with former POWs. His sleeping bag is home, on the gun turret on the fan tail of the ship. While other guys shoot craps and play poker, Jack Blanchfield soaks up the late May sun.

But after four days at sea, they are dead in the water. An engine has failed.

Still, it proves to be only a minor setback, fixed within forty-eight hours, and after eleven days at sea they pull into the naval port of Norfolk, Virginia.

Greeting them on the dock are three GI's, two with horns and one with a drum.

It is the best damn parade Jack Blanchfield has ever seen.

Next morning, at Camp Patrick Henry, they line up to use the phone.

Amsterdam 3014 rings and Teresa Blanchfield answers.

"Mom, it's Jack."

She can't say a word.

They both sob.

"I'll be home soon."

And that is the entire conversation.

On June 8, 1945 he boards a train at Grand Central Station for Albany. Uncle Francis sees him first, then Mom and Dad and brother Porky. They drive to Schenectady to the Blanchfield grandparents and stay up until the wee hours eating western egg sandwiches and talking and talking and talking. They ask him briefly about getting captured, but no one asks about combat or POW camp.

For that, he is grateful.

Nearly fifty years will pass before he finally tells his story.

Near daybreak, they set out for Amsterdam. And promptly get a flat tire.

Into each life some rai ...SCREEEEECCCHHHH!!!

A quick fix, a twenty mile drive, and Jack Blanchfield falls sound asleep in his own bed in his own home at 19 Trinity Place, Amsterdam, New York, USA.

Before long, the smell of bacon frying in the kitchen below rouses him. That morning he eats 14 eggs, along with much much bacon, and toast smothered with fresh butter.

And milk.

Wholesome, natural, Montgomery County contented cows' milk.

.

17. I DON'T CONTEMPLATE LIFE, I LIVE IT

John Sanford is nothing more than an itinerant tin peddler from Connecticut when he passes through what will become Amsterdam on his path from distant farmhouse to still more distant farmhouse at the age of eighteen in 1821. Before there is Horatio Alger, Sanford is the original pluck and luck guy. A chance overnight stay in Log City, in the northwest corner of the town, leads to a job teaching school. He soon takes a wife and settles in. After a while, he decides to go into the business of hand-weaving rugs, finding a used mill on the Chuctanunda Creek, pretty much across from what would become the Sanford Mansion in later times. The business prospers, and twenty years after arriving he gets himself elected to Congress, serving one term that includes in its first months the presidencies of Martin Van Buren, William Henry Harrison and John Tyler.

When the factory burns down in 1854, he retires and turns the whole business over to his son, Stephen, who, before he dies in 1913, builds the company into one of the largest manufacturers of carpets in the world.

Meanwhile, back in Connecticut, John's older brother Nehemiah Curtis Sanford has also been making a name for himself, founding Birmingham, Connecticut and marrying (well) Nancy Bateman Shelton, a direct descendant of Thomas Welles, an early governor of the Connecticut colony.[25] Nehemiah makes his fortune in the manufacture of brass tacks. The Nehemiah Sanfords have but one child, Henry Shelton Sanford, who,

---

25 Other descendants of Welles include Lyman Beecher, Harriet Beecher Stowe, actor Bruce Dern, President Gerald Ford, First Lady Nancy Reagan, poet Archibald MacLeish, Lincoln's Secretary of the Navy Gideon Welles, FDR's Undersecretary of State Sumner Welles, Daniel Wells (one of the first apostles of the LDS church and third mayor of Salt Lake City), Henry Wells (founder of Wells Fargo and Company), a couple of U.S. Senators, and James Phinney Baxter, III, historian of the Office of Scientific Research and Development.

unlike his cousin Stephen, shows little interest in the family business. Educated at Heidelberg University, his career path takes him to diplomacy, beginning in 1847 as Secretary to the American Legation in St. Petersburg, Russia (a position once held by a very young John Quincy Adams), with later posts in Frankfurt and Paris, before being named by President Abraham Lincoln as Minister to Belgium in 1861, where he serves until 1869 when he declines President Grant's offer to be Ambassador to Spain, at a time when his cousin Stephen is serving as a Republican Member of Congress.

While in Europe Henry finally marries (well), at age 41, Gertrude Ellen Dupuy of the Philadelphia Dupuys ("du Puy Place, Banks-of-the-Schuykill") and spends the remainder of his life making bad investments in Florida real estate (including founding the city of Sanford) with an occasional bad investment in the Congo[26]. All seven of their children are born in Brussells, where he remains as an adviser to King Leopold, among other things convincing Henry Morton Stanley to explore the Congo on the king's behalf, and later serving as the king's lobbyist to persuade the United States to recognize his claims in the Congo.

Back in Amsterdam cousin Stephen has been building a family of his own, and wealth beyond wild imaginings. By and by it comes time for his 41 year old son and heir, Republican Congressman John Sanford II, to take a bride and they need look no further for a suitable match than to Stephen's cousin Henry's daughter, eighteen year old Ethel. And thus in 1892 the two branches of the Sanford family merge in a society wedding in Sanford, Florida.

The Sanford-Sanfords return to Amsterdam. Two children are born in Amsterdam in 1899 and 1900, Stephen "Laddie" Sanford (future international playboy and professional polo player) and Sara Jane Sanford. Daughter Gertrude follows in 1902, born in Aiken, South Carolina. According to her obituary she was "reared" in Amsterdam, and in a Manhattan town house on East 72nd Street.

---

26 The respective family fortunes appear to have been significant enough that they were able to avoid the poor house nevertheless.

Around the time of his father's death in 1913, John Sanford has the family mansion on Church Street completely rebuilt and expanded, expending more than two million pre-income-tax dollars. Modern visitors to the building, now serving as Amsterdam's City Hall, are often amused by the ceiling in the third floor meeting room which had served as the Sanford nursery, with its ornamental plaster animals on the ceiling. In fact, it's unlikely the Sanford kids actually spend much time there as the youngest, Gertrude, is already a tween by the time the room is ready.

Still, family friend Philip Barry's hit play *Holiday* (opening in November of 1928 and playing into June of 1929), loosely based on the antics of the Sanfords in their NYC townhouse, has a rather touching moment when the character based on Gertrude (played by Katharine Hepburn in the second, more famous, movie version) retreats to the nursery while a society party is taking place downstairs, because it is the only place where she ever felt happy.

The real Gertrude is no retiring wall flower. While still in her teens she hunts elk in the Grand Tetons. After making her society debut in 1920, she becomes an internationally known explorer and adventurer, hunting big game in South Africa, Canada and Alaska. In 1929 Gertrude Sanford serves as co-leader of the Sanford-Legendre Abyssinia Expedition for the American Museum of Natural History, and has such a good time that she marries the other co-leader, Sidney J. Legendre, in September of 1929 in a wedding that hits the society pages throughout the world, rivaling for space the joining of Charles Lindbergh to Anne Morrow four months earlier.

Six weeks later the hundred year Sanford era in Amsterdam essentially comes to an end, though everyone denies it at the time. On November 4, 1929, the Monday after the stock market crash of October 29, office employees of the Sanford Carpet Company arrive for work to find all the furniture had disappeared over the weekend. Shortly after, an announcement is made that the company has been bought out by the Bigelow Company of Connecticut, and will reopen under the name of Bigelow-Sanford. John Sanford remains as Chairman of the Board, but he is no more than a figurehead. Three years later he gives the family mansion to the city.

Laddie, one of the great playboys of the 1920's (in addition to his own frolics he is one of the many lovers of Lady Edwina Mountbatten), marries a movie actress and manages his horses. Sarah eventually marries an Italian diplomat, and Gertrude settles into a comfortable existence in low country South Carolina society, giving birth to two daughters along the way.

And when the war comes, Gertrude choses the only logical path for someone of her breeding, stature and experience.

She becomes a spy.[27]

They spend one last Christmas together at Medway, their antebellum plantation near Charleston. Their daughters are but eight and one when Sidney Legendre applies for and receives a commission as a Navy lieutenant, and for a few months in early 1942 Gertrude serves in the Red Cross motor corps. By the time Lt. Legendre receives a transfer to Washington, DC in late spring there are not enough servants left on their plantation to run the place, so they shut down the house and ship little Landine and Bokara to New Orleans, to be cared for by relatives and a governess.

Gertrude Sanford Legendre

Once in Washington, Gertrude quickly settles into the whirl of society parties, embassy balls and the like. There are few people among the high and mighty that she does not know personally, and it does not take her

27 For much of the war time experiences of Gertrude Sanford Legendre, I am indebted to Elizabeth P. McIntosh for her splendid *SISTERHOOD OF SPIES: THE WOMEN OF THE OSS,* Naval Institute Press, Annapolis, Maryland, 1998; and Alex M. Rodd's *The Sanfords of Amsterdam,* William-Frederick Press, New York, 1969, both of which draw on interviews with this most remarkable woman, her two memoirs, and her official account of her adventures made in March of 1945.

long to connect to employment in the war effort, though along the way she is shot down by the Red Cross (kids too young) and the Library of Congress (no formal college education).

She lands in the brand-new "Coordination of Information Department," which will shortly evolve into the OSS (Office of Strategic Services, though wags observing the high concentration of Ivy Leaguers and society folk quickly dub it "Oh So Social"), headed by Gen. "Wild Bill" Donovan.

Sidney ships out to the Pacific in August of 1942, and for a year Gertrude works at the cable desk before being transferred to the London office. It takes two weeks by ship from Philadelphia to Lisbon, then follows a harrowing flight on a BOAC flying boat that loses an engine, forcing an emergency landing in Southampton.

The Cable Desk in London organizes and distributes information from around the world from agents, spies, sources, underground networks, etc. Mrs. Legendre has charge of it all, and knows whatever secrets there are in that dangerous time.

Not even the buzz-bombing of London in 1944 holds back her busy social life. Her dinner party guests included Gen. Donovan, Gen. Carl Spaatz, Gen. Lewis Brereton and American Ambassador John Winant (then involved with actress Sarah Churchill, Winston's daughter), among others.

In the aftermath of D-Day and the campaign in France, the Cable Office is moved forward to Paris. Once on the continent, civilian employees of OSS suddenly find themselves in uniforms, though without any unit-identification insignia. With no military training whatsoever, Gertrude Sanford Legendre becomes a second lieutenant.

"I didn't even know how to salute!"

She checks in with the not-yet-up-and-running office every day, but they aren't ready for her, so finally they just give her a five day pass on September 22, 1944 and tell her to have a good time, her first break in a year. Hanging out at the bar at the Ritz Hotel with a bunch of war correspondents, she bumps into OSS colleague Robert Jennings, a Navy Commander, who suggests an adventure: a trip to the front and back in five days, maybe even dropping in on Gen. Patton in the Luxembourg area.

Jennings requisitions a Peugeot recently liberated from some Nazi poobah and off they go the next morning. The auto has some years under its fan belt and a day of rocking over shell-bombed roads brings it to its death. After a night in a Luxembourg hotel, they meet up with Maj. Maxwell Papurt, also of OSS, who has manned himself with a driver and a jeep. He offers to take them along to Wallendorf, a small German village which, according to his maps, has fallen into American hands.

But the intelligence proves faulty. As they approach the village a German machine gun burst stops them in their tracks. Papurt is hit in both legs and crawls toward a hedgerow, pistol drawn. He orders the driver to turn the jeep around, but the driver is hit with a volley in both legs and both arms. Legendre and Jennings take cover behind the jeep and the other two join them, crawling belly-down through the mud. They hoist a white handkerchief of surrender and have just enough time to coordinate cover stories while Gertrude gathers anything identifying them as OSS and burns it, while treating her colleagues' wounds with sulfa powder.

On the second day of her planned adventure, Gertrude Sanford Legendre is a Prisoner of War.

The evacuation of the prisoners takes place while the battle for Wallendorf still rages. Allied artillery shells land nearby, while American planes circle overhead. The wounded are taken to a medical unit while Legendre and Jennings undergo their first of many interrogations.

For the next many months, their story remains the same: Jennings is a Navy ordnance officer and Legendre a clerk in the American Embassy in Paris, sent along as a translator for Jennings. (As time goes by, the cover story becomes so very vivid for Gertrude that she comes to "know" her imaginary fellow-employees and can picture every desk, every typewriter, every file cabinet in her cramped pretend office).

And now begins the wild ride away from the front, through the man-made fireworks and nature's own thunder and lightning, over shell-shocked muddy roads in spring-less seats, through the Siegfried line, to a midnight interrogation in Trier.

What is your job in the American Embassy?
I file requests for typewriters and stationery and office supplies.
Why are you in uniform with no insignia if you have a civilian job?

Regulations.
Tell me, are you frightened?

The first American woman to be captured by the enemy on the European front looks squarely at her inquisitor.

"Why should I be frightened? I understand the Germans treat their prisoners as properly as we do."

Her long day is far from over. Squeezed into a tiny Opel, they are hustled 75 kilometers north to Witlich, where there is no room, and finally thrown into a dirty cell in the village of Flammersheim where for the next twelve days the Mistress of Medway sleeps on a flea-infested straw mat with no soap, toothbrush or toilet paper, kept alive on five slices of bread a day and occasional watery potato soup. She is soon on a first-name basis with a family of lice.

From that fine establishment the Germans escort Legendre and Jennings to a 13th Century castle in Diez. Their host: a Wehrmacht lieutenant who speaks perfect English, as well he should. He had just spent eighteen years in New York City.

A graduate of Columbia University with a Bachelor's degree in Psychology, William Gosewisch had subsequently run a lunch counter, married an American and had two children before coming back to Germany in 1939 to show his homeland to his wife. What he hadn't known at the time was that his short return subjected him to compulsory military service. Going back to America would not be permitted.

None of this matters much now, for he learns that Gertrude Legendre is now considered a dangerous American spy.

Unknown to Jennings and Legendre, Major Papurt had been carrying with him a list of thirty counter-intelligence agents. He hadn't turned it over to her to be burned, and now all of them are in serious trouble.

What does SCI mean?

She knows perfectly well it means Special Counter-Intelligence Unit, a joint operation of OSS and the British MI5. She plays dumb.

She scans the document, recognizing names that had crossed her desk. Nope, no idea.

After six such meetings, the questioning turns to her family background and connections, for by this time Gertrude Sanford Legendre's capture has made headlines around the world. Not only famous in her own right, she has the polo-playing brother and a sister married to an Italian Fascist diplomat who had disappeared underground after the Italian surrender the year before.

Well, of course I know Gen. Patton and Gen. Spaatz and Ambassador Winant socially.

Gosewisch begins to see that there might be some advantage in staying on the good side of this woman.

In the late Autumn of 1944, things are not exactly looking up for Germany. They have been driven out of France and most of Belgium and Allied troops are fighting on German soil. For a German officer with roots in the good old USA, the time has come to prepare for the future.

They become Bill and Gert. When he finishes work for the day, he retrieves her from her cell and they go upstairs to his office. There they chat over cognac or wine from nine pm to the wee hours of the morning. He tells her he will do what he can to keep her out of the hands of the Gestapo, and clear up her case quickly. He loves Germany, but had opposed the war. He allows her to say goodbye to Jennings, who is being shipped to an officers' camp.

After six weeks Gosewisch is ordered to the front for three weeks. The next day Gert is taken to Gestapo Headquarters in Berlin.

Two more weeks of fruitless interrogation, and then a sudden switch again, and a long car ride through bombed-out Cologne and Bonn to a former resort hotel converted into something of a VIP prison camp. No hot water, of course, and a radiator that doesn't work, but a comfortable bed.

At breakfast she meets her fellow-prisoners: one hundred and twenty-nine men and one woman: Mme. Alfred Caillau of Saint-Etienne, the sister of Gen. Charles de Gaulle. The rest are almost entirely retired French Army officers who had been taken into custody to prevent their being recalled to service by the new anti-German government of France. While there, Legendre takes a card with the names of all present and sews the list into the lining of her rain coat.

They play chess, darn socks, mend clothes, give language classes to each other. As prison camps go, this one is pretty good. Lieutenant Gosewisch stops by to visit once, and to tell her that Maj. Papurt had died with other prisoners in Limburg, in an allied air raid.

With the failure of the Battle of the Bulge, Allied forces begin to swarm into Germany and the fall of Bonn to the Americans leads to the closure of the hotel-camp. The French go one way and Gertrude goes to Kronberg, where she is given a room in the home of Dr. and Mrs. Hans Grieme. On the way, she climbs to the hotel at the top of Mount Peter-Hoff, from whence she can see Cologne in one direction and Remagen in the other. They are close enough that on March 6 she can see the American forces coming down the west bank of the Rhine.

The Griemes treat her most kindly, and she even leaves behind a letter of recommendation to be presented to the oncoming Americans. At Gertrude's request, Dr. Grieme uses his connections in the foreign office to establish contact with Lt. Gosewisch, back now at Diez Castle. He comes immediately. And here they arrange her escape.

Not all the Germans are bad guys. In charge of the border police in Konstanz, at the crossing to Switzerland, serves Friedrich Haug. His efforts in smuggling Allies and Jews across the border make his life increasingly precarious as the war draws to a close. In March of 1945 he takes his family to a remote farmhouse and tells them that if on any day he is to not return, they are to flee to that farmhouse and remain until liberated by the U.S. Army. He gives them a code number to give to the Americans to ensure their safety. Night after night his young daughter Ingrid sees him leave in his light topcoat, not knowing what he is up to, or whether she will ever see him again.

On March 22 a Herr Gay from the Frankfurt SS office picks up Gertrude Legendre at the Grieme estate and drives through the wreckage of Frankfurt and Ulm and into the high country where the Danube and the Rhine nearly kiss, taking the ferry to Kostanz and the border. Herr Gay quickly learns that Mrs. Legendre will not be permitted to cross. So he turns her loose.

But before leaving, he tells her of a train from Singen that will arrive that night in Konstanz. Everyone will exit the train, which will then proceed across the border. It is up to Gertrude to figure a way to get on the empty train and make the crossing.

Night falls.

The train arrives, the passengers exit.

Gertrude slips into the center car unnoticed. She crouches behind some seats.

A German guard comes through. She hides in the toilet.

The train starts up again, heading for Kreuzlingen in neutral Switzerland.

And then it stops.

From the door she can see the frontier gates in the moonlight.

She is alone.

She slips out of the passenger car and creeps along a line of freight cars on the adjacent track.

From out of the shadows emerges a stranger in a light topcoat.

He points to the gate.

"RUN!" he whispers.

She needs no further encouragement and sprints for the border.

"HALT!" she hears from a German guard behind her. Footsteps are closing in.

The Swiss guard raises the barrier, all the while shouting for her identification papers.

"American passport!" she claims as she flies under the barrier to freedom, while the German continues to scream at her.

March 23, 1945, the first day of the rest of her long life.

Gertrude Sanford Legendre is absolutely delighted to spend that night in a Kreuzlingen jail cell. Thereafter for several days she is the house guest of Chief of Police Ragganbass and his wife. After a shopping spree she is taken to the American Ambassador in Bern on March 26 and promptly whisked off to Allen Dulles (the future first head of the Central Intelligence Agency), the top OSS guy in Switzerland.

That night, after a splendid French meal with Dulles, she carefully recounts her adventure to Dulles and one of his officers and a secretary who transcribes it all. Then, when describing her time with the French prisoners, in dramatic spy fashion she rips open the lining of her rain coat and produces the list of prisoners. Dulles looks it over, and then chuckles.

Have you read this?
Of course.
No, I mean the part in German.

> *For the attention of Mrs. Legendre:*
> *In order that you will not have a light opinion of the police force of Kreuzlingen and of the Swiss Border Control, we inform you herewith that we have politically examined the enclosed list of names while you were in the custody of the Kreuzlingen police. Since we realize that it is only an act of charity in behalf of imprisoned acquaintances, we are herewith replacing the manuscript in its original hiding place. Travel well, and our greetings to America.*
>   *-O. Ragganbass*

From Bern she is driven to Geneva, given Army orders, then driven to Lyons to pick up the Paris Express. She arrives in Paris on March 29, her birthday, with strict orders not to speak to the press or report to OSS. Her husband, then in Honolulu, is sent similar instructions from Dulles, with a note that she "impressed me as being a person with a great deal of resourcefulness."

Thus ends her career in the spy agency. She returns to New York, reunites with her husband and children, and settles into a daily routine at the Medway Plantation where she will hold court for the next half century and more.

In May of 1945 she, along with quite a few other people, celebrates VE Day on the streets of New York, where, quite happily and accidentally, she bumps into recently-released former prisoner of war Robert Jennings.

In 1950 she is able to arrange for the destitute William Gosewisch and his family to come to South Carolina, where he promptly finds employment with Sidney Legendre. Gosewisch lives until November of 1989 when he leaves this world on the day before the Berlin Wall comes down.

Gertrude Sanford Legendre never learns in her lifetime the identity of Friedrich Haug, the mysterious stranger at the border. In April of 1945 the Gestapo orders him to Voralberg, Austria to make a last stand against the advancing allies. But he has been alerted by his Swiss counterpart that his family will be in danger if he goes. They arrange for the whole family to slip across the border to safety. He dies in 1983 at the age of 85 without ever having written his memoirs.

The *grand dame* of Charleston Society dies days shy of her 98th birthday in March of 2000. At one of the last of her legendary New Year's Eve costume parties, she proposes a toast:

"I look ahead. I always have. I don't contemplate life, I live it. And I'm having the time of my life."

18. PERHAPS NEXT CHRISTMAS

The final year of the war brings some of the most intense fighting, on both fronts. In Europe the Battle of the Bulge finally breaks in a massive defeat for the Nazis, and the next few months consist of a big push across Germany and mopping up operations in Italy and elsewhere, until the final victory in May. As we shall see, the dying of Amsterdam boys on the European front does not stop just because the war does.

Meanwhile, in the Pacific, the liberation of the Philippines which had begun in October continues apace. Island hopping brings the Americans ever closer to Japan, and the resistance which our boys had encountered on Guadalcanal and Saipan and elsewhere grows even fiercer. The 27th Division, including our remaining locals in Company G, are called back into action for Okinawa, and several Amsterdam lads find themselves with the Marines on Iwo Jima.

> ***UPX, December 1944-January 1945, from Sam Sweet in Italy:*** *Just a few lines from a mud-caked, rain-soaked member now spending the winter in "sunny" Italy. As you know, this is no place for beautiful winters like we have home, but I suppose it will have to do. Everything here seems to be leaving or going away except the Germans and the rain. Wish someone would find a better way than "pushing" to get them to leave.*

> ***From Johnny Campbell in the South Pacific:*** *Hope all the fellows are well and holding their own, wherever they are. I'm in the hospital again, had a growth removed from my foot, caused by the sword wound I received last year in the Gilberts. I've been*

here five weeks now and had two operations. I'm finally going to see this war from a back seat – an arm-chair general. I can't say that I'm going to enjoy this non-combatant's duty, but I can say I've had my fill of hospitals. Well, time will tell. I always did make the most of the "social" side of life, and this will be my chance to see the other side of the Army. I doubt if I'll get back home for a while, but I do have one consolation: every day brings the end of this war closer.

From Hank Weidemann: *Yes, they finally caught up with me and here I am in Merrie Olde England. . . .I had quite a boat ride over. Yes, I got seasick, too, as do most people, I guess. It was a rough ride. . . . I certainly appreciated Johnny Campbell's letter. Some jerk ought to be hung for accusing the 105ᵗʰ for some of the things he did, I read some stuff on that before. Some day the whole story will come out and someone's face will be plenty red. I met Benny Drenzek of Harrower's in the Stage Door Canteen in New York and had quite a session with him. He is a member of that outfit and he told me plenty. He looks good, but was kinda shot-up.*

From Harold "Peanuts" Brown in France: *Sorry I didn't write sooner, but it couldn't be helped. The weather was so lousy that you couldn't do anything. Boy, I never thought mud could get so deep and so sticky. . . . I'll have to close this letter. We are back for a rest at the present and we are billeted with a couple of Frenchmen and they have brought out a bottle of cognac. You know I never touch the stuff but these people insist.*

From Frank Cionek in France: *I'm beginning to wonder if I beat my mother years ago and am being punished for it now. Can't say that I remember, though! I've been in France now for the past five and a half months and have enjoyed approximately three weeks of that French weather we read about back home. (Sunny France). The rest of the time has been rain and mud. As a matter of fact, it* *is raining at the present moment and the mud is at least a foot deep. We're in a pyramidal tent with seven other men huddled around a pot bellied stove trying to keep warm and carrying on one of those swell known bull sessions . . . . In exactly seven days, I will have been overseas three long years. . . . Well, I'm going to ask you all to pardon me as the boys have fixed up a broth from a rabbit which I shot this afternoon and my mouth is drooling.*

From S/Sgt George I. Hughes: *Perhaps next Christmas will find most of us at home.*

From Pete Ruback in India: *Haas, on his return from over here, probably told some of you about the brighter side of India because where he was stationed they never had it so good. Take it from us guys here in Assam, it's rough as all hell. In a few days I'll be getting out of this hell hole. You see, I'm leaving for Calcutta on a 21 day furlough. What a place to get a furlough, huh! Anyhow, Calcutta is sorta the New York of India so I really should enjoy myself. There's plenty of good food and scotch in that vicinity, I'm told, so it will be a real treat to get away from this routine way of living for a while and settle down to some good chow and perhaps a wee bit of scotch. Work down here is still as plentiful as ever with no sign of getting back home soon. Looks very much like I'm stuck here for the duration plus.*

From Paul Sykes, somewhere in the Philippines: *No doubt you all read & heard of the landings made here which was a big success so far. Did you see Gen. MacArthur's pictures in the paper making a speech here on D-Day? He sure was a happy man and now he is probably in Australia enjoying a scotch and soda while we're here sweating out the air raids. The Japs sure are stubborn and just about every night we get a call from a few "zeros." Had the pleasure of seeing a few picked off from above. They'll never learn, I guess. I came in shortly after D-day and I was glad to get off that boat. The trip up wasn't too bad but the sea was rough* *and quite a few boys got seasick. No, I didn't lose any meals, but I would have if it lasted much longer. The place we landed isn't the best part of the Philippines. That will come later. However, it isn't too bad here and the natives are much nicer than the New Guinea blacks. The Filipinos were sure glad to see the Yanks. And they are very friendly and good workers. The majority of them speak a little English so it's easy for us to talk to them. The men are all working for us as well as the women and girls. We had a couple boys build us a nice bamboo floor for our tent and you really need one as the weather here is bad this time of year. I never saw so much rain and mud in all my life. And they say it will be like this until Feb. I hope they're wrong. Well, I don't have to do my own laundry. We have a Filipino girl who does it for us. And a real good job for only 2 pesos (that's $1.00 to you). And she also brings us bunches of nice yellow bananas and are they good. Also get fresh pineapple, but I'm not crazy about them. The Japs took all their food, homes and clothes so now they are getting back to normal again. While I was in the hospital I met a guerrilla captain in the Filipino Army. He sure had some tales to tell. He was 60 years old so was one who knows. The guerrillas are up in the mountains and have done a great deal in making this a success. Even the women folk fight the Japs.*

From Mike Niemczyk: Here it is another Christmas come and gone, but we still carry on. I had a rather nice day, in spite of the fact I wasn't able to be with my wife and the son I have yet to see. I'm really thankful, though, for at least I was fortunate enough to be here in America. We had a real nice dinner which lacked nothing at all, only for that home touch and spirit as well. I only wish our other members enjoyed theirs as much. It's pretty hard to enjoy one, you know, where some of our boys are at. I did see some of the conditions they are under and Christmas must have been what we would call another day to them. . . . It must be an awful thing to wake up on this great day and find yourself facing the enemy or even to look at the poverty-stricken people on such a day. Oh, well. We all hope this will be the last one under these conditions. I'm hoping our next will find us all right at home, so we can all be happy once again.

From Gabriel Centi in Texas: The place I am now in is O.K. if you can speak Spanish and like the way Mexico looks. For this place is just like Mexico. Everything you read about in a western story, you know, flat land, sand, cactus plants, and big cowboy boots, for that is all they wear for shoes down here. Even a few soldiers wear them. The reason that I am down here is to go to gunnery school. They are going to try and make a gunner out of me. So far, I am doing O.K. Except for the pressure test. I didn't pass that because of a cold but we will get another chance. Sunday I went up for the first time. I flew in the nose of a B-24. I was scared at first to look down and see that beautiful land below me. (Even Texas looks nice from up there). But after a while I began to enjoy it. We only went up five or six thousand feet, but that was high enough for me. . . . Thanks again for everything. The Ex-Bartender of Lyon Street Grill, Gabe.

From Arnie Eckelman: I know I should've answered sooner but then you will have to excuse me because that was the first mail in forty days and I had a lot of sugar reports to answer. . . . The only news I can pass out is that I am somewhere in the Pacific but as usual, you know I am in a hot action, would like to tell you where but you will have to guess that.

From Harry DeGroff in France: [Y]ou all know by this date that Jerry has been protesting quite furiously lately in regard to the invasion of his homeland. This in turn keeps everyone quite busy, when it comes to holding that line. However, the backs are holding up well and the Jerry goalie can expect to have his hands full with shots from all directions. Met Johnny Hanna recently and although we only had time for a five minute chat, it was a pleasure to meet someone from home. I had Johnny to thank for this meeting as he knew I was coming by and was watching for me. Witnessed some of those head-shaving episodes recently in which women collaborators are the victims, and the immediate public gets quite a kick out of it.

With the Seventh Army in France – (Special). Technician Fifth Grade John Hanna, artilleryman, of 55 Rockton Street, Amsterdam, is one of nine New York State men who distinguished themselves with the 100th Division in Eastern France, division headquarters has announced. Artilleryman Hanna received the Bronze Star for heroic achievement in action on November 4 in the vicinity of St. Remy.

On New Year's Eve Sgt. Alphonse Myers from Eagle Street is holed up in a heavy machine gun nest on a ridge near Rimling France, his company nearly surrounded. He's part of Company M, 397th Rgt., 100th Division, attached to the 7th Army. The 7th Army has been moved up to fill in the defenses when Patton's Third Army swings north to the Ardennes and the relief of Bastogne.

The Germans launch a night attack, pouring over a hill some 700 yards away. The battle goes on for six days.

Sgt. Alphonse Myers, left, with Pvt. Leon Outlaw, Jr.

Myers holds his ground, keeps his binoculars steady and coolly directs his gunner, Pvt. Leon Outlaw, Jr. of Mount Olive, North Carolina, who wears out one gun and shoots off some 5,000 rounds during the engagement. The moonlight and the white snow make the night-spotting easier. Despite their white camouflage uniforms, every movement betrays them. Outlaw maintains there are so many of them, it's hard to miss, especially when they stand upright and yell, "American gangsters!" and "Yankee bastards!"

They kill a hundred, capture six more, and wound untold numbers. Myers gets a Silver Star.

New Year's Day, 1945, in Italy marks the first and only Mud Bowl in the history of disorganized football. Two companies of the Sixth Armored Infantry Battalion of the First Armored Division face off in front of 400 or so cheering GI's. *Uniteds* club member Sam Sweet reports for the benefit of the *Recorder* sports page:

> In a field that lived up to its name as "Mud Bowl" the two teams wallowed through four quarters of clean, hard football. Though the plays were not of college caliber and the blocking was a little off, both outfits showed effects of having played the game before.
>
> With little time to prepare, the men, fresh from the front lines, put on a show few will forget. There were Red Cross girls as cheerleaders and the division band to add to the color. The little field, marked out between two farm lots, took on the aspects of a big-time game.
>
> That's about all that would be interesting. The names of players do not matter, nor do those of the officials. What does is that a group of soldiers took time out to try and forget the war.
>
> Though it looked queer to the Italians passing by, we all had a swell time reliving the things we miss these days, and the things we are fighting to return to. Let's hope '45 turns out as successfully as we started it off yesterday.

Lt. John Leonard Perkins, with the Seventh Army, is leading a tank patrol in Alsace on January 17, 1945 when one of his tanks is hit by German anti-tank fire and bursts into flames. Disregarding his own safety, he dismounts from his own vehicle and assists in evacuating the crew from the burning tank. Meanwhile, his own tank is hit by an enemy shell and is also burning, so he evacuates that crew as well.

While attempting to extinguish the fire he is mortally wounded.

Lt. Perkins is an adopted son of Amsterdam by virtue of his marriage to Shirley Chalmers, daughter of Amsterdam industrialist and sometimes author Harvey Chalmers 2nd, the button king. Shirley and their eleven month old daughter Mary Katherine are residing with her parents at 439 Guy Park Avenue when the telegram arrives. His posthumous Silver Star is pinned on his little girl.

With the collapse of the German offensive in the Battle of the Bulge, the battle for Germany swiftly begins.

1st Lt. Gordon Brooker, with the 48th Engineers, earns his Silver Star leading reconnaissance patrols deep into enemy territory on February 20, 21 and 24, seeking intelligence on troops, weapons and mine emplacements. On the latter day, having reached his objective without enemy contact, he proceeds alone to obtain more information, when he is seriously wounded by small arms fire. Despite his wounds, he manages to safely and effectively withdraw his platoon.

The *Uniteds* add to their medals collection on March 7 when Sgt. Harold "Peanuts" Brown, with the 94th Armored Field Artillery Battalion picks up a Bronze for action near Udersdorf, Germany. Coming under attack, Brown rallies his gun crew and silences the enemy.

Meanwhile, the action in the Philippines has moved to the island of Luzon, and Gen. MacArthur's troops are sweeping southwest toward Manila, but not fast enough. He knows what the Japanese are doing to the prisoners of war, and he knows a major POW camp is between them and Manila. He authorizes a daring raid, well in front of the current lines, to liberate the camp. A select team of army rangers pulls it off, rescuing 513 allied prisoners in February of 1945. These include survivors of Corregidor and the Bataan Death March.

Among those rescued is Sgt. Edward Seaman, who gets a trip to his sister, Mrs. Floyd Brockman's home in Hagaman to complete his recovery. Sgt. Seaman had joined the Army Air Corps in 1938, and while stationed in the Philippines became a meteorologist. His three year term ended, he thought he would be going home in 1941, but all leaves and discharges being canceled, he ends up retreating to Corregidor instead. He is a prisoner for a year and a half before the family is informed he is alive.

I wo Jima. There are 18,000 Japanese soldiers there when the battle begins on February 19. By the time it ends on March 26, only 216 are taken prisoner. It is the first American attack on the Home Islands, and, as can be seen by the statistics, the defense is as fierce as it could possibly be. Our military planners have no idea of the extent of the Japanese defenses, and estimate the island should be completely subdued in five days. They are wrong.

Taking Iwo Jima will serve many useful purposes. The B-29 bomber runs will have their flight time cut in half and, more importantly, they will then have P-51 Mustang fighters to escort and defend them. But it comes at a terrible cost, with 27,909 American casualties, including 6,825 killed, greater than the total allied casualties of D-Day in Normandy.

Cpl. Allen Pileckas of Hagaman serves with Company E, Second Battalion, Twenty-first Marines, Third Marine Division. On March 1 his

platoon is pinned down under heavy rifle, mortar and machine gun fire. They are unable to evacuate their wounded. Pileckas crawls, alone, through the thick of it some fifty yards, outflanking the heavily-defended Japanese emplacement. His well-aimed grenades destroy the crew and silence the machine gun.

Courage under fire is nothing new for Pileckas. Back in August he had been caught up in a night battle in Guam, on top of a landmark the Marines would name Sugar

Bluff. Knowing that a burst of their machine gun would betray their position, he relies instead on grenades. His companion, Silver Star Corporal Manuel Guerrero from Texas, crawls from foxhole to foxhole to gather up enough grenades to keep Pileckas supplied. Pileckas doesn't think he has done anything special, just rolling some grenades down the bluff.

"Any place you dropped a grenade down Sugar Bluff that night you got a Jap. We ran out of grenades about daybreak. We could see that the grenades had done a good job."

Nell's brother had been in action against the enemy in Bougainville, Solomon Islands, November 11 to December 15, 1943; in consolidation of the Northern Solomons December 16, 1943- January 9, 1944; in Guam, Marianas Islands July 21, 1944 to August 3, 1944 (where in addition to the Sugar Bluff evening he is wounded by shrapnel to the arm and awarded a Purple Heart); in patrols against enemy stragglers on Guam August 19, 1944 to November 3, 1944.

And, of course, on Iwo Jima from February 21 to March 1, 1945, when, after earning his Silver Star attacking that enemy position, he takes shrapnel to the head, is evacuated to the *USS Solace* and dies of his wounds two days later without regaining consciousness.

He is 24.

His second Purple Heart comes with a gold star.

Until his final homecoming, he is buried in GRAVE 14, ROW 18, PLOT C, CEMETERY 2, GUAM ISLAND, MARIANAS ISLANDS, the Marines tell his parents.

Eventually his personal effects are inventoried. They consist of:

1 Flashlight
1 Kit, sewing
1 Pad, writing
1 Razor, safety
1 Sweater
1 stamp, name
2 Towels
1 Trunks, swim

Tony Vertucci, far right foreground, adjusts his socks on the beach at Iwo Jima

Back in Amsterdam, brother and sister Al and Marge Vertucci are watching a newsreel of the Iwo Jima battle at one of the local movie houses and recognize their brother Tony wandering through a temporary Marine cemetery.

He's looking for their other brother, Gabriel. While both men join the Marines, they never see each other overseas, even when both are on Iwo Jima.

Gabe is in E Company, 25th Regiment, 4th Marine Division. They have fought in Kwajalein, Saipan (where he is twice wounded), and Tinian. On Iwo Jima, he helps take Mt. Suribachi, then is shot in the eyes, and the bullet ricochets under his helmet causing a serious head injury, his third Purple Heart. Medics operate by lantern light in a tent.

Of the 242 men originally in his company, after Iwo Jima Gabe is one of three survivors.

The war moves on, but the mopping up on Iwo Jima continues. Pfc. Ralph DiCaprio of Vedder Street, with the 147th Infantry Regiment, is out on patrol in April with seven other men, working along the edge of a ravine. He moves to his left about ten yards to get a better view and spots a Jap in a hole below, protected by rocks. A well-placed smoke grenade forces the enemy soldier out in the open and DiCaprio drops him. Two others make a dash for it and are quickly killed by other members of the squad.

A half hour later DiCaprio spots another one and takes care of him as well.

And so it continues, one by one, until the last Japanese soldier on Iwo Jima surrenders.

In 1951.

Palm Sunday falls on March 25 in 1945. Lieutenant Robert J. Gilston, with the 37th Tank Battalion, leads a column of tanks across a bridge into Aschaffenberg, Germany and comes under direct fire, resulting in the death of an infantry platoon leader riding on the rear deck and seriously wounding several of our men. Gilston then moves his tank into the town and sets up a base of fire to cover the entrance of the rest of the tanks. The fourth in line is struck and disabled, leaving Gilston's and two other tanks precariously on the town side of the bridge. They come under heavy attack from German mortar, *panzerfaust* (bazooka) and small arms fire, disorganizing our infantry. Lt. Gilston takes command, ordering the infantry behind an embankment and keeping the enemy at bay with machine guns and cannon. After receiving orders to withdraw, he arranges the safe and orderly evacuation of the infantry and remains behind in a dangerously exposed position to draw fire to himself while directing the freeing of the disabled tank and safe withdrawal of the remaining tanks. For his initiative and daring that day he is awarded the Silver Star. Wounded previously on December 23, 1944, Lt. Gilston is wounded again on March 26, the day after the encounter at Aschaffenberg Bridge.

Private First Class Charles M. Brownell gets the morning off on March 25. He attends Palm Sunday services with his unit in the open country of Germany. For the moment, the war seems a million miles away. He looks around and everything he sees is green and flourishing. No smoke, no shell holes, no thunder of guns.

Just a beautiful, satisfying peace.

He writes a letter home, letting the folks know that the war is passing him by. All's right with the world.

Charles Brownell, 26, of Tribes Hill, a 1938 graduate of Wilbur H. Lynch High School, killed in action April 8, 1945.

Nor is he his home town's only casualty that Sunday after Easter. Tech. Sergeant Frank B. Bujnowski (Benosky), in the army since May 10, 1942, had drawn 19 months duty with the Coast Artillery in Puerto Rico, then in October of 1944 is sent to Europe as a replacement troop in Seventh Army under Lt. General Alexander Patch. On November 18, he earns his first Purple Heart and is hospitalized until January of 1945 when he returns to the front.

On April 8, near Odhelm, Germany, his platoon takes the crest of a strategically important hill, where they come under heavy fire that holds back their advance. Bujnowski moves to the front of the platoon.

He gives the order to attack, and with sub-machine gun blazing charges ahead, destroying a German machine gun nest. He then kills two more Germans, and keeps firing until he runs out of ammunition. Bujnowski grabs a rifle from a wounded man and charges another enemy emplacement.

He's hit by a machine gun burst, gets up and charges forward yet again.

Only the final, fatal bullet stops him.

His leadership carries the day for his company and breaks the back of German resistance in the area.

He is posthumously awarded the Distinguished Service Cross, the third Amsterdamian to be so honored in less than six months.

For Kenneth Garn and the boys left behind in Europe while Malcolm Tomlinson is home playing, the next few months after Christmas aren't pretty. They shut down operations in February, 1945 and proceed to a port for the return home, only to have the orders reversed at the last second, leaving them without equipment or supplies. Some of the men break. The others are just miserable. They end up in Germany, fixing bridges and filling potholes. Camp, however, is not so bad: a castle in Braunfels.

Then one day a truck pulls up and out tumbles a bedraggled mess of a man.

They can't believe their eyes.

Tomlinson has returned.

Recalling his reverse MacArthurian pledge, they berate him mercilessly, questioning his legal skills, his IQ and his manhood.

"The army didn't play fair. They trapped me," he weasels.

Twice he receives telegrams at home instructing him to report back to the camp in New Jersey where he'd been furloughed in order to receive an extension. Each time he reports, each time he receives another two weeks. An identical third telegram arrives, and they have him. Instead of immediately receiving the promised extension, he and others similarly situated are ordered to proceed to a troop train.

Wait a minute. This can't be right.

A master sergeant assures him that hey, this is the army. They're shipping you to a different camp to get your furlough extension from there.

It seems plausible, from what he has seen of the army.

The train stops at the New York Port of Embarkation, they hustle him aboard ship and he is on his way back to Europe.

The army beats him again.

Not until August of 1945 do these beach boys of the army, who had landed on day one and hung on for nearly three months past Hitler, finally get to go home. Malcolm Tomlinson says goodbye to Fort Dix on August 2nd, returns to Amsterdam, finishes becoming a lawyer, and often wonders to himself if he is so smart, how could he ever have been so dumb?

Just a lucky guy.

The first sign for 2nd Lt. Roger Henry's B-17 flight crew that they should have stayed in bed comes when they prepare to take off with their squadron for a raid on the Orlanenburg rail yards in Germany and the plane can't get off the ground. They ditch the plane and scramble into another one, managing to catch up with the formation.

Henry navigates them successfully to their target, but as they line up for the bombing run a flak explosion rips a three foot hole in the left wing, flipping the plane over into a nearly vertical position with the right wing pointing down. The pilot and co-pilot manage to right the craft in time to drop their load on the target as another flak burst punches the fuselage.

The plane shimmies and shakes while the men continue at their battle stations. A steel fragment pierces the co-pilot's window and embeds an inch behind the pilot's head. More flak destroys the top turret, and the uninjured turret gunner finds himself holding a shattered piece of the gunsight. The ball turret gunner is wounded in the arm. There are nine holes in the turret. The tail gunner loses his oxygen supply.

Once clear of the target area, Lt. Henry plots a course for home.

The bomb bays are now just jagged holes. A tire has been flattened by a direct hit. Ripped hydraulic lines make the brakes useless. The pilot lands, nevertheless, using every inch of the runway to lessen the speed, and then deftly wheeling onto soft ground to bring them safely to a halt.

The crew, but for the one man wounded, escape unharmed. They carefully examine their borrowed bomber.

They stop counting the holes when they reach five hundred.

On April 30, 1945 SK 2/c Francis J. Going celebrates his 23rd birthday in Cherbourg, France. The newspaper headlines are all about the death of Mussolini. On the same day, the Soviet Army sweeps through Berlin and Adolph Hitler shoots himself to death and swallows cyanide, just in case.

The days dwindle down to a precious few.

Pfc. Robert Schure is with the 15th Regiment,Third Infantry Division, Seventh Army, now sweeping across Germany. A German soldier surrenders to him, and tells him of a whole bunch more waiting to surrender, so he sets off with his captive to parts unknown, always "just a little farther." Finally, about three miles later, they reach the Germans who, it turns out, aren't actually positive that they want to surrender after all. They start arguing among themselves, and with Schure, who ultimately persuades them to accept his proposal. He gathers and destroys their weapons, and they begin the long trek back. Picking up a couple of more stragglers later, he single-handedly produces 23 prisoners for the day.

UPX, March-April, 1945, From Pete Ruback in India: *Gee, Guy, it must take quite a bit of your own time to prepare this paper each month. Permit me to say that the time you have spent putting the P.X. together has sure put much light into those dull moments a guy runs into over here in the jungle. I can say thanks Guy and all that but still there's that feeling of appreciation deep down inside me that I can't express in words. There'll come a day, Guy, that you shall be repaid for the fine job you are doing. Perhaps we'll not be able to repay you as individuals but the day will come when God shall welcome you into his kingdom with open arms for your thoughtfulness of us guys serving our country during this war-time period. I, for one, in civilian life knew you as just Guy Murdoch, but believe me, since I've been away, a friendship has been set up between us that with your permission will last a lifetime.*

From Arnie Eckelman: *Seeing as the censor has relaxed a little bit in censoring, I will tell you about some of the things I have done out here. When we first came out here we were in the New Guinea campaign, then we invaded the Admiralty Islands, not so tough this one, then we hit Biak Islands and this one was pretty rough for a while, quite a few planes after us, then Hollandia which was fairly smooth, next came the Palau group and I think that Jack Geib was in that landing, then came the biggest invasion that we made so far and that was the invasion of Leyte in the Philippines which I can say was really tough, planes attacking about five or six times a day and night; we entered Leyte Gulf two days before anyone else and on our way in we blew up a mine and that is as close as I ever want to get near one of those again; was in the battle of Surigao Straits which we sank about ten Jap ships and that was something really nice to see; was in the China Sea when the carriers was raiding the China Coast; that sea is the* *roughest water I have ever been in and ever want to be in again. This is all the dope that I am allowed to give out with at present but it does make the letter a little more interesting to read.*

From Art Hartig: *Have been doing quite a bit of flying and have seen quite a lot of Germany.*
Later: *Met up with my brother Carl. Three days of happy talking. Seventeen missions in.*

From Bud McDonald in Germany: *When I think I'm having it tough I remember what we're giving the Jerries.*

From Daniel "Bus" Murdoch: *We are now over the Rhine somewhere in Germany and it sure feels good.*

UPX, May-June, 1945 from Walt Weidemann, somewhere in freedom: *This is truly about the most difficult letter I have ever tried to write, as words are so empty and cold when trying to express my sincere appreciation and thankfulness for your kindness and generosity to my mother and myself while I was taking the rest cure back there in Germany. I cannot find the words to tell you all how happy I am that my home was and is on "Dutch Hill," where lives the finest people in "God's Country," these United States. People who are ever ready to lend a helping hand to one who may need it and who do not forget one far away in some strange land. It is my one earnest hope and wish that some day I may be able to show indeed how grateful I am to all of you folks. Guy, I had written several letters to you and am very sorry that you could not have received at least one of them. I wish to congratulate you on a truly wonderful piece of work, your P.X. It is in my humble opinion "the paper for our boys." I have read all of the papers that you so thoughtfully gave to Mother for me, and never have I had so much pleasure as in them. As so many of the fellows have previously stated, you certainly have missed your calling, Guy. I also wish to add my congratulations to the "True*

Blues" for the job that you all have done and are doing. One day you all will be repaid, I know, for work such as yours does not go unrewarded. Just think of that great day when all of the fellows will be back and a reunion is held at the "Uniteds." Can you all picture the grateful faces trying to find words, as I am now, trying to express their gratefulness to you all for such a fine job so well done. If you can do this you will have then had a small part of your reward. And last, but not least, I wish to thank you all for accepting me once again as a member of that Club of Clubs, the "Uniteds." It seems a person doesn't realize until sometimes too late that he or she, as the case may be, has wandered away from all that is best in life, their own friends and neighbors. I realize how I had wandered away from my hill back there in England even before visiting Germany, and am determined that never again will I make such a mistake. All of this jumble of words, if written by someone who can express themselves, as I cannot, means simply this: I thank God for my Home, my Mother and our Neighbors and Friends. May God Bless you all, now and always. Sincerely yours, Walt.

From Sam Sweet in Italy: Right now the infantryman is located in a town about the size of Amsterdam called Alessandria. . . . I'm on detached service with AMG and it sure is a racket. Anything we need, we take – or, as they call it, "requisition." Got the home of an ex-Fascist big wig for quarters, and those boys really had the homes. With two Italian signorinas as waitresses, and a chef, this is some change from the front. Don't know how long it will last, but it really is the life. Reminds me of home, a lot, as the local yokels are region soccer champs.

From Val Webb: I have just received the Feb. issue of the P.X. . . . .One part in particular hit me right between the eyes, that was the address of Robert G. Murdoch, A.S. It doesn't seem possible that it is the same Bobby Murdoch who used to play with my son, when I lived next door to you. These kids growing up, *makes me realize that I'm not getting any younger. I have been in the service just one year today and have been out here in the Pacific for four months. . . . Photography in the Navy is much the same as in civilian life, except there is more of it and the working conditions are much worse due to the lack of space and shortage of fresh water.*

From Walter Campbell: I know what Pete Ruback means when he says it's a lot of work to keep a flying coffin in the blue. They have four engines to work on and our boys have but one. If any of you soccer fans want a real thrill, just climb in the seat of a dive-bomber and go for what we call a rat chase.

From Harold Brown: We moved out of Czechoslovakia and are now in Germany doing occupational duty. We met the Russians in Czech. Boy!!! They are a rugged bunch. If you want to taste something strong, you should taste that vodka. The first time I drank some of it, my helmet jumped off my head and spun around six times, or maybe it was me that was spinning and my helmet was standing still. That was enough of that stuff. . . . Right now I'm sweating out a trip home. I happen to be one of those 85 pointers. Here's hoping I make it.

From Harry DeGroff in Germany: Well, over here in this country where the figures on banknotes are big and the value little, the Nazi flag is continually being displaced for something white and the folks are using everything from handkerchiefs to bed sheets to indicate their surrender. Some of the towns have shared the fate of those we saw in Italy and France, and by having the war in their back yard this time, maybe they won't be as quick to get war minded in the future.

Later: On seeing Dachau, I can assure you the inmates of that prison camp probably welcome a quick end, were they unfortunate enough to come there alive.

The 65th Infantry Division, attached to Patton's Third Army, is in Efferding, Austria by May 4, 1945, having covered six hundred miles through Germany and upper Austria in the previous sixty days.

Corporal Charles Christian, of 240 East Main Street, is armed with a Browning automatic rifle when he enters a barn and surprises a German SS soldier. The man refuses to surrender, so Christian kills him with a rifle burst. He then spots a German machine gunner in a nearby house taking aim at an American. He shouts to get the German's attention and quickly takes care of him as well. Three others promptly surrender.

Moving with two comrades to a large house commanding an intersection, he breaks into five rooms alone while the others cover him, capturing 40 SS troops.

Using the captured building as a firing point, he then assists in the annihilation of three truckloads of German reinforcements.

He is awarded the Silver Star. Prior to the war he had been a student at Rensselaer Polytechnic Institute.

Pfc. Emil Fleszar of 267 Forest Avenue gets to nab one of the big boys. He is assigned to a squad to pick up multi-millionaire industrialist Alfried Krupp, the head of Germany's war-manufacturing operations. Fleszar is serving with the 79th Division in the 9th Army when sent to Krupp's estate, "bigger than Amsterdam itself." He finds the place manned with 275 servants. Fleszar notes in a letter home, "I've been in many museums, homes and mansions, but I've never seen anything like that before."

Krupp will trade his estate for a jail cell for the next six years.

VICTORY IN EUROPE!

May 8, 1945, the complete, total and unconditional surrender by Germany to the Allies.

Frank Going is lucky. He is one of the thousands of guys hanging over the rails in June of 1945 when the first voyage of the *Queen Mary* sails home from Europe into New York Harbor, crammed with men no longer needed on that front.

There are plenty of cheers for and from them.

The joy is tempered only by the issuance a short time later of light-weight Pacific uniforms.

.

19. THE HELL WHERE YOUTH AND LAUGHTER GO

Though no one knows it at the time, including even those planning the big experiment in Los Alamos, the siege of Okinawa will be the last significant battle of World War II, and it stands far and away as the fiercest of the fierce Pacific War. Only 350 miles from the home islands, Japan considers Okinawa to be sovereign Japanese territory, and, as they have at every stage of the war thus far, they make us fight for every square inch of it.

The Allied naval fleet alone is enormous, over a thousand vessels: some 39 American aircraft carriers, 17 battleships, 29 cruisers, countless destroyers and destroyer escorts, mine-sweepers, landing craft, support ships; even the British are able to provide an additional 4 carriers, 2 battleships, 5 cruisers, 14 destroyers and their fleet train. And while our side has complete dominance of the seas (actions against the fringes of our fleet are quickly swatted down like so many tropical gnats), *kamikaze* airplane attacks, some two thousand individual attacks over the course of the battle, send twelve Allied destroyers and fifteen amphibious ships to the bottom. Another 120 amphibious boats and 248 others receive various levels of damage. As horrendous as the casualties on land will prove to be, the U.S. Navy actually suffers more killed (4,907) than either the Army or Marines. Japanese naval losses amount to 16 ships, the battleship *Yamato* being the most prominent.

Amsterdam's Seaman First Class Karol Krajewski is aboard the *USS Nevada*, a veteran ship commissioned in 1916, bombed and beached at Pearl Harbor (she was the only battleship able to get underway during the attack) and reborn to fight again, providing support for the landings at Attu in the Aleutians, the Normandy invasion and the D-Day landings in southern France in June and August of 1944, and the Iwo Jima operation. Krajewski had participated in all but the Aleutians campaign.

Those ghost ships of Pearl must be especially unnerving for the Japs, for they put the *Nevada* in their sights and score five direct hits from a shore battery on Tuesday, March 27, 1945. At the same time, the on-board terror is compounded by the arrival of a *kamikaze* plane that smashes into her. The dead include twelve enlisted men and one officer; another 65 wounded.

The *Nevada* is back in action within four hours.

Seaman First Class Harold Gotobed serves aboard the battleship *New York.* The 31 year old ship pours her big guns at Okinawa steadily throughout the campaign without relief, cannoning more than five million pounds of shells at the enemy. Though there are more than two hundred air raid alerts adding up to the equivalent of two solid weeks of air defenses, they emerge without a scratch on ship or man.

Meanwhile, still with his flight deck crew on the escort carrier *USS Marcus Island*, CPO Sylvester Foltman helps launch fighters and bombers to Okinawa from March 26 to April 29, pounding enemy airfields, gun emplacements, supply dumps, and troop concentrations. His pilots are credited with shooting down 11 Japanese aircraft and eliminating another 13 on the ground. Each Japanese plane taken out of action results in many American lives saved.

While Easter Sunday Mass is being celebrated from the summit of Mt. Suribachi on Iwo Jima and broadcast across the world, the landings on Okinawa begin, on the western shore at the narrow waistline of the island, with the plan being to establish a beachhead, and then have the 6th Marine Division heading north and the 7th and 96th Army Divisions sweeping south and east.

The Marines, familiar with D-Days on Guadalcanal, Saipan, Guam, Tinian, Tarawa, Iwo Jima, Peleliu, and all those other places, are expecting the worst. Amazingly, there is virtually no resistance. Lt. Stanley J. Litwa, USMC, is among the first ashore.

It was a beautiful day for Easter, but instead of going to church we
carried our weapons to the enemy. We took Youtan airfield and
pushed northward after the Nips, of whom we have taken our
share.

Litwa is in the front lines for 23 days, and has two narrow escapes. A
mortar shell almost gets him, and then a sniper bullet passes right
between his legs.

The Marines manage within a week to isolate the bulk of the Japanese
defenders on the northwest Motobu Peninsula, but on the southern front
the army's irresistible force soon meets an immovable object and
casualties mount without much forward advance along the outer Shuri
defenses, where the relatively flat central part of the island begins rising
to a series of well-defended ridges, escarpments, hills and mountains. The
decision comes down to call the floating reserve into action, and so the
27th Infantry Division, originally composed of New York National Guard
regiments, finds itself back in action on the front for the first time since
Saipan.

When the Boys of Company G marched out of Amsterdam on October 23,
1940, they'd been led by their second in command, 33-year-old Charles
DeGroff, a man who had entered New York's National Guard as a private in
January of 1928 and climbed steadily up the ranks to first lieutenant.
When his boss, Capt. Peter Rogers, gets promoted to Executive Officer of
the Third Battalion of the 105th Infantry, DeGroff takes over as captain of
Company G in mid 1941, where he serves through the next two years of
training in Alabama and Hawaii, before again succeeding Rogers and being
promoted to Major in 1943, taking him through the hard fighting on
Saipan.

And when the Battle for Okinawa begins, DeGroff is himself the boss of
the Third Battalion.

They also give him his own island to capture.[28]

---

28 As with the Saipan chapter, the story of the Amsterdam men on Okinawa
could not have been told without the aid of the excellent historian of the 27th
Division: Love, Edmund, *The 27th Infantry Division in World War II*, Infantry

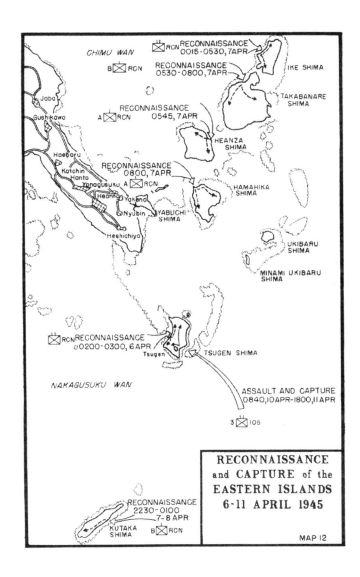

RECONNAISSANCE
and CAPTURE of the
EASTERN ISLANDS
6-11 APRIL 1945

MAP 12

Tsugen Shima is the fifth of six islands running north to south off the southeastern coast of Okinawa and sits opposite the entrance to Nakagusuku Bay, extending but 3,000 yards from tip to tip. Marine reconnaissance has shown it to be the only one of the Eastern Group of islands to be significantly occupied. The island is mostly flat, with the exception of a high ridge on the western side with two knobs. Tsugen

Journal Press, 1949.

Town rests on the slope of the ridge and has been mostly destroyed by air and naval bombardment which commenced at 0700 on April 10, 1945.

The Japanese soldiers are well aware of their pending fate. They clothe themselves in full dress uniforms with ribbons and medals displayed and fight to the death in the manner of their comrades before and after them across the Pacific. They center themselves primarily on the two knobs and the village, the hillsides carefully tunneled and natural caves utilized to the full, facing the landing beaches and overlooking the town.

DeGroff lands his men (including amphibian tanks of the 780th battalion) on the south beaches beginning at 0840 with not much opposition and marches his Third Battalion north with two companies abreast, I company on the west and L on the east, K in reserve. By 0930 they establish the first phase line, running east to west across the island and through the center of the village, in a cold, driving rain. L company reaches the next phase line, six hundred yards north of the village, by just after noon, while I company gets pinned down by machine gun fire from a triangular trench system toward the northern outskirts of the village.

When one of his company commanders reports that they are being mauled by mortars and can not advance, DeGroff replies, "The hell you can't. If you're going to lose men, you might just as well lose them advancing as standing still. The mortar fire isn't any worse ahead of you than it is where you are. Now get moving!"

Major DeGroff then utilizes K company, moving them around the east side to take up I company's second phase line, leaving I to mop up while K and L sweep to the north end of the island, reaching the beaches by 1805.

Early the next morning the mop-up re-commences and becomes a full-blown battle by noon. One hill has been taken completely and the other under fire when the Third Battalion is ordered back to the ships, over the protest of Major DeGroff, leaving about fifteen Japanese soldiers on the island. All known enemy positions except the one hill have been taken at the cost of thirteen Americans killed or died of wounds and 79 wounded.

Two hundred and thirty-nine Japanese soldiers lie dead.

Major Charles DeGroff receives a quick promotion to Lt. Colonel.

Meanwhile, the rest of the 105th Infantry Regiment begins landing the next day, April 12, on Okinawa, including the boys of Company G. As they move into place, the 27th Division takes over a line running from the west coast with the left boundary being a road running from Futema to Kakazu to Nakama, where they link up with the 96th Division on their left. That road is used as the supply line route for the 96th, while the 27th is assigned the west coast road.

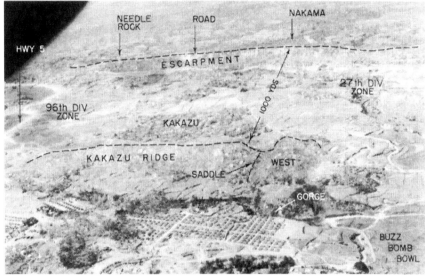

Looking south. (USA photo, LOC)

By April 16 the 105th Regiment anchors the west end of the line with the First Battalion in front facing Kakazu and the Second Battalion under Major Holman Grigsby, including Company G, behind them with Lt. Col. DeGroff's Battalion in regimental reserve by April 17. Nakama Ridge (later called "Rotation Ridge") runs for some 2,000 yards across the front in an East-West direction, the most prominent feature of which is a high tower of rock rising about forty feet in the air above the escarpment of Nakama Ridge (itself about two hundred feet above the plain approaching it), nick-named "The Pinnacle," which proves to be a great observation post for the enemy, guarding the eastern approach over the boundary road running over Kakazu Ridge and through Kakazu village. A second, smaller Pinnacle (shown on the above photograph as "Needle Rock") rises up farther east on the ridge and becomes known as the "Eastern Pinnacle" and the larger as the "Western Pinnacle." Between the pinnacles lies a secondary road, blocked with brush and mines.

The orders given to the 105th on April 15th are to bypass all strong points and advance, but, as Col. Halloran of the 381st regiment of the 96th division on their immediate left notes, "You cannot bypass a Jap because a Jap doesn't know when he is bypassed."

Kakazu Ridge now stands about two hundred yards to the front between the 105th and the village of Kakazu. On April 19 tanks move up the road to the right and through the ridge to the village while the First Battalion is expected to cross over the ridge and meet up with them, but the First, under Lt. Col. Raymond Miller, becomes bogged down. The Second Battalion's Major Grigsby and Capt. William Evans-Smith move up to look over the field. Grigsby gets hit four times and is given up for dead while Evans-Smith gets pinned down. Capt. Ernest Fleming, executive officer of the Second Battalion, takes command in Grigsby's absence. Col. Winn, regimental commander, tries to reach Grigsby, not knowing of his injuries, and Fleming has gone out looking for Grigsby and is himself out of contact. Finally at around 1225 the Second Battalion is ordered to bypass Kakazu Ridge on the left and maintain contact with the 381st. (The Kakazu Ridge lies between the zones of the 27th Division and the 96th Division on their left, proving to be considerable trouble for both).

Meanwhile, DeGroff's Battalion has been ordered onto Crocker's Hill (west of Kakazu Ridge) to protect the right flank and put fire on Kakazu Ridge to support the First Battalion advance, which, as noted, never happens. The tanks, meanwhile, destroy Kakazu village, but when the troops fail to arrive over the ridge, the tanks go back the way they came. Only eight of the thirty tanks return. The rest are disabled.

At noon DeGroff is ordered off of Crocker's Hill and sends I and L companies to bypass the ridge on the right and after about twenty minutes they run into fire from the west wall of Kakazu Ridge. Tech. Sgt. Richard Ben fires eight rounds from a borrowed bazooka, then borrows a BAR, charges 150 yards across open ground and completely destroys the enemy positions. In three hours DeGroff reaches his objective line on top of Rotation Ridge (Nakama Ridge).

Meanwhile, Capt. Fleming moves the Second Battalion out at 1225, with Companies F and G to move abreast to assault the east nose of Kakazu Ridge, pivot southwest, to bypass the village on the east. But first they have to get past the First Battalion's C company, still pinned down on the saddle, and F company quickly gets bogged down in the same fire.

Part of Company G does manage to get around the ridge, though. Lt. Charles Thompson's platoon makes it through the Route 5 road cut, moving west to where they can see the tanks in the village. But the Japanese open fire on them, Thompson is killed and the platoon cut off. Tech. Sgt. Edward Wojcicki, now in command, tries raising Capt. Louis Cudlin for instructions but is unsuccessful. The rest of Company G is gone, having retreated back to the departure line. Wojcicki moves his men to the nearest tank (then in the process of withdrawing from the village) and is able to thus safely extricate his platoon. But the whole left flank of the 105th now is right back where it started.

Capt. Fleming then sends the Second Battalion around to Col. DeGroff's side, and after tying in at 1800 they settle on the north slopes of Rotation Ridge. The First battalion then follows and is in place by dark, but with a huge gap between the 27th Division and the 96th Division on their left, with the 27th a full 1600 yards forward.

So by the night of April 19 they have taken and held Rotation Ridge, except for the Pinnacle, which is riddled with tunnels, caves and pill boxes. It stands right on the division line between the 105th and 106th regiments. The next morning begins a five day battle for its possession.

On April 20, the First Battalion of the 105th moves to the left to mop up Kakazu Ridge, along with the 27th Reconnaissance Troop, which includes in its number a former Company G man, Lt. Thomas Quigley. They are ordered to clean off the ridge by nightfall.

The Reconnaissance Troop arrives at 1400 and by 1800 has found no resistance on Kakazu Ridge, though they have yet to reach the eastern nose.

The Pinnacle (USA - LOC)

The morning of April 20, 1945 finds the 105th stretched across Rotation Ridge with the Second Battalion looped under the north slope. Col. Winn orders the Second and Third forward to seize the road cut between the Pinnacles, with E and I companies leading. At 0730 they are immediately pinned down. Winn personally assesses the situation, then orders Fleming and DeGroff to advance at 1230 regardless of fire conditions. When the time comes, DeGroff moves and Fleming doesn't. Winn replaces Fleming on the spot with Maj. John Purcell, the regimental supply officer, and in the interim takes personal charge, ordering Companies F and G to move along the base of the ridge past the East Pinnacle, and then straight up the steep cliffs into the north end of Nakama, to sweep through the town and await orders.

Capt. Louis Cudlin of Company G and Capt. Edward Kidd of Company F make quick progress, advancing to the top of the ridge within an hour. With F on the left and G on the right they move down a gentle slope to a road running from what would be called "McKenna's Cut" into Nakama. In the process they surprise and knock out from 8 to 10 enemy positions from the rear.

Capt. McKenna's E company, meanwhile, has not yet made it through the road cut. This leaves Company G's right flank a hundred yards away from Company E, with the East Pinnacle between them.

And the maps are wrong. Instead of being just north of Nakama when they come over the ridge, they are 400 yards west of the village, forcing them to change the direction of the attack, and with F having an exposed left flank, the two companies are way out there on their own. Col. Winn nevertheless orders the attack on Nakama to continue.

While the two captains communicate by radio phone, F is attacked by mortar fire, and Capt. Kidd signs off for half an hour to deal with the problem. At about 1700 they agree to swing Company G around like a gate to face east to present a front rather than a flank to the enemy. Company G is to follow F's lead in the maneuver.

Unknown to Capt. Cudlin, as soon as Capt. Kidd signs off he is hit by enemy fire and evacuated and his radio destroyed. While Cudlin awaits Kidd's move, the Japanese work themselves around to the rear of Company F.

Within minutes all the remaining officers and most of the NCO's of Company F are killed or wounded. The 27th Division historian compares it to Custer's Last Stand. All organization is lost. All except the platoon nearest Company G flee to the rear and back over the cliffs.

A runner from the lone platoon remaining comes up to Capt. Cudlin and asks, "Where the hell is Company F?"

Cudlin understands the situation and immediately executes the gate-swing maneuver.

It is too late.

Enemy soldiers from the East Pinnacle, as well as the troops that had wiped out Company F, close in on Company G's rear. Cudlin deploys his two assault platoons along the south edge of the road. Jap machine guns on each flank sweep over the open slope, firing at anything that moves. Cudlin and Company HQ are cut off from their men in reserve on the ridge (the third platoon and weapons platoon). In a fog of war mix-up, Cudlin intercepts a radio message giving Second Battalion HQ permission to withdraw and interprets it as an order for Company G to withdraw and passes that on to his men on the ridge. When the messenger from F company is hit, Cudlin loses time evacuating him and misses the opportunity to climb over the bluff.

His First Sergeant is killed by machine gun fire, his Executive Officer Lt. Donald Spiering is hit in the knees (seriously wounded several times more, he manages to hide out behind enemy lines for three more days until rescued). Cudlin and his ten remaining men are surrounded by a Japanese platoon. They make a concerted rush straight through the enemy lines. Cudlin himself leaps over the crest of the ridge and falls thirty feet to the mouth of a cave. He crawls to safety. The rest of the men hide in bushes and ledges through the night, until the next day when they stumble upon Cudlin's cave. They are rescued by a patrol late in the afternoon on April 21.

By the end of the day on April 20, fifty men of the Second Battalion are dead and another forty-five wounded, mostly from Company F and Company G. None of the original officers are left, though Cudlin manages to return to duty two days later.

Meanwhile, at the western end of the 105th's line, Lt. Col. DeGroff's Third Battalion can not move Company K forward at 0730 as planned, because Company E on his left has failed to move and protect his flank. While awaiting developments, he keeps Company L busy blowing up caves and working on the West Pinnacle, which, though surrounded, continues to be a problem. What follows is a deadly game of hide and seek, as the caves and tunnels of the Pinnacle are cross-linked to give the defenders the maximum advantage. Casualties mount, including L company's commander, Capt. Robert Spaulding, hit in a mortar attack.

On Col. Winn's orders, DeGroff's battalion advances at 1230 over the crest of the ridge and by 1500 are 200 yards SW of Iso, moving into the zone of the 106th Regiment to avoid the fire from the Pinnacle.

The prize of the day is the discovery on the body of a Japanese officer of a map of all the mine fields along the road running east from Machinato, the west coast anchor of the 27th Division. As a result, by 0900 of April 21, the entire road has been cleared, opening up a direct supply route for the 105th, and a mined roadblock on the cut through to Iso has also been cleared, allowing tanks to pass through southward from Rotation Ridge.

April 21 also witnesses an additional command shuffle as DeGroff's Executive Officer, Capt. Carl Roehner, takes over the Second Battalion command from the temporary assignment of Major Purcell, and the former Second Battalion commander Capt. Fleming returns to take over Company G from the still-missing Capt. Cudlin, with orders to "attack and seize the East Pinnacle," then move across the ridge to connect with Capt. McKenna's E company. Company F, meanwhile, decimated by the previous day's battle, is placed under Capt. Walter Sluzac, the regimental communications officer, and spends the rest of the day reorganizing.

Neither Company G nor the assisting First Battalion is able to make much progress, but the line holds solid and well-protected for the remainder of the day. Considering the hits Company G had taken on the 20th, that is about as much as can be expected of them.

On the right, DeGroff renews his attack on the West Pinnacle, a fight of steady attrition, aided now by tanks which cross the cut to Iso by 1400, and fresh supplies dropped in before dark. Skirmishes continue through the night, with organized attacks of the scattered enemy advancing on bugle calls from the West Pinnacle.

During a lull in the fighting, Company G veteran Dominick LaMori, who jokingly claims to be the oldest Private First Class in the 27th Division, having held that rank without advancement since October of 1940, hears a cry from no-man's-land between the lines.

"Come help me, I'm hurt!"

LaMori instinctively moves forward to aid his wounded comrade.

The "wounded" man leaps to his feet in his Japanese uniform and fires at LaMori. Simultaneously, from farther back, a mortar shell launches in his direction.

The rifle bullet whizzes past his head.

The mortar shell drops short, right on top of the Japanese soldier with the perfect English.

"I've got to hand it to those Jap mortarmen. They certainly helped me out of a tight spot."

On April 22, though the West Pinnacle still holds out, Lt. Col. DeGroff manages to reduce all of the machine gun nests, opening up a fire-free supply route for the troops south of Iso. This enables DeGroff to pull his troops back to the ridge while the 106th Regiment fills in for the advance.

Meanwhile, Company G and the re-grouped Company F continue the attack on the East Pinnacle, suffering extremely heavy casualties, including Company F's new Capt. Sluzac, riddled with machine gun bullets. By nightfall on the 22nd, the Eastern Pinnacle remains fully entrenched.

April 23rd finds the front basically quiet, as a task force of officers from the 27th and adjacent 96th Divisions coordinate their movements, resulting in a major thrust on April 24, with the First Battalion advancing below the East Pinnacle and attacking directly to the ridge and a Japanese stronghold, where it quickly becomes bayonets, clubs, grenades and hand-to hand combat, with over a hundred Japs killed in an hour, and with Staff Sgt. Nathan Johnson of Company C taking out thirty or more himself, at one point shooting eight with his rifle and clubbing four to death. The East Pinnacle is secure.

At midnight, a Japanese bugler signals a *banzai* attack, and the thirty remaining defenders of the West Pinnacle charge straight into the lines of the 106th Regiment where they come to a swift end.

The 105th regiment pushes through Nakama on April 26 and holds a line south of town until May 1, when they are relieved by elements of the 1st Marine Division.

The following day, the 27th Division moved north to Nago for mopping up operations beginning May 10, 1945. The "mopping up operations" are not without risk. Between May 19 and August 4 the 27th Division kills over a thousand of the enemy and captures another five hundred.

Under a point system developed by the government, men with 85 points are now eligible for discharge, but if put into full effect, that would leave only 2,500 men in the division, and nearly all of them are combat replacement troops.

So they get selective, and in May a small number return home, including all the survivors of the advance party that had landed in Hawaii on March 10, 1942.

Which includes many of the surviving men in the division who had marched out of Amsterdam on October 23, 1940 to the thunderous cheers of their families, friends and neighbors for one year of active military duty in the United States Army.

But not everyone. The officer corps has been so wrecked that Lt. Col. Charles DeGroff stays on until July 26, and then goes home, with the seven remaining members of the original Company G following shortly thereafter.

Except First Lt. Thomas J. Quigley, Jr., who never makes it at all.

He is killed in action on June 11 while operating with the 27th Division Reconnaissance Troop.

He had joined Company G of the National Guard on December 31, 1932, been promoted to corporal in 1934, reenlisted, promoted to sergeant on December 13, 1937 and honorably discharged on March 15, 1939.

When it becomes clear that his old company will be called up in preparation for war, Quigley re-ups on October 7, 1940, so that he can be with his boys when they leave two weeks later.

Okinawa brings him his fourth battle star, a Purple Heart, and, for his wife of six months, a Gold Star. He is the last of the guests at the Freer/Pileckas wedding to die in combat.

The 5th Marine Regiment, as part of the 1st Marine Division, lands on the first day and spends the next couple of days sweeping across the waist of Okinawa. While other units turn north or south, they spend the month of April mopping up the middle, taking few casualties. They are amazed at their luck. They had landed unopposed, walking off the landing barges fully erect. But luck like that does not last forever on Okinawa. On the first of May they replace the 27th Division on the line, and for the next fifty days are in virtually continuous combat, fighting for ridge after bloody ridge.

With them, in Company B, is Pfc. Donald James of 63 Forbes Street, Amsterdam, New York. Soon comes the rain. Cold, miserable rain, and they slog through mud and maggots and the decayed remains of their enemy. Foxholes fill quickly with water. What little sleep they get is in fits and starts, hunched over in a sitting position. Combat is around the clock. They go weeks without even being able to change into dry socks. They take care of their personal sanitary needs in their own foxholes. There is no alternative.

When the roads and trails become too bogged to support any motorized transport, the men have to slop and slide, often under fire, to bring munitions and supplies to the front. Replacement troops are brought up and many are wounded or killed before anyone learns their names. All the men are exhausted, physically and mentally.

The rains last into June. Shiru, the most strongly defended outpost, falls at last and little remains of Japanese resistance, but as with every previous step, the Marines still face death from instant to instant.

By the 18th of June they are battling for Kunishi Ridge, the final obstacle to total victory, and Pfc. James is leading a squad of his rifle platoon. Seeing several of his men wounded and lying in an exposed position, subject to a sweeping and extremely dangerous cross-fire, James crawls forward and fires on the enemy emplacements.

But it is not enough, so he pulls back and locates a tank, which he then brings forward. He walks directly in front of it, so that he can point out the enemy positions, completely disregarding his own safety.

The tank dispatches the enemy emplacements, the corpsmen are able to move forward and give medical assistance and his squad members' lives are saved, which is far more important to him than the Silver Star he is later awarded, or his own Purple Heart. He is twenty years old.

When it is over, the bean-counters find 107,539 dead Japanese soldiers. Another 10,000 have surrendered. Estimates suggest another 20,000 are sealed in caves or otherwise buried by the Japanese themselves. And some 42,000 civilians die as well.

Among the dead is Pfc. Erwin George Hudson, of Star Route Hagaman, who suffers severe gunshot wounds and burns in the battle and is evacuated to the hospital ship *USS Solace*, where he dies of his wounds on May 9, 1945. Initially buried in the American cemetery on Tinian Island, after the war his body is returned to his native Galway. Among the pall bearers listed is his friend Melrose Freer.

Originally declared "missing in action" in May of 1945, Pvt. Ralph H. St. Clair of the 29th Marines, Sixth Marine Division is declared dead a year later. His father, suffering in a tuberculosis sanitarium, dies ten days after receiving the telegram that his son is missing. Pvt. St. Clair is eighteen years old.

On June 14, 1956 the family receives word that an Okinawan farmer plowing his field had discovered his body. At his mother's request, he is buried in the military cemetery in Hawaii.

Among the Amsterdam-area wounded, and the circumstances suggest that this list is not exhaustive, are Company G veterans Pfc. Louis Aldi (who returns with two oak leaf clusters attached to his Purple Heart) and Pfc. Stephen Bielecki, wounded in the action of April 20. The latter recuperates in an Army Hospital with the ever-reliable duo of Tech. Sgt. John Polikowski and Staff Sgt. Joseph Ochal, men who had nothing to prove after their valor on Saipan, but do it all again anyway.

Sgt. Frank J. Martuscello, of the Carmichael Street Martuscellos, had been transferred out of Company G to the 7th Division shortly after war broke out. He takes part in the re-capture of Attu island in the Aleutians a year later, then Kwajalein atoll, and Leyte in the Philippines. Okinawa brings him his fourth battle star with his landing on the first day. Shrapnel wounds in the face, arm and leg bring him a Purple Heart.

Army Sgt. Salvatore Gatto is wounded on May 13 from mortar shell fragments that land in a hole he is using as a forward observation post while serving with the 77th Infantry Division, who had replaced the 96th Division on the front lines. Gatto is a portrait artist before he becomes a soldier. He has suffered a number of close calls before he is wounded:

One morning we were moving along a trail and I saw a Jap so close that in another step I would have been on him. He started reaching for a hand grenade and I raised my rifle, but it jammed. Maybe you think I didn't sweat then.

But the Jap must have been more nervous than I was because he jumped up and ran. He stumbled over a man we had left behind us for rear security and he killed the Jap with one shot.

Prior to Okinawa, Gatto had fought in the Marianas and the Philippines as well.

Among the Marines, Cpls. Walter H. Selby, Jr. and Martin V. Conway, are both hurt in June.

American ground casualties in the 82-day battle which ends in mid-June include 7,613 killed and missing and 31,807 wounded in action. Neuropsychiatric patients (shell-shock, etc.) are an incredible 26,221. The latter figure is difficult to comprehend in cold print, but if you want a first-hand look at what those men went through, pick up a copy of *With the Old Breed* by E.B. Sledge, a Marine who saw it all. Sledge serves in K company of the same 5th Marine Regiment as Donald James.

Read the book. You will never be the same.

Here's a sample:

The stench of death was overpowering. The only way I could bear the monstrous horror of it all was to look upward away from the earthly reality surrounding us, watch the leaden gray clouds go scudding over, and repeat over and over to myself that the situation was unreal --- just a nightmare --- that I would soon awake and find myself somewhere else. But the ever-present smell of death saturated my nostrils. It was there with every breath I took.

I existed from moment to moment, sometimes thinking death would have been preferable. We were in the depths of the abyss, the ultimate horror of war. During the fighting around the Umurbrogol Pocket on Peleliu, I had been depressed by the wastage of human lives. But in the mud and driving rain before Shuri, we were surrounded by maggots and decay. Men struggled and fought and bled in an environment so degrading I believed we had been flung into hell's own cesspool.

. . . I imagined Marine dead had risen and were moving silently about the area. I suppose these were nightmares, and I must have been more asleep than awake, or just dumbfounded by fatigue. Possibly they were hallucinations, but they were strange and horrible. The pattern was always the same. The dead got up slowly out of their water-logged craters or off the mud and, with stooped shoulders and dragging feet, wandered around aimlessly, their lips moving as though trying to tell me something. I struggled to hear what they were saying. They seemed agonized by pain and despair. I felt they were asking me for help. The most horrible thing was that I felt unable to aid them.

At that point I invariably became wide awake and felt sick and half-crazed by the horror of my dream. I would gaze out intently to see if the silent figures were still there, but saw nothing. When a flare lit up, all was stillness and desolation, each corpse in its usual place.[29]

Sledge, writing of Okinawa, quotes a World War I English officer and poet, Siegfried Sassoon:

> *You smug-faced crowds with kindling eye*
> *Who cheer when soldier lads march by,*
> *Sneak home and pray you'll never know*
> *The hell where youth and laughter go.*[30]

---

29 Sledge, E.B., *With the Old Breed*, Presidio Press, N.Y. 1981
30 Sassoon, Siegfried, "Suicide in Trenches" in *Collected Poems,* Viking Press, N.Y. 1949

20. KEEP RIGHT ON TO THE END

P vt. Robert Crouch, at 32, is a little old to be getting into the war in late 1944. He has a wife and three small children at home. An ordinary guy, like so many of the others. He used to drive bus for the Vollmer line. But the demands of the Selective Service System finally reach him, and he is called up on October 9. He doesn't even leave for Europe until March 19, 1945 after a six day furlough in Amsterdam. Right away he sees action in Belgium and Holland with the 10th Tank Battalion and then sweeps into Germany with the conquering Army. After VE Day he is mostly assigned to guarding prisoners.

On June 17, he and four others attempt to clear an ammo dump. It goes off (some reports suggest it had been booby-trapped), and they are all killed instantly. He is survived by his wife Esther and children Barbara, 5, Robert, 4, and William, one and a half. William had been named after his uncle, William Hasenfuss.

William Hasenfuss.

Yes, that William Hasenfuss.

In the Amsterdam Tragedy that is World War II, Esther Hasenfuss Crouch's life forms terrible book ends, for she not only loses her brother at Hickam Field, Territory of Hawaii, on December 7, 1941, as the war begins, but her husband as well, on the other side of the world more than a month after the war should have been over.

She serves as a figure for the thousands of wives and sweethearts and loved ones of our Amsterdam boys of World War II. Those who sit and wait are rarely given much thought, or notes in history books, but war's destruction reaches those who never see a bomb fall or hear a shot fired.

The Japanese Navy has been pretty much rendered useless by the conquest of the Philippines, which cuts off their principal fuel supply from southeast Asia, and what's left of their air force has been decimated, confined now mostly to suicide missions. The American Army and Navy planes now hit Japan at will, hundreds of missions a day. MacArthur's weatherman, Col. Theodore Gillenwaters, passes on his forecast for Japan: "Generally clear tomorrow, followed by B-29s."

The sheer numbers make one overlook the danger of those missions. The round-trip to Japan from the bases in the Marianas takes some fourteen hours, only at most an hour of which is over Japan, the rest being over open water. Crew members take turns napping along the way, mostly in their seats as the planes are so loaded that there's no room to lie down, but for a cramped tunnel that runs just beneath the roof of the fuselage. Over Japan they have to face fighters and anti-aircraft flak, while over the ocean they have to deal with the limitations of their own machines, which are being pressed to the limit. They pride themselves with the recovery rate, some twenty per cent, of crews who are forced to ditch before getting back to safety.

Tech. Sgt. Edward F. Gawron is with the crew of a B-29 targeting the city of Kochi on the island of Honshu on July 3, 1945. The plane, appropriately nick-named *Miss Hap*, is caught by anti-aircraft flak and crashes in its target city.

Gawron becomes the last Amsterdam combat death of World War II.

Company G's Pasquale Mercadante is now a civilian, discharged after years of hard service that had seen so many of his friends die. While overseas, he is transferred to the 24th Division, where he participates in fighting the Japanese in New Guinea at Biak, and in the landings at Leyte Gulf and the Philippine campaign. He is in a party that rescues 130 Catholic and Protestant missionaries in Hollandia, Netherlands East Indies.

Coming home through the Albany train station, he has a chance meeting with his little brother, now reporting for duty in the Navy after graduating in the class of 1944, the fifth brother in that family to serve. They have not seen each other in four years.

Death touches him one more time, when the brother, Seaman First Class Frank Mercadante, 19, dies in Okinawa on July 11, 1945 after a long illness.

Japanese war actions range from the incredibly brave to the astonishingly pointless. In the latter category is a late-war effort to launch balloons to randomly fly on the winds heading toward the United States. Amazingly, a few of them actually reach the Pacific Northwest and cause some casualties.

A vigilant sky-watcher from Albany calls the State Police in Fonda to report that he has seen what appears to be one of these Japanese balloons flying high over Amsterdam.

A teletype message is then sent from Fonda to the Amsterdam Police Department, which also makes its way to the Schenectady Police Department, which sends a detail of their own men to Amsterdam to track this weapon before it can reach the General Electric and American Locomotive facilities in their city.

The various police agencies gather on roof tops and determine that there is indeed a flying object, somewhere over the fields beyond Kreisel Terrace. APD dispatches Officer Adamski to investigate.

What he finds is a bunch of kids from Reid Hill flying a box kite, albeit a rather large one, six feet by four feet.

Corporal Jack Blanchfield's seventy day furlough takes him through the summer, much of it spent at Galway Lake. His near-constant companion is his SMI classmate Bill Burns, another former POW. They understand each other, share an experience few others could understand. And yet, they never talk about it.

He avoids meeting people. There's that old "survivor's guilt" again. He thinks of Tom Cronin, Bill Hoppy, Andy Hopkins. Others he knew well, knew of, knew their families, or knew they came from Amsterdam.

More than 175 of them. He came home. They didn't.

But he doesn't let any of this show. He plays army with his little brothers, attacking the outhouse at the lake. He rescues a couple of boaters. He lives the summer as though nothing had happened, and ignores the war in the Pacific which still might be calling him.

On August 14, 1945 he joins his parents at Saratoga Raceway, for an evening watching the trotters.

And suddenly, the war is over.

They go home to find downtown Amsterdam alive with joy, triumph, hilarity.

War's swift end becomes quite obvious after Hiroshima, and the exclamation point of Nagasaki begins the countdown. Amsterdam readies itself for the explosion to come, with the merchants chipping in to buy brand new 48 star flags to line downtown and factory and retail holidays being planned and police department contingencies developed (some of the older members of the force can recall the 1918 festivities that had ended with an unfortunate homicide). Most important of all, the city's noisemakers are firmly in place.

Promptly at 7:00 PM on August 14, 1945 the FLASH comes over the AP wire at the *Evening Recorder*. Immediately the newspaper passes the word to Superintendent James Donnelly at the Bigelow-Sanford plant and to the Central Fire Station on Pearl Street. The huge siren at the carpet mill goes off, and audible fire traffic signals at street intersections. Other mills join the cacophony. The chimes at St. Mary's Church begin to play, and every church bell in town rings gloriously.

Front doors fly open. Neighbors hug and tears flow. Everyone, EVERYONE heads for downtown, on foot, or, much more slowly, by car, as the roads to downtown quickly back up a mile or more. Now the big whistle at the Chalmers knitting mill takes over, blowing exultantly for a half hour or more, barely heard above the din of honking horns. Kids jump on the hoods of cars. Home-made confetti appears spontaneously, and the various drum and bugle corps from the local veterans groups start to make their own impromptu parades. A Mohawk Mills truck appears with a quickly-assembled brass band playing patriotic airs. Horns, cowbells, housewives bashing pie tins, all add to the merriment.

Over at the New York Telephone Company every available operator reports for duty to handle the 50,000 local calls and double the usual number of long distance calls. Some wait as long as a half hour to get their turn. Reporters wonder who could be making all those calls, since the entire universe seems to be on Main Street.

It won't stop. The Fort Johnson All-Girl drum corps arrives, and the WBA Girls' drum corps. Even Adolph Hitler shows up, or at least some Amsterdamian looking like him, being carried around as one of our victory trophies. "What's *he* doing here?" some of the biddies want to know.

The tumult continues downtown past midnight, and then spreads to the neighborhoods where non-regulated fireworks and drinking and laughing and cheering go on until heavy rains at 2:30 in the morning finally drive everyone indoors. By then the Bergen Post boys had marched to the Wyszomirski Post to salute their comrades and together they continue to salute to the last man standing.

The next morning breaks calmly, quietly, serenely. The only sounds heard are of municipal workers cleaning up the streets and parishioners of the seven Catholic churches heading for Mass on the Feast of the Assumption. By order of Bishop Gibbons, the Blessed Sacrament remains exposed for thanksgiving prayers after the last Mass in each church for the remainder of the day. The various Protestant churches open their doors as well and celebrate services of gratitude to the Almighty for the war's end.

And in an otherwise deserted downtown, nameless volunteers carefully and proudly unveil the new American flags, no doubt a few of them recalling the refrain from John Philip Sousa's most famous march:

> *Hurrah for the flag of the free!*
> *May it wave as our standard forever,*
> *The gem of the land and the sea,*
> *The banner of the right.*
> *Let despots remember the day*
> *When our fathers with mighty endeavor*
> *Proclaimed as they marched to the fray*
> *That by their might and by their right*
> *It waves forever!*

Amsterdam Evening Recorder
AND DAILY DEMOCRAT

PEACE!

Japan, Bitter in Defeat, Hints at New War; Was Defeated, Not Beaten, Premier Asserts

White Plane to Carry Jap Surrender Envoy To Manila Conference

World Celebrates Defeat of Japan, Return of Peace

New Bomb Responsible, Emperor Hirohito Says In First Radio Address

UPX, July-August 1945:
"V-J Day" IN LI'L OLD New York, by Mary W. Murdoch

"....First atomic bomb dropped on Jap city .... Russia declares war on Japan.... The *Domei News Agency* has reported that the Japanese government is ready to accept the terms of the Potsdam Agreement, provided that the sovereignty of the Emperor is retained .... The United States, Great Britain, Russia and China are willing to start peace negotiations with the Japanese government, granting them their proviso ... The Swiss Embassy has reported that a coded message from the Japanese government is on its way to Switzerland .... The world still awaits expected Japanese surrender."

After August 6, when the first atomic bomb caused such havoc in Hiroshima, the entire world was held in suspense .... It hardly seemed possible that the war was actually drawing to a close.... Reports came over the radio at 10-15 minute intervals.... We read the papers from front to back.... At the office little work was done.... Everyone gathered at the teletype.... Friday, August 10, the teletype issued an 8-bell bulletin.... We ran from our desks, shaking with tension, and learned the best way to prepare an appetizing meal of fish.... The days dragged on.... Why do they torture us so?.... When?.... What's holding it up?.... And then the false report.... If we could only forget about the whole thing... Tuesday, August 14, a particularly trying day at the office... And in the evening a quick meal so as to waste no time in getting back to the radio.... At 6:30 P.M.- a bulletin.... "At 7 P.M. Prime Minister Atlee will speak over this station".... 7P.M. - dead silence while we waited.... Big Ben in London striking solemnly – midnight in England.... And then Atlee saying, "The Japanese government has accepted...."

All around us New York let out the emotion held in so long.... A synchronized roar echoed throughout the city.... automobile horns.... Noisemakers.... shouts.... Whistles.... Sirens.... Bands.... Horns on harbor boats tied down....

We sat for a moment in silence.... Stunned.... "It's over." ..... "the boys will all be coming home".... And a silent prayer, "Thank God!" .... A short visit to the neighborhood church ... Surprisingly few people there.... A bonfire in the middle of 16th Street ... Effigies of Hitler, Mussolini, and various Japs being burned....

The gathering of the cohorts for a visit to the Crossroads of the World.... Times Square.... Funny how New Yorkers gather there for every important event.... People from small towns always wish they could be there for such occasions... The Square was teeming with people.... Thousands of voices were raised and thousands of hearts were happy.... Soldiers .... Sailors.... Marines.... Merchant seamen... civilians... Men.... Women.... Bobby-soxers.... babes in arms.... People kissing total strangers.... Slapping of backs.... We were shoved from 43rd Street to 45th .... A half-hour of very close contact with thousands of curious New Yorkers.... And then the final effort to get off the square.... Mounted policemen trying to keep the crowd in check.... The papers the next day reported very few accidents... It was an experience never to be forgotten.... V-J Day in Times Square.... Many years from now, I can look back on it and recall all the days, weeks, months, years – of waiting for just that time ....

It wasn't what I had expected.... I was too stunned.... During the week of waiting for the end of hostilities after the first atomic bomb, I tried to visualize just how I would feel when that glorious day did at last arrive.... Deliriously happy?.... Relieved?.... Stunned?.... Thankful?.... Yes, all of that – and more, too.... Hopeful for the future... Joyful at the prospects of an early reunion of the family which hasn't been all together in peace for over three and a half years.... PEACEFUL....

But this V-J Day was merely the beginning of a series of private V-Days celebrated by individuals when the boys close to them return for good.... That will be the time to be celebrated and remembered by all of us ... The day that Johnny returns .... or Bus

…. or Bob …. or Peanuts …. or Lindsay … or Pierce and Harry … Dynesie …. and all the rest … And best of all – the day when the clubhouse begins to operate in full swing again, with Uncle Sam's Champions joining again the ranks of the Uniteds, defeating "tribe after tribe in the arena" …. Till then, boys, so long …. We're waiting for you and praying that our wait will not be too long.

From Francis Mosher: Our crew has joined a new squadron, and we were operating prior to the end of the war down around northern Borneo, and the Philippines. But now, we're on the move once again, and this time from all the scuttlebutt on the ship, we're bound for up around the China Coast and Korea. I ran into a fellow from down "Dutch Hill" way, out here about two months ago. It was up at "Jinamoc" in the Philippines and he was Archie Kinowski's older brother. It sure is a big morale booster to see someone from the old home town, especially out here, and it goes to prove that the boys from the Uniteds Club are spread all over the world.

From Carl Hartig: Boy, the old gang is sure scattered, but it'll be together again one of these days. I'm waiting for that old conductor to say, "Next stop is Amsterdam," and I'll bet most of the other fellows are, too.

From Bruno Petruccione, on Okinawa: Now that the war is over & censorship has been lifted I can tell you where I am and what I've been doing. I am now at Machinato on Okinawa, about three miles north of Naha, the capital. Before that I was at Hagushi where the original landings were made. I'm operating a freight barge. Bringing supplies in from the ships in the harbor. Pretty choice stock – such as beer or whiskey – and in such cases we do alright. Brought whiskey in two days ago, 1000 cases, all kinds. And the gold braid snapped for a drink for once, tho they didn't know about it. I haven't enough points for discharge. With the set-up the Navy has a single guy hasn't much chance. If you weren't fortunate enough (or unfortunate enough, all according to the individual's point of view) to be married you have to be so old to get out, that you were probably too old to get in in the first place. . . . Bruno, The Great Petroosh.

P.S. There's a load of beer tied up to me now but the S.P. that's watching it thinks that the war was on the level and won't turn loose of any of it. However, he can't watch everything at once as he will soon find out. B.A.P.

Journey's End [by the editor of the *Uniteds PX*]

During the First World War, Sir Harry Lauder, the famous Scots comedian, sang a very stirring song, which met with popular approval. The chorus of that song ran something like this--

Keep right on to the end of the road,
Keep right on to the end,
Tho' your heart be weary, still journey on
Keep right on round the bend.
Tho' you're tired and weary, still travel on
Till you come to your happy abode
Where all your love and you're dreaming of
Will be there at the end of the road.

The words of that song came back to me when World War II broke out and we were faced with the need of traveling another rough road. It was with the idea of doing something about this rugged traveling that the writer first became interested in the *Uniteds P.X.* While we could not help you in your difficult journeys, we tried the next best thing which would help you to forget it, even for a few minutes. We hope, and we are encouraged to believe, that that purpose was accomplished. As a paper or magazine it had no literary merit, and perhaps that fact gave it whatever appeal it had. Dutch Hill is just an ordinary corner in our city and our country, but out of such corners came the extraordinary effort which brought our side the Victory which, in our minds, never was in doubt. The only question was, "How long?" It was a long, long time for all of us. Ninety-six of you went away, sixty-two of you have returned and are now honorably discharged, the other thirty-four are still away, but we expect that before too long you will all be back home again. After seeing those of you who have come back, we are of the opinion that you are pretty much the same as when you went away, only older and more experienced. We have been very fortunate, for we have not lost a member as a result of war activities. While we would not like to be charged with flying in the face of Divine Providence, we have always been confident of your ability to take care of yourselves under all circumstances. Your active participation in all forms of rugged sports was a good education for what you had to meet during your war service.

The war is now over. The war for the Peace is now in progress; so far, a vocal war, and we are quite sure it will continue to be only vocal. That kind of war won't cause many casualties. The real need for the *P.X.* has been served and this is the last copy which will be printed. We are pleased that there is no further need for it, but it seems like saying goodbye to an old friend. We are grateful to all who have helped make it possible and interesting. Particular thanks are due to the young ladies who did the typing and mimeographing; without them there would have been no *P.X.* To Howie Dynes we extend our gratitude for the use of his scrapbooks from which we borrowed the write-ups for the Soccer games of the past. Johnny Page, Sports Editor of the *Amsterdam Recorder*, voluntarily contributed the page known as the "Sports Canteen." We owe Mary Murdoch a thank-you for her peppy little contributions and novelty items. Frank Dean of the Recorder Job Printing Dept. was very helpful and patient in supplying us with the printed covers which made the *P.X.* Look quite official. The greatest of all help came from all you fellows who wrote and filled the P.X. With your letters and words of high praise, and the war-time officers of the club, the good old Blues who denied me nothing.

It is finished. This is the end. You have all been most generous and indulgent, you Doughfoots and Gobs and Leathernecks, and my association with your *Uniteds P.X.* will always remain one of my most cherished memories.

-Guy Murdoch, Editor

The Bigelow-Sanford Uniteds finally get a chance to thank Gavin "Guy" Murdoch in person, March 9, 1946.

Many Amsterdamians take part in the first acts of peace. Tech. Sgt. James H. Gardner, serving with the 124th Cavalry Unit, drives one of the official cars to Chungking, China to witness the surrender of Japan's troops in that country. Cpl. Walter Selby shares the distinction with four of his Marine Corps 4th Division mates as being the first to set foot on mainland Japan as occupiers. Following shortly after is Pvt. Edmund Swierzowski, who had fought with the Sixth Marine Division through the Battle of Okinawa.

But the real first guy ashore is actually Navy Radioman Louis Coluni, Jr. of 105 Florida Avenue, a member of Underwater Demolition Team 21, whose men swim ashore a full 24 hours ahead of the Marine landings on Futtsu Saki Peninsula in Tokyo Bay. Their job is to check the beaches for mines, booby traps and other impediments. Their commander accepts the first surrender of a Japanese fort to the Allies.

After former Prime Minister Hideki Tojo, the man who plunged his country into war, attempts suicide, Staff Sgt. Harry Hemingway is assigned to closely guard him. Tojo survives long enough to be convicted and executed for war crimes.

Photographer's Mate Velmer "Val" Webb, in peacetime a staff photographer for the *Recorder*, takes advantage of the opportunity as a crew member of the destroyer *USS Suwanee*, lying off of Tokyo, to take a small boat ride through the harbor of Nagasaki, Kyushu Island, Japan as part of the occupation forces. Later he gets an army truck ride through the city as well. Also sharing the experience is Amsterdam orchestra leader Tony Brooks, a brother of Ray Brooks who had been at Pearl Harbor, now serving as Musician Second Class aboard the *USS Wichita*.

They are stunned.

The area hit most directly by the atomic bomb blast is completely leveled, but for a few concrete buildings, and even these are gutted with nothing but the barest framework standing. The zone of devastation is several miles square. All that is left of factories and shipyards is twisted masses of blackened steel. There are no homes, just a reddish rubble where they used to be and a strange odor wafting through the air.

There is no evidence of fire or wood.

Everything is just completely and utterly vaporized.

"One Jap commented that the gods were angry," Brooks writes home. "It took us about an hour to go through the entire devastated area, about as large as the City of Amsterdam. Those buildings had just disappeared, blown off the face of the earth.

". . . Even after seeing the devastated area, I can't believe it is true, or how it could be possible. Thank God that bomb is in American hands, and I hope we can hang on to it."

Brooks has been in the Nagasaki area helping to evacuate 10,000 prisoners of war, placed near the military target of Nagasaki so that they could share in the misery of the American bombing. By blind luck of the topography, they are shielded from the atomic blast. Among those rescued in Nagasaki is Chief Watertender George Ulrich, who had been a prisoner since the fall of Corregidor.

A 25 year Navy veteran, Ulrich has not seen his Amsterdam area siblings in almost twenty years. He and his wife of then some seven years, an English missionary in the Philippines, both had been taken prisoner when the Philippines fell.

Their fate is a complete mystery to their relatives until George is transferred to a hospital in Manila, where, on October 4, 1945, his niece, Pfc. Margaret Lasher, WAC, finds him, and finds his wife as well shortly after. Suffering from malnourishment and maltreatment, he is still receiving care the following July, in the Brooklyn Navy Hospital, when he has a happy reunion with his five siblings.

On the second day of September, 1945, at noon, Miss Anna Marie Fratianni becomes the bride of Chief Electrician's Mate Arnold Eckelman in St. Michael's Church, Rev. Joseph C. Beck presiding. Though he will have another year of service to go in the Navy, added to the ones he's been piling up since a year before he'd witnessed the attack at Pearl Harbor, for now war is just a memory, with a proud reminder pinned to his chest: eleven battle stars. Three from the Guadalcanal campaign. One in the Bismark Archipelago. One for New Guinea. Two for Leyte. One for Palou, one for Iwo Jima, one for Okinawa. Another for the China Sea.

While the Eckelmans celebrate at Isabel's Restaurant, across the globe in Tokyo Bay, Seaman 2/c Richard Wawrzonek and Seaman 1/c Wai Hong

Wong can not have a better station, aboard the battleship *Missouri*, where General of the Army Douglas MacArthur presides over the colorful formal surrender ceremony, punctuated by the flyover of 500 Superforts and 800 assorted navy planes. Hanging off the rail of the nearby destroyer *USS Haven*, fellow Amsterdamian MM2/c John Fitzgibbons has a similar ringside seat.

The formalities concluded, MacArthur then steps to a microphone and addresses the American people:

> Today the guns are silent. A great tragedy has ended. A great victory has been won. The skies no longer rain death; the seas bear only commerce; men everywhere walk upright in the sunlight. The entire world is quietly at peace. The holy mission has been completed. And in reporting this to you, the people, I speak for the thousands of silent lips, forever stilled among the jungles and the beaches and in the deep waters of the Pacific which marked the way. I speak for the unnamed brave millions homeward bound to take up the challenge of that future which they did so much to salvage from the brink of disaster.

As I look back on the long, tortuous trail from those grim days of Bataan and Corregidor, when an entire world lived in fear, when democracy was on the defensive everywhere, when modern civilization trembled in the balance, I thank a merciful God that He has given us the faith, the courage and the power from which to mold victory. We have known the bitterness of defeat and the exultation of triumph, and from both we have learned there can be no turning back. We must go forward to preserve in peace what we won in war.

. . . And so, my fellow countrymen, today I report to you that your sons and daughters have served you well and faithfully with the calm, deliberate, determined fighting spirit of the American soldier, based upon a tradition of historical truth as against the fanaticism of an enemy supported only by mythological fiction. Their spiritual strength and power has brought us through to victory.

They are homeward bound.

Take care of them.

21. THE EVIL MEN DO

Even before war's end, some of the mysteries of World War II begin to unravel. With the liberation of the POW camps in the Philippines, the American government starts to piece together the fates of our men who had been left behind. Some thought dead turn out to be quite alive, and, unfortunately, *vice versa*. Early reports find 3,485 live men previously listed as missing in action. Several American fliers reported by the Japanese government to have been executed walk away unharmed. Every such story hitting the press becomes the source of hope, and sometimes despair, for the anxiously waiting families back home.

The war years have been cruel to Mrs. Jenny Federowicz. Her nine year old daughter had drowned in the Amsterdam City Pool at Harmon's Field in June of 1943, and some eighteen moths later she receives word that her brother, Edward Knapik, has been killed in the war.

They, and another sister, had been orphaned at a young age and separated, with Edward being raised in an orphanage in Lodi, Massachusetts run by the Felician Sisters. It is the orphanage that gets the telegram announcing his death, and the Sisters pass on the information to Jenny.

Then, in January of 1946, an Amsterdam Police officer knocks on her door with more news. He reads a letter to her and she becomes hysterical.

The letter is from her brother.

Edward is alive, and in New York City.

All he knows of his sister is that her last known address is somewhere in Amsterdam. The cops work out the rest. This time, it's good hysteria. They leave her smiling.

In March of 1945 the family of Capt. Christopher Heffernan III learns indirectly that an officer who had been held prisoner in Manila had heard from another prisoner that Heffernan had been seen alive as recently as the previous November.

Judge Heffernan makes immediate inquiries of the War Department. Four subsequent responses show that the Amsterdam boy had died in Bataan of malaria in April of 1942. And that he had died on April 9, 1942. And April 8, 1942. And definitely on April 7, 1942 according to the chaplain who had been with him when he died. By the time his body is returned to Amsterdam in 1949, the Heffernans have discovered that their son is one of the first victims of the notorious Bataan Death March, a certified war crime of the Empire of Japan.

Pvt. William Thatcher's family back in Hagaman had been told in February of 1943 of his prisoner of war status in the Philippines. And that is it. What the Empire of Japan neglects to mention to the Red Cross is that Thatcher died of pneumonia the very day that they finally announce his existence. This the family learns only after the Japanese surrender, in September of 1945.

Likewise Sgt. Joseph Revelia's family waits until the surrender ceremony in Tokyo Bay before learning that he had died in a Jap POW camp on June 26, 1942. Revelia, born in 1900 in Italy, is a veteran of both World Wars and, at 42, the oldest Amsterdamian to die in World War II.

Pvt. Walter S. Slavek, on the other hand, survives the atrocities of the Japanese POW system and remains a prisoner in the Philippines until October of 1944 when advancing American and Filipino forces threaten to liberate him. Rather than allow such a thing, the Japanese military diverts vital cargo ships to carry the remaining prisoners to mainland Japan and Formosa. One of these vessels, containing Pvt. Slavek and one thousand seven hundred and seventy-four other Americans, is targeted by an American submarine in the South China Sea and sent to the bottom. Four are picked up by other Japanese vessels, and five manage to escape to the coast of China, two hundred miles away.

Pvt. Slavek is not among them.[31]

Chief Radioman Lawrence W. Covert has been a Prisoner of War since 1942 when captured in the Philippines[32] For over three years the prisoners suffer from nutritional deprivation, reduced to skin and bones, all the while having their eyes on a 700 pound bull the Japanese use as a work animal. When the war ends and the tables are turned, they convert the bull into one enormous stew, and eat it for six days straight. Their former guards ask to join in the feast. They are denied.

---

31 Lee A. Gladwin has painstakingly put together American and Japanese records to tell the stories of these POW ships for the National Archives (*Prologue* magazine: Winter 2003, Vol. 35, No. 4). He found a survivor's story of the ship carrying Pvt. Slavek:

The *Arisan Maru:* A Navy Boatswain Survives

On the eve of and during the Battle of Leyte Gulf (October 23–27, 1944), intercepts and intelligence summaries focused upon the movements of "#1 Diversion Attack Force," "#1 and #2 Replenishment Force," and other sea, air, and land units. Occasional references to patrol boats, merchant ships, and convoys are found. On October 24, 1944, the following message was decrypted: "The Luzon Straits Force is assigned to 2 unidentified Convoys and the Naval Air Force is assigned to 2 other unidentified Convoys."

One of these convoys may have been the Harukaze Convoy, which departed Manila for Takao, Formosa, on October 21, 1944. In that convoy was the *Arisan Maru*. Its cargo: 1,783 American prisoners of war. **[Sources vary as to the total number of POW's aboard, ranging from 1,775 to 1,783 -rng]**

Boatswain Martin Binder was among the prisoners compressed into hold two of the *Arisan Maru* on October 11. There was standing room only. On the following day, the Japanese mercifully moved about 800 prisoners to hold one, which was partially filled with coal. Mercy did not, however, extend to providing water, and several died of heat exhaustion.

To the surprise of the POWs, the ship took a southerly route, away from their Formosa destination, narrowly missing a devastating Allied air attack on Manila airfields and harbor. The *Arisan Maru* returned to Manila a few days later when it was thought safe to do so, joined the convoy, and departed on October 20.

It was nearly dinnertime on October 24. About twenty prisoners were on deck preparing the meal. The ship was near Shoonan, off the eastern coast of China. Binder and the others suddenly "felt the jar caused by hits of two torpedoes." *Arisan Maru* stopped dead in the water. After severing the rope ladder leading

In 1916 Joseph Orapello had left Amsterdam to "Join the Navy and See the World." And boy, did he. Even after World War I he stays in, finally retiring as CPO in 1930, after which he puts down roots in China, purchases a grill in Shanghai, marries a Chinese girl and brings a son into the world. When he comes home to Amsterdam for a visit in 1939, he knows that political developments are not blowing favorable winds in his direction. Not long after his return a Japanese bomb lands in front of his house. With the Japanese occupation of Shanghai comes the loss of his home and bar as ethnic cleansing of their neighborhood forces them across a bridge into another sector, where he starts over. Then, on November 5, 1942 he and 40 other Americans are arrested as political criminals, charged as being a Menace to the Order of East Asia and accused of being spies. He is placed in an internment camp, and Joe's Bar, a little piece of Amsterdam in Shanghai, ceases to exist.

For two years and ten months Orapello remains in custody. Once every fourteen months his wife Anna and son Michael are allowed a fifteen minute visit. Because the camp is not far away, however, Anna begins staking out the periphery and observes that her husband's work crew passes within a few hundred feet of the fence at the same time each day, so she begins bringing young Michael to wave to his father. Even that small touch of humanity becomes too much for the Japanese captors, who chase them away at bayonet point.

---

down into the first hold, the Japanese abandoned ship. Binder was first to escape from hold two and assisted in lowering a ladder down to those in hold one. Ropes were thrown down to those in hold two, as well. Wearing life belts and clinging to rafts, hatch boards, and any other flotsam and jetsam, the prisoners struggled in the rough waters of the Pacific.

Japanese destroyers deliberately pulled away from the men struggling to reach them. Binder survived by clinging to a raft and was later rescued by a Japanese transport that took him to Japan. On October 25 a Japanese army shipping message was intercepted stating "that the *Arisan Maru* had been loaded with 1,783 men (presumably prisoners)."

32 Covert has the rather unique distinction for a sailor of receiving the Army Distinguished Unit Badge, with oak leaf cluster, for his service in defense of the Philippines.

Many prisoners die from ill-treatment, and Orapello is convinced that his wife and son suffer greatly in order to send him food in prison. On July 8, 1945, the Japanese move the prisoners eight hundred miles north, with the intent to transfer them to Japan and place them in areas targeted by American bombers.

"Their motive purely revenge," Orapello writes in a letter to his mother. "But, on our arrival in Peking, there was no transportation available so we stayed there one month awaiting a ship from Korea. Anna, Mike and I were convinced we would never see each other again. But the atomic bomb saved us."

Not long after the surrender, American Marines enter the camp and former Petty Officer Orapello returns to his family. [33]

Lt. Col. Rene Juchli, an Amsterdam physician who served in both World Wars, probably thought he had seen and heard it all. And then they appoint him Chief Medical Officer in charge of the Nuremberg prison, responsible for the health of the most notorious war criminals the world has ever put on trial.

Juchli makes front page headlines in October of 1945 with his allegation that Rudolf Hess, Hitler's number two, who had inexplicably parachuted into Great Britain early in the war to present his own peace plan, has been faking amnesia. Juchli's position is the minority one among the examining physicians, but it also proves to be correct when a few weeks later Hess announces that he had indeed been faking for strategic reasons.

The Amsterdam doctor has an advantage over his British colleagues who join in the exam. He speaks fluent German and is able to also read the Hess diaries. Showing no respect at all for the prisoner's rank, Juchli takes immediate control.

"I said to him, 'Sit!' Well, he sat. 'Strip,' I said, but he did not comply very rapidly. 'If you need some help you will get it.'" He stripped.

---

33 A few years later as Mao's Communists march across China, Orapello reasons that the time is right to return to Amsterdam. They lose all contact with their relatives in China and years later learn that Anna's father, a lay Catholic leader, had been killed when the Reds took over.

After the two hour interview, Juchli informs Hess that approximately fifty times he has forgotten to forget, "And one big thing you forgot to forget, and that was to forget to be anxious about your amnesia." Juchli knows that a true amnesia victim wants to remember, wants help remembering, whereas Hess would just arrogantly say, "How can I be expected to remember? I have lost my memory."

At the end of the session, Juchli says to him, "You and I understand each other now, Hess. Let there be no more nonsense between us." And, according to Juchli, there never is.

For Reichsmarschall Herman Goering, Lt. Col. Juchli is actually the second-highest ranking Amsterdamian he has to deal with. The first is Amsterdam-born Brig. Gen. Robert Stack, to whom he offers his surrender quite ostentatiously in May of 1945. Ever gregarious, Goering tries to establish a one-general-to-another relationship. When Eisenhower, who had seen Nazi death camps in person, hears about it, he orders Goering stripped of all military insignia and treated like a common criminal.[34]

Goering suffers from heart disease, obesity and drug addiction. Dr. Juchli determines he has a thyroid problem and in treating him for that causes rolls of fat to fall off. As for the drug addiction, solving that problem is easy, he tells the Amsterdam Kiwanis Club when he returns home in 1946.

Brig. Gen. Robert Stack

"I wish to God that those dealing with the habit here would practice the method. It is jail. No one brings drugs to jail. They just don't get it."

Thanks to the excellent care of the Amsterdam doctor, Goering probably is healthier than he'd been in years when he commits suicide.

One of the newspaper articles of the period suggests that the top Nazis appear to be all "4-F," and Dr. Juchli's records seem to reflect that. Foreign

---

34 Although Gen. Stack had moved with his family to Schenectady from their Lark Street home soon after the turn of the last century, his mother still retained close ties with the town. His Stack ancestors were among the first Irish immigrants in Amsterdam and earliest parishioners of St. Mary's Church.

Minister Joachim von Ribbentrop suffers from a variety of neuroses. A former champagne salesman, he adopts the "von," to which he had no birth entitlement, to puff himself up. Says Juchli, "He wanted to appear crazy, and he may at one time have been crazy, but not now." He is the first of the Nuremberg prisoners to be hanged, on October 16, 1946.

Robert Ley, who suffers from acute bronchitis and laryngitis, as well as being somewhat nuts, had been the head of the German Workers' Front, a successful Nazi effort to nationalize the trade union movement under the party. Extravagant worker benefits, such as family cruises, are financed out of the dues of the workers themselves. When Ferdinand Porsche is unable to offer the Volkswagen at a low enough price for Hitler's taste, Hitler simply takes over the company and puts Ley in charge, who then blasts the malevolence and greed of the business class. Using his slush fund of union dues to pay a big chunk of the manufacturing costs, Ley is able to offer the "people's car" at a price everyone can afford and 344,000 are sold on the installment plan. Not one is ever delivered.

Despite his perpetual drunkenness and erratic behavior, Ley remains part of Hitler's inner circle, in no small part due to his fanatic loyalty to Hitler himself. He encourages the use of Slavic slave-workers during the war and special brutality against the Russian prison laborers.

While under Dr. Juchli's care, this virulent anti-Semite Nazi begins reading the Bible and claims he had never understood it before. He confesses to the doctor his friendship for the Jewish people. And he then commits suicide by hanging himself in his cell, using strips of cloth ripped from a towel as a noose and attaching it to a radiator pipe.

And then there is Julius Streicher. Germany's leading Jew-baiter, who claims that he had only ordered the destruction of the Great Synagogue of Nuremberg because he disapproved of its architectural design. He suffers from partial paralysis of a leg due to an old skiing accident and thinks about attempting suicide at war's end, but changes his mind and marries his secretary instead. A few days later he is captured in Austria by a Jewish-American officer. He is still screaming anti-semitic slogans as the hangman's noose catches his neck on October 16, 1946.

Not all doctors are kindly physicians. The *Recorder* account of Dr. Juchli's Kiwanis speech includes this:

> The next portion of the address was devoted to the experiments in the German concentration camps, where men were placed naked in ice water to ascertain how long it would take for a human being to freeze stiff and what were the chances of resuscitation. Some were thawed out, the Doctor observed dryly, one of the methods being contact with a woman, generally one of the gypsies confined to the concentration camp.
>
> Other experiments dealing with cold were conducted by placing the human guinea pig naked in the cold air, where it took nine to fourteen hours to freeze stiff, as compared with five minutes in the ice water.
>
> "None of these were ever resuscitated," said the speaker. "I talked with both physicians who conducted these experiments," said Dr. Juchli, "and incidentally one of them later hung himself. I don't know whether it was because of his contact with me or not."
>
> Reduced to the lowest terms, the justification for these terrible things done to human beings was that everybody confined in a concentration camp died eventually anyway, and they could die to better advantage in experiments that might benefit the German army.

Returning POWs need no indoctrination on the brutality of the enemy. Tales quickly emerge from them of the starvation, the beatings, the inhumanity of the camps, the Bataan Death March, enforced slave labor. Jack Blanchfield sees Russian prisoners begging for bread. Paul Dirsa sees worse.

Pvt. Dirsa, an employee of the Sweet Ice Company before the war, spends fourteen months in German POW camps after being captured at Anzio. The reporters try to drag the experience out of him.

"Everything was just about as you are reading it," he says when he returns home to Hagaman. "We would have almost starved if it had not been for the extra food we received through the Red Cross and I saw plenty of the brutality you read of.

"I once saw three or four hundred Russians machine-gunned; the dead, and any who might have been alive, dragged into an empty barn which was set on fire and the bodies burned."

Captain Arthur Carter comes home with his own stories, some of which he passes on at a Kiwanis Club luncheon.

On one occasion he had been called upon to take care of a health threat in Italy: a dozen decaying bodies lying in a field. They had been prisoners of the Germans, and when they proved unable to keep up with the retreating German army, they had been simply machine-gunned and left there.

And then he tells of the incident where a German colonel gets into a brawl in a bar in Italy and is killed. Those responsible head for the hills. One hundred and forty innocent civilian villagers are then lined up and summarily executed in retaliation.

> I want to tell you, now that it's all over, before we get all soft and say this is all propaganda, that these things never happened, that they *did* happen. I was too close to them, too close to others who witnessed similar things, not to know that they happened.

Norman Lowenstein before the war had been a member of the Temple of Israel synagogue in Amsterdam. Though a veteran of Utah Beach, the

Normandy Campaign and the Battle of the Bulge, he is still completely unprepared when his 13th Field Artillery Observation Battalion happens into the horror of the Mittlebau Dora Concentration Camp in Nordhausen, Germany.

Slave laborers no longer able to keep up with the work of building V-1 and V-2 rockets, had been sent to Mittlebau Dora to be starved to death.

In an interview with the *Desert Sun* in Palm Springs, California in 2010, sixty-five years later, Lowenstein recalled:

> I remember vividly taking pictures of the common graves where they were burying the unfortunate ones in the concentration camp. There were mothers holding babies. German soldiers we caught as prisoners — we used them to do this mass burial. One German soldier was carrying bodies and was laughing at what he was doing.
>
> I remember going over to him, I was so mad. Why I didn't shoot him, I don't know.
>
> I pushed him into the grave. I don't know if he ever got out.
>
> He was screaming.
>
> I hope he got buried alive.[35]

---

35 http://www.mydesert.com/article/20100526/NEWS13/5250347/Vet-saw-Utah-Beach-concentration-camp

22. HOMECOMING

Every town loves a parade, and never more so than when its boys are coming home from war. Amsterdam, New York is no exception, and the parade they throw together in a hurry for Saturday, September 15, 1945 is the biggest, the brightest, the brassiest, the most fantastic parade ever thrown together anywhere, any place, any time.

That, at least, seems to be the observation of the *Amsterdam Evening Recorder*'s intrepid reporter Hugh P. Donlon, a veritable *Mr. Chips,* who has, nearly singlehandedly, kept the hometown paper going through the war as the younger staff members take their turns working for Uncle Sam. Though by no means an old man in 1945, he already has emerged as the Dean of Montgomery County Journalists, an informal title he will continue to hold for several more decades.

As the bands and floats cram the side streets in the city's East End in preparation for the start of the parade, Donlon drifts back to his youth, before the turn of the century, when the area east of town bore the name "Ross Flats" and all the big players pitched their tents there: Ringling Brothers, Barnum and Bailey, even Buffalo Bill's Wild West Show featuring Annie Oakley and Frank Butler. Here again, in 1945, the color, the excitement, the thrill of the day the circus comes to town.

He can not be faulted for his enthusiasm.[36] By actual count the parade contains over four thousand participants; by reasonable estimate more than 30,000 bystanders cheer; by metes and bounds the parade stretches over three miles, from the east city line to the old Post Office at Division and Wall. It takes an hour and twenty minutes for the parade to pass any given point. Nineteen bands, dozens of floats, every ethnic group and society represented.

Home on leave, the newly appointed Intelligence Officer for the soon to be disbanded 27th Division, Lt. Col. Charles DeGroff, who had led Company G out of town on October 23, 1940, serves as Grand Marshal, and leads the parade behind the police motorcycle escort and a mass of American flags. John P. Curran, the postal clerk from the 27th Division Veterans who

---

36 Though he is, this being Amsterdam. Competing letters to the editor in subsequent days challenged whether this really *was* the biggest parade ever.

had escorted Company G in 1940 and later re-upped himself and prayed over the graves of his boys on Saipan, leads the returning veterans, escorted by every veterans organization in the area and the Amsterdam High Band.

Next comes the Polish division, accompanied by the newly re-constituted Mohawk Mills Band, making their first formal appearance since Flag Day in 1942. The Third Division contains the exhilarating notes of the British Empire War Veterans Bagpipe Band, various fraternal organizations, and the Kiwanis float re-creating the raising of the flag on Iwo Jima. Then follow the Italian and Lithuanian Divisions, the latter featuring eight champion beautiful Suffolk horses weighing over a ton each.

The final division, commanded by Mrs. Mary Going, features the American Legion John J. Wyszomirski Post 701 Drum and Bugle Corps, followed by car after car of Gold Star Mothers. Donlon does not say how many.

Upwards of 180 mothers are eligible to participate.

And then, thirty more floats.

Bigelow-Sanford has three floats, one containing an Honor Roll of their employees who served, another remembering the millions of blankets produced for our boys and a third actually containing a working loom producing duck cloth as it passes through downtown.

And when the cheers from the thirty thousand fade away, "Cheers!" becomes the salute of the day as the veterans organizations open their doors to hours and hours of conviviality.

And then it is over.

In the natural rush to celebrate, overlooked is the fact that the vast majority of the men of World War II haven't come home yet. Many, probably most, of them never see a parade, though as the months pass by the various organizations, churches and neighborhoods take turns welcoming home the sons of Amsterdam.

Back in December of 1941, Hank Greenberg of the Detroit Tigers had been delighted to learn that an act of Congress had terminated his six month draftee service in the army due to his advanced age. December 7 had changed it all back. After more than four years of service to his country, he is finally released to his team in time for the American League pennant race. At 35, his prime years are behind him, lost forever.

On the last day of the season, he belts a grand slam home run to win the pennant. In the World Series that follows he bats .304 for the seven games, with two home runs and three doubles. He scores seven runs and knocks in seven in leading Detroit to victory. Sportswriters immediately dub it the "Hank Greenburg World Series."

The same day the series ends, in an Army Air Force field in the greater Tokyo area, the tattered American flag that had flown over Hickam Field, Territory of Hawaii on December 7, 1941 is raised over the base and solemnly saluted. It is the very flag that flew over William E. Hasenfuss, Jr. when he gave his life for his country.

On November 23, Louis A. Opelia takes out an ad announcing that after three years in the service, including 28 months in the Pacific with the Sea Bees, he is back operating his Mobil Station at the corner of Market and Meadow Streets.

Nearly every day for quite a while thereafter, the newspaper contains brief notices of returning servicemen. On December 7, 1945 those included Pfc. George M. Platt, Cpl. Charles P. Ilnicki, Pvt. Florenzo Tambasco and Pfc. M.R. Dumar of Fonda and T/5 Millard N. Hansen of Ft. Johnson. On the social page we learn that Cpl. W. Hicks Nadler of 18 Phillips Street, had arrived home a couple of days earlier after having been discharged.

The world and national news tell of the conviction and death sentence for Lt. Gen. Tomoyuki Yamashita, the military commander of the Philippines, for war crimes, and the continuing investigation of the events leading up to the Pearl Harbor attack.

The Regent theater is closed for renovations, but the Strand is showing *River Gang*, starring Gloria Jean and *Springtime in Texas* with Jimmy Wakely, while over at the Rialto a sexy Deanna Durbin stars in *Lady on a Train* with Ralph Bellamy and David Bruce, with a side bill of *Mexicana* with Tito Guizar and Constance Moore. Albany's Palace Theater advertises the upcoming live, in person, Victor Borge.

Five guys are drafted and inducted and have their pictures taken: William S. Ratajczak, Chester F. Krzynowek, Albert R. Hammond, Bruno J. Murdico and Emil W. Sievert.

The downtown merchants are all bracing for the Friday night Christmas traffic. Salamack's Liquor Store on Forest Avenue advertises *Roma* wine for $3.70 a gallon, and up in Perth at the Big Maple Tavern you can spend a fine night of dinner and dancing to the tunes of "Pals of the Saddle."

The *Recorder* runs the children's serial *Santa and the White Bunny* six days a week. NBC Radio suspends their normal programming for a day of remembrance with military-related interview shows and a massive promotion for the Victory Bond drive.

Both Terry's Tavern at 47 James Street and the Bayard Street Grill at 3½ Bayard Street advertise "La Pizza," while over on the South Side, Lanzi's Restaurant, which started the fad, has been handling it long enough now that they feel comfortable taking off the quotes and just calling it pizza.

And up on Lincoln Avenue "Sam" Fariello is selling *Genuine Double Balsam Christmas Trees, All Sizes, the Largest Assortment in the City!*

The Army had taken Cpl. John J. Blanchfield back for a bit, sending him down South to do some clerical work. He is eligible to vote for the first time that year, and in the November election proudly casts his ballot for his father, James A. Blanchfield, who is elected alderman of the Second Ward.

On December 6, 1945 he receives his final discharge, and in the early hours of December 8 he comes home for good, in time to join his family at St. Mary's Church for Mass for the Holy Day of the Feast of the Immaculate Conception.

A former altar boy, the 21-year-old veteran knows well the prayers that are being muttered quietly by the priest and the server at the foot of the altar.

> *Introibo ad altare Dei.*
> *Ad Deum qui laetificat iuventutem meum.*

> I will go to the altar of God.
> To God who gives joy to my youth.

For the Blanchfield family, a Mass of most perfect thanksgiving.

Sy Foltman finds himself dumped on the west coast of the United States, and dropped down a stripe from his temporary CPO status, while the *USS*

Marcus Island begins its last voyage, through the Panama Canal and up to Connecticut where it will be decommissioned, parked, and finally scrapped. He boards a crowded train for the long ride east, where, in February of 1946, he receives his discharge from Lido Beach, makes his way to Grand Central Station in New York and grabs the first train to Amsterdam.

No brass bands. No big parades. No one even aware that he is coming home.

He throws his sea bag over his shoulder and walks alone up the long hill

to the family homestead on Vanderveer Street, where he kisses his mother, tosses the sea bag in the corner, plops down in a chair and begins the serious business of getting on with the rest of his life.

A month later, the 1940 graduate of Wilbur H. Lynch Senior High School with a technical degree in textiles is back in a high school classroom, this time cramming up on academic courses so he can get an academic diploma and go on to college, which he does, as do all six of his family's World War II veterans.

Alexander Kilinski duly reports to the Draft Board on his eighteenth birthday, April 25, 1946, and registers for the Selective Service System as required by law. Nothing unusual about that. Probably about five thousand Amsterdam guys had done that, including more than 4,000 in the first registration in 1940 alone. What sets Kilinski apart is that he had just been discharged from the Navy a few months earlier after more than two years of service, mostly aboard ships in the South Pacific.

Three years earlier he had done the same thing, shown up at the Draft Board and filled out his registration form, and although he had told them truthfully on April 26, 1943 that yesterday was his birthday, he neglected to mention that he had just turned fifteen. He fudges his year of birth on the registration form and in due course is called up and reports for duty on September 8, 1943. At five feet nine and 165 pounds he is passable and at no time in the entire course of his service does anyone question his age.

He just wanted to do his part, and had figured that if he waited until 1946 he would miss the whole thing, and even if he got parental permission, the earliest he could get in would be April 25, 1945. So he submits the false document when he's even too young to be prosecuted for it.

And his mother never tattles.

It's only after he's discharged and becomes eligible for benefits under the GI Bill that it occurs to him that the time has come to set the record straight. The Draft Board considers the situation and decides that by registering on his 18th birthday he has fulfilled the requirements of the law and on review of his military record they promptly classify him as 1C as a discharged veteran.

Having entered the service after his sophomore year, he goes back to Wilbur H. Lynch High School to finish up.

Sgt. Melrose Freer comes home safe and sound to his beloved Nell and, as promised, they produce a dozen kids.

Sue and Kris Freer at the Pileckas
homestead, c. 1957

In the Spring of 1945 and again in 1946, members of the Student Council at Wilbur H. Lynch Senior High School plant trees on the school grounds, each a memorial to a graduate of Amsterdam's High School who died in the service of his country in World War II. They cover the hillside in front of the school and all the way up Brandt Place and around the tennis courts. A forest grows up on the west side of the football field, and still more trees along the east driveway.

There are eighty-eight of them.

Photographs appear in the paper of individual families with their tree, and Memorial Day in 1946 marks the formal dedication of the living memorial. Each family receives a chart showing the exact location of each tree.

Allen Pileckas gets number 65, the third from the end as Brandt Place approaches Lindbergh Avenue (Bunn Street Extension does not yet exist), almost to the east tennis court.

Over the years the trees grow tall and full, but gradually their purpose is forgotten. Expansions, reconstructions, maybe even traffic safety factors come into play. The trees begin to disappear.

No one notices.

Not many more than a dozen still exist.

On the side where once stood a tree dedicated to the Silver Star hero of Iwo Jima there are none at all.

Capt. Frank Olander stays in the army, the only man from Company G to do so. It takes over a year to recover from the wounds received in the *banzai* charge on Saipan, and for a while they have him doing soft desk work in recruiting stations, and then training new infantrymen. But as his strength returns, he decides in 1950 to train for an airborne unit. The Korean War interrupts and instead he goes back to work in the line infantry.

Now a major in the 24th Division, he is in Korea but a few weeks when he is shot and wounded again, twice in the left leg and once in the cheek, on October 30, 1950 in Kusong, about twenty miles from the border with Manchuria. Though qualified as a mountain Alpinist, ski trooper and paratrooper, the injuries disqualify him from the United States Para-Rescue Team, his dream. When he retires he settles in his wife's home town of Gooding, Idaho.

On September 22, 1946, for the first time in over four years, the Bigelow-Sanford Uniteds Soccer Team takes the field on Dutch Hill, opening their (1942) National League Title Defense against Galicia of New York City. Johnny Campbell, who will be hobbled by that Makin Island sword wound to his foot for the rest of his life, can no longer play, so he coaches the team. Pierce and Harry Tolson participate, and Bill and Edwin McKnight. And that intrepid builder of the Alaska-Canada Highway Walt Slagus. Howie Dynes returns as well, and Walt Campbell, and Peanuts Brown and Skip Holland and Bus Murdoch. They play as they had always played, with a smothering defense and aggressive offense, coming out with a 3-0 win.

No one on Dutch Hill had expected anything less.

Beginning in late 1947 and for the next eighteen months or so, the somber reality of war comes back to Amsterdam, literally, as dozens of the war dead are returned to their final resting places from distant shores. The *Recorder* once again recaps their stories.

Pvt. Norman Briskie arrives first, from Europe. Nearly three years after his death his grieving parents at last have their opportunity to say goodbye. The paper carries a photograph of the crowd outside St. Stanislaus Church honoring his mortal remains.

Then follows a pattern eerily reminiscent of the advancing news from the war years: first a trickle, then a flood of casualties, until the town grows numb again from the sheer magnitude of it.

Bill Hasenfuss never comes home.

In the chaos of the Pearl Harbor attack and its aftermath, the body of Amsterdam's first war hero gets misplaced. He's remembered at the National Cemetery in Hawaii, and presumed to be there, but exactly where, well, Uncle Sam can't say.

His mother had done her duty, attending Honor Roll unveilings, parades, the dedication of a city park in memory of her son. She'd even launched a Navy Cruiser in the name of the City of Amsterdam. When her son-in-law dies as well in the service of his country, she helps raise her grandchildren, when their mother can't. Most every year she appears at the patriotic service on December 7 at Hasenfuss Field.

Then, in the 1950's, with the war an increasingly distant memory for most but very current in her heart, she is approached by a city official. Amsterdam's recreation director has died, and the official wants to know if it would be alright with the Hasenfuss family if Hasenfuss Field were to be renamed for the recreation director.

She thinks it over.

"No, it would not be alright."

"I'm sorry to hear that," he says, "because we're going to do it anyway." He points out a long list of things the recreation director has done for the city over the years, a very true and most impressive collection of civic accomplishments.

"Really, what did your son ever do for Amsterdam?"

The answer to that question is contained in this *Recorder* editorial :

HE DIED FOR AMERICA

Amsterdam has felt the first real impact of war —the death of one of its sons in the treacherous attack of the Japanese upon Hickam

Field near Honolulu, while their emissaries were still dickering for peace with Secretary of State Hull.

William E. Hasenfuss, Jr., son of Mr. and Mrs. William E. Hasenfuss of Northampton Road, has died that the American way of life, which is the way of freedom, civilization and all the decencies of a peaceful existence, might be preserved. Greater love than this hath no man.

Nothing that we can here set down through the medium of the printed word can express the deep sense of regret and sympathy for the family which pervades the city as the news of our first great contribution to the cause of freedom reaches us. Perhaps it does not need expression, for we are a small community and therefore neighborly. That which brings sorrow to one, brings sorrow to all.

First Class Private Hasenfuss will have his name inscribed on Amsterdam's new Roll of Honor. There will be others as the conflict grows more intense. It is the supreme sacrifice that these boys and their bereft families make. Then let none of us who remain at home be less steadfast in keeping faith with them than they have been in serving us. Nothing that we can do can equal their contribution.
-*Recorder December 11, 1941*

Homecomings don't always have a timetable. "Oh, Boy! Ain't it Great to Be a Soldier!" the caption had read when the private had his picture snapped for the *Evening Recorder* on October 23, 1940 when the boys of Company G shipped off to prepare for a war that hadn't even come for us yet. He had climbed up through the ranks and made officer.

Then, in an obscure corner of France, where his valiant rearguard defense of his own troops earned him a Distinguished Service Cross and his own death, Lt. Lewis Dilello had been hastily laid to rest by a retreating enemy in a forgotten field.

He became a statistic, another small piece of unfinished business of World War II. After a while, few outside his family even recalled him much.

In 1991, more than half a century after he had marched out of Amsterdam, a collateral descendant of his, with no personal memory of the hero and only stories and pictures to know him, has a strange dream. A very strange dream, indeed.

Uncle Lewis appears, the broad smile of his officer's portrait spread across his face.

"I'm coming home," he says, matter-of-factly.

Days later, a telegram arrives.

A year and a half earlier French soldiers had come across the traces of the dead. A lengthy investigation had taken place, and, finally, the body (and a companion) properly identified.

The family opts to have him returned to Amsterdam. In the very first group of the home town lads to leave, he is the last, thus far, to return.

Dilello receives a well-deserved hero's welcome on Saturday, August 17, 1991. Originally expecting a small family funeral at St. Michael's, interest grows so fast that the venue is moved to the much larger St. Mary's. An honor guard from the 10th Mountain Division at Fort Drum, New York escorts the mortal remains.

Traffic stops as crusty veterans fill East Main Street in front of St. Mary's Church, snap to attention and salute their forever-young comrade, then file in behind the flag-draped coffin and fill the pews of the church.

Many glance up at the magnificent stained-glass Liberty Window, at the western end of the transept. Some had even been present at its dedication on June 10, 1945 when the Company G Color Guard, veterans old and new, Knights of Columbus in full regalia, church choirs and buglers, Gold Star Mothers and Blue Star Mothers, and the congregation of St. Mary's, met in solemn remembrance.

Very Reverend Edward Walsh, then Pastor of St. Mary's, had conceived of the window and overseen its development. By the time of its installation, the war in Europe had ended and the Japanese surrender was barely two months away.

It remains a fantastic work of art.

At its peak, worshiped by two angels, is the Holy Spirit in the form of a dove, directly over God the Father, and beneath Him, Jesus Christ, "*VIA*

VERITAS VITA," the Way, the Truth and the Life. To His right is Mary, "QUEEN OF PEACE," and to His left, Moses, "LIBERATOR." Above Mary is the *Pieta,* and in the quarters surrounding her the Old Testament heroines Judith and Esther, and the somewhat more modern Sts. Joan of Arc and Catherine of Siena. The quarters of Moses contain King David, St. George, Don Juan of Lepanto, and Christopher Columbus. On the next level below are tableaux of the signings of the *Magna Carta* and the Declaration of Independence, flanking a lion lying down with a lamb, surmounted by the legend, "*Agnus Dei Dona Nobis Pacem.*"

Lamb of God, Grant Us Peace.

At the feet of Jesus, a quote from 2 Corinthians: *Where the Spirit of the Lord Is, There Is Liberty.*

And at the bottom, women and men marching in already quaint uniforms of the 1940's: nurses and WACS and WAVES; Army, Navy, Marines and Army Air Force.

And between them, the dedication:

THIS LIBERTY WINDOW IS ERECTED
IN MEMORY OF ST. MARY'S
HEROES WHO FIGHT THAT
THE FREEDOM OF OUR
COUNTRY BE FOREVER PRESERVED

The *Evening Recorder* preserved Father Walsh's brief words of blessing.

In the name of the most Holy Trinity the Father, Son and Holy Ghost, we solemnly bless this Liberty memorial window. In the name of our most Holy Lady, Mary, Mother of God, and spiritual mother of the children of God, we affectionately in Christ dedicate this memorial to the sons and daughters of this parish who belong to the great host of American patriots defending the life and liberties of our beloved country.

To their memory and to the memory of all St. Mary's gallant sons and daughters living or dead, who in this war or any other war, have fought that the liberties we now enjoy, and have enjoyed, might not perish from the earth, we affectionately offer this memorial.

It is the gift of St. Mary's congregation and is the symbol of our grateful appreciation; the voiceless tribute of our measureless pride; it is memory's beautiful promise of a remembrance that shall not die with the years.

It is a memorial that has come to find its home in the Temple of God, not upon the highways of a restless fitful world where men so soon forget, but rather here in this temple of Him whose memory is the fadeless memory of God.

It is our dear, deep hope that children yet unborn shall come to look upon this window, this vision of apocalyptic beauty of color and light, and then kneel to adore and thank God for the noble, gallant, intrepid sons and daughters of this historic parish of St. Mary's; to thank God that this parish has had an honored part in the matchless achievement that has wrought the salvation of our country's high destiny; and to thank God that our sons and daughters are worthy of a memorable place in the mighty epic that shall one day be written of the imperishable glory of American youth.

May the streaming rays of its light be a symbol of God's shining glory, and may its radiant beauty be an unfailing index to the measure and quality of the dear deep thought that sweet remembrance shall forever carry in our heart of hearts.

The remains of Lewis Dilello are rolled up the middle aisle, and come to rest before the altar.

There are present, that day, old men who had served with Pvt. Dilello in Company G, who had marched with him in the big parade of 1940, who had seen him become First Sergeant of the company, and who had said goodbye when he went off to become an officer, while they went on to Saipan and Okinawa.

Even those who had never known Lewis Dilello still find themselves flooded with memories, memories of youth and laughter and music and love and friendships fused by the shared terror of war and its horrible consequences.

They are, for the moment, once again on distant shores, in sand and mud and cold and relentless heat and fear. They wonder how they had survived at all, when so very many had not.

Rev. James Gulley, only the second Pastor of St. Mary's since Msgr. Walsh, celebrates the Mass of Christian burial. He lifts his eyes to the Liberty Window, and the open-armed Jesus, "Welcoming Lewis," he says, "at an unknown place forty-seven years ago. . . . Why one person lives and another dies in the same situation is a mystery. The men who lived, they too are our heroes, those who were wounded and are now in veterans' hospitals and often forgotten. That's why a day like today is so important, so we never forget, and so we learn to appreciate the freedoms that have come at such a great price."

The Mass over, the funeral procession moves on to St. Michael's cemetery where the honor guard fires a salute and the bugler plays *Taps*. Uniformed men carefully fold the flag that had draped the coffin and present it to his brother Anthony.

Not a few ponder the miracle that has finally brought Lewis Dilello, after all this time, from across the far sea to Amsterdam and home.

Home, at last, to the consecrated earth of the family burial plot.

Father Gulley had chosen the Old Testament reading for the funeral Mass from the Book of Deuteronomy:

> *Though you may have been driven*
> *to the farthest corner of the world,*
> *even from there will the Lord,*
> *your God, gather you.*
> *Even from there will He bring you back.*

ABOUT THE AUTHOR

Robert N. Going is a graduate of St. Mary's Institute and Bishop Scully High School in Amsterdam, NY. He received his BA degree from the State University of New York at Albany in 1973 where he majored in History. After being awarded a *Juris Doctor* degree from Albany Law School in 1979 he entered the practice of law.

He is the author of several books, including a companion to this one, *Honor Roll: The World War II Dead of Amsterdam, NY*; a murder mystery, *The Evil Has Landed*; and a collection of essays, *The Judge Report: Musings of a Conservative Republican Pro-Life Catholic Red Sox Fanatic Currently Hiding Out in Amsterdam, NY USA*. He maintains a popular blog, *The Judge Report*, found at rgoing.livejournal.com.

He remains in Amsterdam with his wife Mary. They have four accomplished children and a sweet granddaughter.

Comments, criticisms, corrections, suggestions and reviews may be addressed to the author at rgoing@yahoo.com.

Thank you.
We will remember. Always.